## DATE DUE

| | | | |
|---|---|---|---|
| | | | |
| | | | |
| | | | |
| | | | |
| | | | |
| | | | |
| | | | |
| | | | |
| | | | |
| | | | |
| | | | |
| | | | |
| | | | |
| | | | |
| | | | |
| | | | |
| | | | |
| | | | |

DEMCO 38-296

# The Culture of Protest

# Conflict and Social Change Series

Series Editors
Scott Whiteford and William Derman
*Michigan State University*

R

# The Culture of Protest

## Religious Activism and the U.S. Sanctuary Movement

Susan Bibler Coutin

**Westview Press**

BOULDER · SAN FRANCISCO · OXFORD

*Conflict and Social Change Series*

Copyright © 1993 by Susan Bibler Coutin

Published in 1993 in the United States of America by Westview Press, Inc., 5500 Central Avenue, Boulder, Colorado 80301-2877, and in the United Kingdom by Westview Press, 36 Lonsdale Road, Summertown, Oxford OX2 7EW

The cover design is taken from a square on the "Sanctuary Quilt," made by the Boise Peace Quilt Project in 1988. The square was designed by Patricia Hall. The Peace Quilt Project is a determined and hopeful group of people creating a peaceful world one stitch at a time. These activists use quilts to honor peacemakers and to make the world a better place. They are stitching on their thirtieth quilt since 1982. Full-color greeting cards and postcards of the quilts are available. Please send a SASE to: BPQP, P.O. Box 6469, Boise, Idaho 83707, or call (208)378-0293.

Library of Congress Cataloging-in-Publication Data
Coutin, Susan Bibler.
   The culture of protest : religious activism and the U.S. sanctuary
movement / Susan Bibler Coutin.
      p.   cm.—(Conflict and social change series)
   Includes bibliographical references and index.
   ISBN 0-8133-1553-0.—ISBN 0-8133-1554-9 (pbk.)
   1. Sanctuary movement.   2. Refugees—Central America.   I. Title.
II. Series.
BV4466.C63   1993
261.8'32—dc20                                                                      92-45553
                                                                                       CIP

Printed and bound in the United States of America

∞   The paper used in this publication meets the requirements
    of the American National Standard for Permanence of Paper
    for Printed Library Materials Z39.48-1984.

10    9    8    7    6    5    4    3    2    1

*To Jesse*

# Contents

# Acknowledgments

My deepest debt of gratitude goes to all who participated in this study. I am grateful for the time people took from busy schedules to talk to me about the sanctuary movement, for the rides from bus or BART stations when I didn't have a car, for the trust and openness with which people discussed sensitive information, and most of all, for the friendship, colleagueship, and fellowship I found. I hope that this book provides a useful reflection on the movement, and I apologize for not writing in Spanish as well as English. I would particularly like to thank the East Bay Sanctuary Covenant, the EBSC office volunteers and staff, the West Coast portion of the 1987 Central America Caravan, the Tucson Ecumenical Council's Task Force on Central America, Tucson Ecumenical Council Legal Assistance (TECLA), the January 1988 Borderlinks group, and the congregations that allowed me to participate in their sanctuary work as part of this project.

Through a 1987–1988 American Fellowship, the American Association of University Women Educational Foundation generously provided the financial support that made this research possible.

A number of individuals provided invaluable assistance. My father, Neil Bibler, first suggested that I write about the sanctuary movement. Ben Paul, Herb Schmidt, Marilyn Chilcote, and Ron Parker encouraged my initial explorations of this topic. William Walker gave me access to his copy of the official transcripts of the 1985–1986 sanctuary trial, without which Chapter 7 could not have been written. The Tucson office of the American Friends Service Committee allowed me to read through and copy portions of their extensive file of newspaper articles about the sanctuary movement. Irene Litherlund sent me a tape recording of the service commemorating the tenth anniversary of the original sanctuary declarations. Lisa Amsterdam devised the pseudonym "Congregation Aron Kodesh" and commented on my interpretations of Jewish participation in the sanctuary movement. My mother-in-law, Luxy Miller, helped invent some of the pseudonyms used in this manuscript. Nara Diniz's attentive care of my son freed me to concentrate on revising the manuscript.

The ideas out of which this manuscript grew were formed during conversations with mentors and colleagues too numerous to name but whose contributions deserve better acknowledgment than they are getting. Jane Collier taught me the importance of theoretical rigor and holistic analysis. Her intellectual guidance and her interest in my work have been a source of inspiration and support throughout this project. She, along with Sylvia Yanagisako, first encouraged me to look at the political implications of culture in the way that led to my research on the sanctuary movement. Mary Pratt also encouraged me to explore directions that proved more than fruitful. Renato Rosaldo asked difficult questions, encouraged me to take risks, and made criticisms that struck at the heart of an analytical problem. His advice on reshaping the manuscript proved invaluable. When I was a graduate student at Stanford, my fellow students taught me a great deal about the connections between theory and practice. In particular, Tamis Renteria listened to many of these ideas before they were written down, and she and Diane Weiner provided encouragement while I was writing. In addition to these individuals, Bev Chaney, Curt Coutin, Steve Hays-Lohry, Ken Kennon, Irene Litherlund, Kamala Visweswaran, Ellen Willis-Conger, and an anonymous reviewer for Westview Press commented on drafts of individual chapters or of the entire manuscript. Part 2 benefited from comments on papers I presented at the annual meetings of the American Anthropological Association in 1988 and 1989, the joint meetings of the Law and Society Association and the Research Committee on Sociology of Law of the International Sociological Association in 1991, and the meeting of the Southwestern Anthropological Association in 1992. I am extremely grateful for all of the detailed and helpful criticisms that have shaped this work.

I would also like to thank Dean Birkenkamp for his interest in this manuscript and Westview's editorial staff for a smooth publication process.

Finally, I would like to thank my family. My parents, Vada Binick and Neil Bibler; my sister, Debbie Bibler; and my in-laws encouraged me throughout my studies, research, and writing. My son, Jesse, proved a joyous distraction while I was revising this manuscript. Last but far from least, I am grateful to my husband, Curt Coutin, for his loving support throughout this project.

*Susan Bibler Coutin*

# 1

# Introduction

One warm September morning in 1987, I was sitting in a folding chair in the crowded sanctuary of "All Saints"[1]—a Tucson, Arizona, Protestant church that had declared itself a sanctuary for Central American refugees in 1982 and whose pastor had been convicted in 1986 of conspiracy, transporting, and aiding and abetting the transportation of illegal aliens. This particular Sunday was unusual because other convicted sanctuary workers and their attorneys had gathered in Tucson to plan their appeal and had joined the 200 or so church members at All Saints' regular worship service. At the beginning of the service, the lawyers and others active in the defense effort were asked to stand so that they could be honored. When the pastor thanked the defense attorneys for their hard work and commitment, he spoke as though the congregation itself had been on trial. I found myself wondering how many of the "unindicted co-conspirators" named in the indictment were from this congregation.

The sermon that Sunday morning wove together trial, truth, tilling, and tax collecting to ask how one could *denounce* injustice while *benefiting* from injustice. The sermon was based on a parable from the Gospel of Matthew in which a father asks two sons to till the fields. The first son agrees but never follows through. The second son refuses but later does the work. Jesus (the teller of the parable) then asks the Pharisees (his audience) which is the better son. When they choose the latter, Jesus tells them that the prostitutes and tax collectors will enter heaven before they do. The minister drew two conclusions from this parable: first, that lies, such as claiming to promote peace while aiding the Contras, are the root of evil, and second, that God judges individuals by their actions rather than their words. Declaring that the modern church had become too comfortable, the pastor positioned himself and his audience among the Pharisees. He told his congregation, "The question before us today is whether the *poor in spirit* will go to heaven before the *preachers* and the *lawyers* and the *powerful* in society." The minister went on to portray sanctuary, the trial, and the appeal as actions that were *uncomfortable* and that therefore could redeem the powerful. Using words evocative of human rights violations in Central America, the pastor reminded the congregation that only one week after he told the ruling families of his day that the despised

*1*

would enter heaven before them, Jesus was betrayed, denounced, captured, tortured, and killed on a cross. The minister thus likened sanctuary work and the trial to Jesus' act of denunciation, to the truth that undermines the reign of the powerful, and to the persecution that awaited both Jesus and Central American activists.

Coincidentally, that particular Sunday morning—when I heard a pastor who was a convicted felon encourage individuals to proclaim truth at the risk of imprisonment or death—was my first visit to All Saints. I had been involved in the sanctuary movement in the San Francisco Bay Area for more than a year and had been conducting fieldwork and interviews among participants since January 1987. I'd been in Tucson for about a month and had already met this pastor, attended meetings, interviewed a rabbi, and done volunteer work. So, on that Sunday morning when I stood to introduce myself to the congregation along with other new visitors—a weekly ritual in this well-known church, which one member described as a "goldfish bowl"—the pastor told church members, "She's here to help us with our sanctuary ministry, and she's very welcome. Glad to have you with us."

And I was glad to be there. Despite my fears that this church, which had been infiltrated by undercover government agents, would not welcome an anthropologist in its midst, no one reacted suspiciously to my presence. Rather, after the service, several churchgoers greeted me, asked about my research, and invited me to worship with them again. Nor, I soon discovered, was I alone in my quest for knowledge of the movement. During the brief period after the minister lifted a Salvadoran boy to ring the church bells and before church members divided into Bible study classes, I met a young man from the East Coast who was being funded by his university to work with the sanctuary movement. When I asked why he'd taken on this task, he told me that his father was a minister, he was a church member, and he didn't want to give up on the mainstream church.

And why was I there, talking to a young man who didn't want to give up on the mainstream church, looking at wall-hangings that commemorated the martyrs of Central America, feeling the echoes of this sermon, and mentally comparing All Saints to congregations in California where I had worshiped and attended sanctuary meetings? I was analyzing the culture of protest within the U.S. sanctuary movement; a grass-roots religious-based network whose aid to undocumented Central Americans had unleashed the state's power of surveillance.

## The Culture of Protest

Protest movements, like societies, have cultures; however, unlike societies, cultures of protest are created when individuals and communities deliberately invoke, recombine, and reinterpret preexisting practices and meanings in light of particular social causes and notions of justice. Constructing and reshaping culture is not, of course, limited to protest movements. Whenever individuals act, they choose between, reformulate, and sometimes improvise on available cultural options. Moreover, these choices often have political implications. For example, enrolling one's child in a public high school that has just instituted busing can be a political act. However, whereas everyday actions can and do intentionally and unintentionally contest and reconstruct social norms, these processes are often buried in the onslaught of social life, their implications, though significant, difficult to ascertain. In contrast, to form the construct known as a social movement, actors create discourses and actions that coalesce around particular political causes and at particular historical moments. Because of their visibility and their explicit link to political issues, protest movements provide a uniquely unmuddied window on the ways that individuals produce culture and on the political nature of such processes.

The sanctuary movement formed during the early 1980s when religious volunteers devised methods of assisting and advocating for undocumented Salvadoran and Guatemalan refugees. The sanctuary movement had a particularly rich culture.[2] Its name derived from the prototypical movement practice: congregations giving sanctuary to Salvadorans or Guatemalans at risk of being detained and deported by the U.S. Immigration and Naturalization Service (INS). In addition to this action, movement members brought Salvadorans and Guatemalans into the United States, traveled to Central America to accompany displaced communities, organized caravans to transport Salvadorans and Guatemalans to other parts of the United States, held ecumenical prayer services and vigils focusing on Central American issues, enabled undocumented refugees to testify publicly about their experiences, sent telegrams protesting human rights abuses in Central America, lobbied Congress, provided social services to Central American refugee communities, sold and distributed Central American crafts and literature, organized press conferences, arranged visits and public presentations by visiting Central American activists and religious leaders, raised bail bond money for detained Central Americans, helped detainees file for political asylum, and more. As they performed these activities, sanctuary workers invoked and reinterpreted legal, cultural, and religious practices in unique ways. These reinterpretations as well as the practices through which they were enacted made up the culture of the movement.

My own involvement with the sanctuary movement was occasioned by the trial of which All Saints' pastor spoke. During fall 1985, as I was designing my doctoral research, the prosecution of eleven sanctuary activists—including All Saints' pastor—began in Tucson. Articles about the trial made front-page headlines, and newspapers around the nation featured in-depth stories about the movement and its history. As I learned about the movement, I realized that not only would sanctuary's unique fusion of religious and political activism afford material for analyzing how people manipulated cultural concepts and practices, but that, in addition, the movement struck a personal chord. I discovered that a Protestant church that I had attended sporadically as a U.C. Berkeley undergraduate was one of the original sanctuary congregations. The movement aided Central Americans, and I spoke Spanish, had lived and studied in Colombia and Argentina, and had focused on Latin America in my graduate studies. Sanctuary was designed to combat human rights abuses, and while I was in Argentina, I had worked with the mothers of the disappeared—an experience that had exposed me to the atrocities of state terrorism and deepened my commitment to oppose such abuses in the future. Doing fieldwork within the sanctuary movement would not only further my academic ends, it would also reconnect me to some of my religious roots and enable me to take practical action on human rights issues.

As I began reading about protest and resistance, I became aware of a schism that obscured the similarities between organized protest movements, such as sanctuary, and the continual, though often implicit, acts of resistance that occur in everyday life. Studies of organized social movements viewed protest as an exception to the normal state of affairs (Piven and Cloward 1977; Gusfield 1970; McCarthy and Zald 1973, 1977; Marwell and Oliver 1984; Hannigan 1985; Melucci 1989; Klandermans and Tarrow 1988), an aberration that occurred when resources became available to aggrieved groups, permitting them to act. What came to be known as "resource mobilization theory" assumed that when it *did* occur, protest consisted of rational, strategic action designed to accomplish clearly explicated goals (Jenkins 1983; Zald and McCarthy 1979; Gamson 1975; Oberschall 1973; Tilly 1978). In contrast, analyses of what Scott termed "*everyday* forms of resistance" (1985: 29, emphasis in original) considered resistance an *ongoing* facet of social life, the inevitable consequence of social asymmetry (Scott 1985; Comaroff 1985; Taussig 1980; Limon 1983; Ong 1987; Price 1983). These theorists contended that, in addition to being strategic action, protest could take the form of seemingly apolitical cultural practices that implicitly critiqued the structures in which they occurred. To understand the political implications of such practices, these researchers argued, protest had to be placed in its social, cultural, and historical context.

In order to analyze how sanctuary practices that did not appear rational, strategic, or goal-oriented were an integral part of the protest enacted within the movement, I have drawn on the analytical tools that were developed to study everyday forms of resistance. By placing sanctuary within its cultural context, I discuss how this movement, like other acts of resistance, engaged discourses of power that were much more pervasive and insidious than the movement's stated cause. In other words, sanctuary addressed not only U.S. foreign and immigration policy but also power-laden facets of middle-class U.S. cultural, religious, and legal life.[3] The movement's challenge to power-laden discourses occurred not only through strategic actions but also through the informal, "nonpolitical" yet nonetheless insurrectional practices participants developed alongside prototypical movement practices. Therefore, in addition to analyzing movement strategies, such as sheltering undocumented Central Americans, I examine sanctuary rituals, the jokes and stories told by volunteers, the interaction between sanctuary workers and refugees, the forms of community created within the movement, and the "conversions" that some participants experienced as they became acquainted with Central American reality. Along with explicit strategies, these seemingly superfluous aspects of movement culture commented on the social context in which they were formed. By its very existence, the sanctuary movement incrementally changed society.

This book is divided into three parts, each of which focuses on a different facet of movement culture. Part One, "Crossing Borders," analyzes how movement culture was created, reproduced, and made authoritative to participants. Part Two, "Sanctuary," examines the ways that power and resistance pervaded both the movement's and the government's deployment of U.S. immigration law. Finally, Part Three, "The Culture of Protest" brings together these discussions of social and political processes in order to investigate the ways that movement culture enacted participants' visions of a more just social order.

## The Research Subjects

My portrayal of the sanctuary movement is based on fieldwork and interviews conducted from January 1987 to March 1988 in sanctuary communities in the San Francisco East Bay in California and in Tucson, Arizona. The San Francisco East Bay is made up of a number of cities, including Oakland, Berkeley, Albany, Hayward, and San Leandro, whose populaces range from affluent to impoverished. Though the twenty-six participating congregations came from many of these locales,[4] the East Bay sanctuary community was centered in Berkeley, a city noted for its political activism. The sanctuary congregations in the East Bay were organized into a covenant body that worked with other local covenants (for example, the San Francisco Sanctuary Covenant), all of which belonged to the Northern California Sanctuary Covenant. In addition to sheltering undocumented Salvadorans and Guatemalans, the East Bay Sanctuary Covenant (EBSC) provided social services to the approximately 60,000 to 80,000 Central Americans who had settled in the Bay Area, sent delegations to Central America to accompany displaced communities, and performed other advocacy work. The legal risks of these activities were minimal, and no East Bay participant had been indicted for doing sanctuary work.

Tucson, located 64 miles north of the U.S.-Mexico border, is a sprawling desert city. Unlike the San Francisco East Bay, Tucson—which is buttressed only by South Tucson, a largely Chicano barrio; Oro Valley, a more affluent community; and Marana, an outlying farming town—is at least an hour's drive from any other major town. In Tucson, sanctuary and related work was carried out by what one participant labeled "agencies," most of which worked under the auspices of the Tucson Ecumenical Council (TEC). These agencies included the TEC's Task Force on Central America (the TECTFCA, or simply "the Task Force"), the Tucson refugee support group (Trsg), Tucson Ecumenical Council Legal Assistance (TECLA), and the TECHO Interamerican Center (an educational and community group focusing on Central America).[5] Though participants worked closely with colleagues in Nogales, Phoenix, San Diego, and elsewhere, Tucson sanctuary groups were not structurally connected to a larger regional body as were their East Bay counterparts. Moreover, with the exception of one or two extremely active congregations, most participants worked through the aforementioned community groups rather than their own congregations. Due to its proximity to Mexico, the Tucson branch of the movement focused on bringing Central Americans across the border and helping them reach safety in the United States. Because of this focus, the U.S. government had infiltrated the local movement and in 1985 indicted movement members on conspiracy and alien-smuggling charges. The grueling six-month trial that followed the indictments had affected not only the eleven sanctuary workers who were prosecuted but also their supporters and the approximately 100 other individuals that the indictment termed "unindicted citizen and alien co-conspirators."

My fieldwork in Tucson and East Bay sanctuary communities consisted of what anthropologists call "participant observation"—living among and joining in the activities of the people one is analyzing. Among other things, I lived in middle-class areas in Oakland and Tucson, attended services at two Protestant churches and a synagogue, interviewed approximately 100 participants, volunteered with social services programs, attended community-wide sanctuary meetings and events, and answered phones in an office. It was through such everyday and seemingly mundane experiences and conversations that I learned of the cultural depth of the movement. As Gerlach and Hine noted, "There is a quality of experience in any movement which cannot be imparted by rational means but must be communicated through existential means" (1970: 197). By sharing the activities of movement members, I was able to analyze this "quality of experience" as well as the types of activities more commonly designated as social protest.

The first congregation where I did fieldwork was "First Church," a Protestant church I had attended erratically my senior year at the University of California, Berkeley, unaware that the congregation had recently declared itself a public sanctuary for Central American refugees. Founded in the late 1800s, First Church was a well-established middle-class church with a large sanctuary (leased to another congregation), a small chapel where church members worshiped, and a separate building that housed church offices and meeting rooms. The church's proximity to a major university and a local seminary lent an intellectual cast to the congregation. Once a congregation of 1,200, First Church's membership had dwindled during the 1960s and 1970s to approximately 300 people. After this loss, First Church had defined part of its ministry as making its facilities available for community use. First Church's commitment to social action dated at least to the civil rights movement. Rev. Henry Carson, a former pastor, recalled that during the 1960s, "it got pretty bad in the neighborhood. I remember coming back to the office, and the secretary would have tears in her eyes because of the tear gas that was coming in the window." First Church's pride in diversity was reflected in creative worship services that invoked a variety of new and old traditions. The excellent choir, which included some professional singers, performed beautiful, complex religious music that sometimes shook the rafters.

In some ways, First Church was not a typical Protestant church. It had joined the movement of Reconciled Congregations, which publicly affirmed the value of homosexual men and women in the life of the church. The announcements that preceded services were as likely to mention a demonstration at the Concord Naval Weapons Station as a luncheon for new members. During coffee hour one winter morning, there was a letter-writing campaign to support the Moakley-Deconcini bill (legislation that would temporarily prevent the deportation of Salvadorans and Nicaraguans) and a petition drive to oppose harboring the *U.S.S. Missouri* in the San Francisco Bay. However, First Church was not entirely atypical either and had its share of potluck dinners, Bible studies, bake sales, and church committees.

First Church was one of the most active congregations in EBSC. Its representatives to the EBSC Steering Committee participated in EBSC meetings and activities, acting as liaisons between the congregation and the local sanctuary community. First Church had its own Sanctuary Committee—approximately ten church members who met monthly to organize such projects as funding a refugee house, writing to members of Congress, and holding potluck dinners with church members and Central Americans. Members who were not on the Sanctuary Committee participated in First Church's sanctuary work through worship, sanctuary-related events, and occasional donations of time and money. The few people who performed most of First Church's sanctuary work did so with the backing of the entire congregation.

The second congregation where I did fieldwork was "Congregation Aron Kodesh,"[6] a small Berkeley synagogue that had declared itself a sanctuary congregation in 1984 when Jews joined the local movement. Congregation Aron Kodesh was part of the Jewish Renewal Movement[7] and had been founded so recently that the congregation had yet to secure a permanent building. Congregation Aron Kodesh was organized in the late 1970s to embody an alternative vision of synagogue life. The synagogue's purposes included commitment to social justice, renewing the depth of Jewish spirituality, and creating community. Congregation Aron Kodesh members—who, at the time of my research, numbered between 100 and 200—were committed to their young synagogue and, in choosing to join this particular congregation, had explored what it meant to be Jewish. Congregation Aron Kodesh sought to include people whom synagogues had traditionally excluded, such as interfaith couples, single-parent families, and lesbian and gay individuals, couples, and families. The congregation was run on an egalitarian, democratic basis, and services were innovative yet traditional. Uniting politics and spirituality, Congregation Aron Kodesh members had formed committees on Black/Jewish relations and sanctuary and had performed a Passover Seder at the nuclear test site in Nevada.

One Shabbat service that I attended conveyed Congregation Aron Kodesh's commitments to community and to renewed spirituality. After lighting the Shabbos candles, the twenty adults in attendance formed a circle around the burning candles, put our arms around each other, and shared aloud the blessings we had experienced during the previous week. We then returned to our seats to chant and read prayers in Hebrew and English. The rabbi led the prayers, sometimes clapping, stomping rhythmically, or moving around the room. At one point the prayer books were set aside and the rabbi asked us each to reflect on times when we had had contact with the mysterious, the connection to the universe. Participants broke into small groups to read and reflect on rabbinical writings about finding the holy in everyday life. After about fifteen minutes, we reassembled to meditate, pray, break the *challah,* and bless the wine. The service concluded with participants chanting, holding hands, and moving about the room in a line dance.

Synagogue members' sociopolitical work (including sanctuary) was a vital part of the congregation. Like First Church, Congregation Aron Kodesh was one of the more active sanctuary congregations in the East Bay. The Sanctuary Committee sent representatives to EBSC meetings and used the synagogue's newsletter to keep the congregation informed of local sanctuary events. Sanctuary Committee meetings, attended by seven to ten participants, were held monthly. The congregation's sanctuary work had included housing refugees, paying the bail for a detained Guatemalan family, and funding a synagogue member's trip to Central America. Synagogue members who were not on the committee participated in sanctuary activities by issuing a public declaration of sanctuary, donating money and other items, and attending sanctuary-related activities (such as a worship service focusing on the congregation's sanctuary work).

In Tucson, I conducted fieldwork at All Saints, the Protestant church widely regarded as the origin of the sanctuary movement. All Saints was a small white adobe church located in a Tucson barrio. The cactus-studded yard and gravel parking lot seemed appropriate for the church's desert surroundings, while a children's playground attested to the vitality of the congregation. All Saints services struck me as surprisingly traditional after those of First Church and Congregation Aron Kodesh. Though sermons often distilled liberation theology, much of the liturgy proclaimed such fundamental Christian beliefs as that Christ died for humanity's sins so that people might have eternal life. The choir was led by a gospel-singing Baptist who reportedly could not read music but whose spirited voice and direction brought the music to life. Merlin Wynn, a church member, eloquently described why he joined All Saints:

> The actions were what drew me to it, not the words. I would come here, and especially the first four or five times, what I came for wasn't the talking, it was [_____]'s music. I would let the words go by, and someone would be up there talking, and it would wash right over me, and then I would hear the singing, and I would cry. I

didn't go there for the talking, but for the sadness and the joy and the awareness of the world's needs and what to do about it. There, I learned about having faith and truth, rather than simply having a beautiful opinion.

Services at All Saints were informal. Children often played on the floor in the midst of the abundance of chairs—there were no pews—that had been squeezed into the small sanctuary to accommodate the 200 or so churchgoers. The services were lively and participatory but less deliberately so than at First Church or Congregation Aron Kodesh. For instance, one Sunday morning the pastor ended the Bible reading for the children's sermon, saying, "and let the women present be silent, for they don't have permission to speak." He then looked around expectantly, and a young man who worked with a squatter settlement in Mexico yelled out, "Amen!" The minister commented, "Hah! I thought I'd get an amen from someone, but I didn't think it would be you." As congregants laughed, the minister continued,"I just added that last part to make sure that all of the adults were paying attention."[8] All Saints was a close-knit congregation, and services celebrated that community through announcements and prayers about members' concerns, joys, and activities. At the end of each service, the minister scooped up one of the children, lifting him or her high to ring the church bells.

All Saints' commitment to social action had historical depth, as one church member explained: "All Saints was founded seventy-five years ago to minister to the Indians, who were pretty oppressed in those days. Even then, it was a challenge to the status quo and a ministry to the oppressed." All Saints had traditionally focused on local issues, such as assisting prisoners' families and working for a community park, rather than the national issues that First Church and Congregation Aron Kodesh usually confronted. It was ironic that All Saints helped to spawn a national movement.

Unlike First Church and Congregation Aron Kodesh, All Saints' sanctuary work was not carried out by a committee. Rather, the All Saints members who were active in border crossings and related work participated in meetings of local sanctuary groups, such as Trsg and the Task Force. However, sanctuary was an integral part of the church. The entire congregation had endorsed the movement by declaring the church a public sanctuary. All Saints' administrative body made decisions about how to accommodate the Central Americans who regularly slept in the church building. Almost every church service, in one way or another, referred to the congregation's sanctuary activities. As previously mentioned, All Saints' pastor had been convicted on alien-smuggling charges, and numerous congregation members were listed on the indictment as "unindicted co-conspirators." Though their methods, faiths, and organizational forms differed, All Saints, First Church, and Congregation Aron Kodesh were linked to each other and to more than 300 congregations nationwide that had declared themselves sanctuaries for Central American refugees.

In addition to conducting fieldwork in these congregations and the larger sanctuary communities of which they were part, I also interviewed 108 individuals, including 52 East Bay sanctuary workers, 39 Tucson sanctuary workers, 10 Central Americans who were connected to the movement, 3 former pastors of First Church, 3 of the attorneys who defended sanctuary workers during the 1985–1986 Tucson trial, and an attorney who represented Central Americans applying for political asylum. Instead of constructing a statistically representative sample, I sought to interview a large enough proportion and wide enough variety of participants to ensure that the views expressed during interviews were indicative of the range of perspectives among Tucson and East Bay sanctuary workers. I sought out people who were heavily involved, peripherally involved, movement founders, recent participants, college students, retirees, working people, Catholics, Jews, Protestants, Atheists, Unitarians, and so forth.[9] I approached these individuals in three ways. Most often, I met participants through meetings, church services, volunteer work, or sanctuary activities and then, during a meeting or other event, requested an interview. In the East Bay, I also interviewed people whom I had not met but whose names were listed on volunteer and Steering Committee representative rosters used in the EBSC office. When I called to request an interview, I identified myself as a researcher, volunteer, and First Church member and explained that I had gotten their names and numbers through the office. Finally, in both Tucson and the East Bay, I also interviewed individuals whose names and phone numbers had been given to me by other members of the movement. When I called, I was careful to mention the contact who had given me the name, particularly in Tucson, where participants were concerned about infiltrators. No one in Tucson or in the East Bay refused to be interviewed.

This interview sample reflected the predominantly white, middle-aged, middle-class, religious composition of the movement. Yet it is difficult to generalize, because participants—whose ages ranged from twenty to eighty-eight—came from diverse religious backgrounds, espoused a variety of political views, performed different occupations, and so forth. Therefore, I allow sanctuary workers to emerge as personalities in the pages that follow and here limit myself to discussing the demographics of this interview sample. In the East Bay, one-third of the sanctuary workers I interviewed were Protestant, one-third were Jewish, and the remaining third was composed of Catholics, Unitarians, and unaffiliated individuals. In contrast, in Tucson, two-thirds of the interview sample were Protestant and the remaining third was Catholic, Jewish, Unitarian, or unaffiliated. The larger number of Jews and smaller number of Protestants interviewed in the East Bay was due to my fieldwork within Congregation Aron Kodesh and the fact that five of EBSC's twenty-six publicly declared sanctuary groups were Jewish, whereas in Tucson, there was only one publicly declared synagogue. In both Tucson and the East Bay, approximately two-thirds of the participants interviewed were working professionals, with clergy constituting 36 percent of the Tucson sample but only 8 percent of the East Bay group. The remaining third was made up of students, retirees, housewives, and blue-collar workers. In the East Bay, 58 percent of the sample was female and 42 percent was male, but in Tucson, these percentages were reversed, with 44 percent female and 56 percent male. The higher percentages of clergy and men in the Tucson sample were interconnected, as when clergy (most of whom were male) were excluded from both groups, the percentages of men and women interviewed were parallel. I attribute the higher number of clergy in the Tucson interview sample to two factors. First, in the East Bay, most sanctuary work was performed by the laypeople who served on congregational sanctuary committees, rather than by clergy. In contrast, in Tucson, where border workers regularly risked encountering INS agents, the proportion of participants who were clergy (and who, because of their religious status, might not be prosecuted if apprehended) was higher than in the East Bay. Second, clergy were more public about their sanctuary participation than were laypeople. As a result, I may have had greater access to the participants who were clergy than to those who were not.

One other segment of this book's cast of characters remains to be introduced: the refugees. Both Tucson and East Bay sanctuary communities regarded the sanctuary movement (excepting the Mexican and Central American segments of the underground railroad) as *North* American. Salvadoran and Guatemalan immigrants participated in the movement by giving testimonies, living with sanctuary workers, coming across the border, performing ritual roles at movement events, and advising and instructing movement members in countless ways, but although their influence on the movement was profound, neither they nor North American participants considered sanctuary *their* movement. Instead, Central Americans formed their own organizations, such as CRECE (Comité de Refugiados Centroamericanos, Central American Refugee Center) in San Francisco and TECHO and El Comité (The Committee) in Tucson. The relationship between sanctuary workers and members of these organizations was often one of colleagueship. For example, a CRECE representative attended EBSC Steering Committee meetings to update committee representatives on Central American issues. Movement members often credited Central Americans with suggesting new directions for the movement, and North and Central Americans (particularly individuals who had lived together for long periods of time) often formed close personal ties. Sanctuary itself, however, remained a movement about, rather than of, Central Americans.

The location of Central Americans within my account of the movement reflects their positions within Tucson and East Bay sanctuary communities. In describing the movement, I have largely sought to represent and analyze the perspectives and experiences of North American sanctuary workers rather than those of their Central American colleagues. The ten Central Americans whom I interviewed were not drawn from the immigrant community at large but rather were connected to the movement in various capacities. They included Clemente Rivera, a young Salvadoran living in private sanctuary in Oakland, California;

José Martín, Esperanza de la Cruz, and Erica Castillo, three Salvadoran refugee organizers who were active in both San Francisco and the East Bay; Angel Muñoz, a Salvadoran who had settled in Tucson where he had played an important role organizing a Salvadoran community group; Felipe Arguelles, a Guatemalan who had served as a staff member of the Task Force and who was very active within the Tucson sanctuary community; Gustavo Alvarez and Marta Rodriguez, a Salvadoran couple who had entered the United States with the aid of Tucson sanctuary workers and had been sheltered in a Tucson congregation before renting their own apartment; Marisol Hernandez, a Guatemalan who, like Gustavo and Marta, had been aided by Tucson sanctuary workers and who was trying to maintain her culture by participating in a local refugee group; and Ramon Palacios, a Salvadoran who was also active in the Tucson refugee community, who had entered the United States with the aid of sanctuary workers, and who was the first Salvadoran to file affirmatively for political asylum with the movement's aid. While these and other Central Americans are quoted throughout this book, Chapters 5 and 6 go furthest in depicting their experiences.

## The Ethnographer

Throughout fieldwork, my position within East Bay and Tucson sanctuary communities was ambiguous and shifting. On the one hand, I was a member of the movement like any other participant. Not only was I a white North American who opposed human rights violations and agreed that most Salvadoran and Guatemalan immigrants deserved refugee status, I also had attended and eventually joined a sanctuary congregation. On the other hand, I had not become involved in sanctuary work until *after* I decided to do research about the movement, and my volunteer activities were also a means of gathering data. The tension between my roles as researcher and participant pervaded my participation in the movement. As a sanctuary worker, when I listened to the minister at All Saints Church condemn the hypocrisy of denouncing injustice while reaping its spoils, I had to question my motives. Was my "fieldwork" (which was also to a large extent "volunteer work") the form of resistance that some have called "activist anthropology"? Was it primarily an act of religious service? Or was I, like many anthropologists before me, merely *assuming* the role of a participant, in the name of science, to acquire knowledge that would earn me a Ph.D. and provide material for research articles and eventually a book? Should I refer to sanctuary workers as "they" or as "we"?

As I negotiated the answer to this question, I was largely free to position myself within or outside of the movement. Every time I requested an interview, introduced myself at a sanctuary gathering, explained my involvement in the movement, or responded to a request for volunteers, I had the opportunity to construct an identity. On these occasions, I attempted to occupy a dual position as a researcher and a participant. During introductions, I identified myself as a member of a sanctuary congregation and a Stanford graduate student who was doing research about the movement. When asked about my motives for participating, I discussed my commitment to human rights as well as my interest in how people shape their own societies. While volunteering, I conceptualized my work as simultaneously practical action, a means of repaying sanctuary workers for their participation in this project, and a method of learning about the movement. My discomfort with defining myself *solely* as a researcher stemmed in part from my awareness that this identity claimed an expertise to represent sanctuary workers' lives,[10] a representation that could have legal ramifications for movement members in the event of future indictments.[11] When I asked permission to conduct fieldwork at First Church, one Sanctuary Committee member honed in on the power-laden nature of this request by asking if participants would have a chance to disagree with my interpretations of their behavior.[12] However, despite my desire to be both researcher and participant, there were times when this was impossible, when one role slipped into the other, or when my ground for claiming a particular identity dissolved. When this happened, I (sometimes unwillingly) found myself occupying or prioritizing one or the other position.

One of the conditions that led me to situate myself *within* the movement was my fear of being taken for an infiltrator. As I learned about the U.S. government's undercover investigation of the movement, I realized that there were disturbing parallels between that covert operation and my own research methods. Beginning in 1982, undercover agents collected literature, handouts, and newspaper clippings about sanctuary work—probably a collection similar to the one that fills a box and several file drawers in my apartment. Like this anthropologist, undercover agents began their investigation by attending public meetings, seminars, and events organized by the movement. According to government prosecutor Don Reno, the agents' next step was to "gain the confidence" of local sanctuary leaders (U.S. v. Aguilar 1986:2643)—an objective not unlike the anthropological concern with establishing rapport. This accomplished, INS informants began to work more closely with sanctuary workers, worshiping in their churches, volunteering with the movement, and befriending participants. I engaged in similar activities, though with different motives. All the while, the informants were taking notes, tape-recording meetings, and reporting to their superiors about sanctuary activities. Similarly, I taped and transcribed interviews, recorded my observations about meetings and events, and submitted reports to my advisers and a granting agency.

Conscious of these similarities, I continually sought to avoid seeming like an undercover agent. As one of the distinctions between myself and government infiltrators was the sincerity of our claims to support sanctuary, I frequently rejected the role of a disinterested investigator. For example, when one Congregation Aron Kodesh member asked whether my interest in sanctuary was primarily research or commitment, I answered that I did not separate the two. The fact that I belonged to a sanctuary congregation substantiated this claim and gave me access to participants who might otherwise have refused to be interviewed. I also took care not to act like an infiltrator. In Tucson, because undercover informants had secretly recorded conversations between sanctuary workers, tape recorders—an anthropological tool of the trade—symbolized surveillance. Because of this symbolism, I did not tape-record sanctuary gatherings and, in Tucson, generally transcribed interviews from notes rather than recordings.[13] I also avoided noting potentially sensitive or incriminating information (such as the details of particular crossings), a decision that, particularly in Tucson, limited the material that I could consider when analyzing the movement. Finally, I do not refer to people I interviewed as "informants" because, within the movement, this frequently used anthropological term connoted infiltration, deception, and betrayal.

While my commitment to the movement and desire to allay participants' concerns led me to position myself as a sanctuary worker, self-interest and the norms of ethnographic research led me to situate myself outside the movement. Though my credentials as a member of the movement gave me access to some participants, my status as an *outsider* opened doors to others. For example, one sanctuary congregation member who was somewhat critical of the movement agreed to be interviewed precisely because she saw me as uninvolved and therefore unbiased. Participants sometimes assumed that my portrayal of the movement would be more accurate than one written by one of them. The pastor of All Saints told me, "We need people like you to come in and tell us what you think. We need observers to do analysis, because we're too close to it." It was during interviews that I saw myself most as a nonparticipant, in part because these constituted "research" more unambiguously than my other fieldwork activities but also because my authority to question movement members derived from being outside the movement (see Pratt 1986). During one interview, when a participant who had told me about his own religious background asked me to describe mine, I actually turned off the tape recorder, placing my own life outside the bounds of the "research data." However, even during interviews, there were moments when I ceased to be a researcher and became a participant. For example, Anya Fischer, an East Bay participant whom I interviewed, interrupted a description of her sanctuary work to ask:

*Anya:* I'm really not up right now on what is going on with the [EBSC] group. Tell me!

*Susan:* Do you want me to tell you what's happening?

*Anya:* Yeah, I really do!

*Susan:* Well, one thing that's happening right now is ...

Anya's query had taken me by surprise. Since I had previously been the questioner, I hadn't expected her to question me, and I found it necessary to verify that she had done so. I'd been a researcher interviewing a sanctuary worker, when suddenly our roles shifted and she became a *former* participant asking me, a *current* participant, for an update on the movement. I, the "interviewer" was actually somewhat better informed than my "informant."

The differences between myself and those whose lives I was analyzing were further blurred by the fact that, just as I was both a participant and a researcher, so too were many sanctuary workers both movement members and intellectuals. In contrast to the anthropological norm that, while in the field, the ethnographer is the sole expert in social theory, most of the people I interviewed were college graduates and many held master's or doctoral degrees. Those who had written dissertations had already completed the qualifying exercise that I was in the midst of, and thus they had a greater claim to the production of academic—if not specifically ethnographic—truth than did I. For example, Charles O'Brien, whom I interviewed in Tucson, was a scholar and academician who had written extensively about Latin America. My interview with him began when he asked, "Well, what more do you want to know about me besides what I've written? " During interviews, I sometimes found sanctuary workers using the kind of language that I had been accustomed to hearing during graduate seminars. Carl Fonde invoked a "Hobbesian notion of political," cited the political theorist Karl Schmidt, explained the Greek root of the word "political," and critiqued positivist definitions of the law. Gloria Murdock defined conversion using Paulo Freire's notion of praxis, Larry Hauffen cited author Jim Wallis to criticize the institutional church, and Samuel Durand used Scott Peck's philosophy of evil to analyze his congregation's reaction to his sanctuary work. The "research subjects" whom I was interviewing were actually quoting authors I had read for the university examinations that had constituted my official preparation for Ph.D. research.

Because the sanctuary movement had more than its share of scholars and theologians, I found that I was not only a researcher but also a pupil. The fact that I was a young student interviewing people who, in most cases, were older than I was and who, in some instances, were clergy or other professionals made me feel less an expert than a novice. When I interviewed Jamie Porter, a Tucson professor and sanctuary worker, at his campus office, he began the interview by asking me to describe my theoretical perspective. As I discussed recent anthropological interest in the political implications of culture, I found myself in the familiar role of "student" meeting with "professor" during office hours. Similarly, when I asked Joanna Spoakes, an East Bay Quaker, several abstract questions about her religious beliefs, Joanna did not simply assume that I, as a researcher, had a good reason for seeking this knowledge. Instead she challenged me, querying, "Why are you asking that? What does that have to do with sanctuary?" The incident that placed me most fully in the position of a novice occurred when Simon Portnoy, pastor of a Tucson sanctuary church, redefined not only my research but also my anthropological career in movement discourse. After I asked him to explain which aspects of U.S. society would have to change in order for (as he advocated) the kingdom of God to come into fruition, Simon commented, "Some people at my church are yuppies. They were baptized and confirmed, but they don't serve the kingdom of God. You either serve the kingdom or you don't. I'll give you an example. If you get your Ph.D., work to be powerful and influential within anthropology, and pursue your career, then you're not serving the kingdom." As Simon defined my career goals as failing to serve the kingdom of God, our identities shifted from "ethnographer" and "research subject" to "religious believer" and "pastor."

Though I sometimes felt uncomfortable defining myself as an anthropologist, only a few movement participants openly questioned the value of my research. For instance, when I called David Hoffman, a San Francisco volunteer, to ask for an interview, he initially balked. David said, "I'd like to help you, but I give lots of time to volunteer work, so I like to limit the interviews I do to things that will have a practical effect, like newspapers, because then you get the publicity." Similarly, in a comment that she later reassured me was not aimed at me but that I nevertheless took to heart, Katherine Baerman of First Church said that she admired "people who *have* put themselves on the line and have had to suffer criminal consequences. ... They have done what they believed. And instead of talking about it, or maybe writing a paper about it, *did* it. *Those* are the kind of people I want to know." However, while movement members esteemed action, they also valued analysis. The pastor of All Saints told me repeatedly that sanctuary workers needed people like me to make sense of the movement. Peter Lockhart, a monk who volunteered with EBSC, commented flatteringly that my work would, in its own way, support participants' efforts to shape their futures. He told me, "I'm really interested in your dissertation. You're making history. Liberation theology teaches that we are agents of history, laying stone upon stone. You can provide a reflection and understanding about what is happening." Most people I interviewed seemed to appreciate the opportunity to reflect on their sanctuary work, and many asked to see my analysis when it was finished. I hope that this representation of the movement does justice to their trust.

## Notes

1. Although those familiar with the sanctuary movement will easily recognize its identity, I have chosen to use a pseudonym for this and all congregations mentioned. I also use pseudonyms for sanctuary workers, Central Americans, and others connected to the movement. The only exception to this convention is when I draw on published material from newspaper articles, trial transcripts, and other sources. For example, in Chapter 7, which analyzes the 1985–1986 Tucson sanctuary trial, I refer to defendants, attorneys, government informants, and so on by their real names.

2. I use the past tense not because the movement is over, but rather, in contrast to the "ethnographic present" of many cultural accounts, to situate my representation of the movement in historical time.

3. I am not using "middle class" in an analytical sense. Rather, I use this term because this is how sanctuary workers characterized their own privileged positions as distinct from those of "the poor" or "the oppressed."

4. Since I completed fieldwork, another four East Bay congregations have declared themselves sanctuaries and joined EBSC, making for a current total of thirty participating congregations.

5. "TECHO"—not an acronym—is Spanish for "roof."

6. I would like to thank Lisa Amsterdam for inventing this pseudonym. "Aron Kodesh" means "Holy Ark" and refers to the ark where the Ten Commandments were kept within the tabernacle from 955 B.C.E. to 586 B.C.E. This ark was in the Holy of Holies, the inner sanctuary that was the spiritual center of the tent of meeting where congregations came together for ritual and worship.

7. For a description of the Jewish Renewal Movement, see Waskow 1983.

8. This joke worked because praising a sexist statement was extremely out of character for both the pastor and the young man.

9. In contrast to resource mobilization theorists, who analyze movements from the perspective of movement leaders (Miller 1983; Pichardo 1988), I examine sanctuary from the perspective of average participants. I chose this perspective in part to analyze the culture of the movement and in part because sanctuary was a grass-roots, decentralized movement. The movement did have leaders who were more influential, better informed, more closely connected to regional, national, and international networks, and more likely to speak publicly for the movement, but leadership was also relative to individuals' positions within the movement. The most influential member of a congregation's sanctuary committee might only be somewhat influential within the local sanctuary community and even more peripheral within regional and national networks. I was interested in the views and experiences of the entire range of sanctuary workers, not merely the organizers. Therefore, rather than distinguishing binarily between leaders and rank and file, I term all movement members "participants" and, when quoting particular individuals, usually specify their positions within the movement (e.g., EBSC Steering Committee representative, Task Force member, member of All Saints).

10. Anthropological concern over the politics of representation arose during the 1970s as, due to the 1960s protests, ethnographers became increasingly aware and critical of social inequality (see, for example, Nash 1979; Godelier 1977; O'Laughlin 1975; Reiter 1975; Rosaldo and Lamphere 1974) and the relationships between imperialism, colonialism, and the anthropological project (e.g., Asad 1973; Deloria 1969; Said 1979). By portraying ethnographers as positioned subjects rather than omniscient scientists and by including the voices of the people being represented, "reflexive" ethnographies attempt to undermine the hierarchy between investigator and investigated (e.g., Clifford 1988; Clifford and Marcus 1986; Rosaldo 1989; Abu-Lughod 1986; Narayan 1989).

11. For example, if I wrote that most participants in the movement were not religious, this conclusion could be cited in court to undermine participants' claims that sanctuary merited the First Amendment protection accorded religious practices.

12. I answered that I would circulate a copy of my dissertation before I submitted the final copy to my advisers at Stanford. Four movement members read a draft of the manuscript, and their comments were incorporated into the dissertation and this book. Additionally, I gave copies of my dissertation to EBSC, the Task Force, and the Tucson office of the American Friends Service Committee. I invited movement members to submit critiques of my dissertation, but no one responded to this invitation.

13. In the East Bay, interviews were tape-recorded unless the participant requested otherwise. In Tucson, I only sought to record interviews with well-known individuals who spoke publicly about their sanctuary work and who had, presumably, already come to the government's attention. In other cases, I did not even bring a tape recorder to the interview.

# PART ONE

# CROSSING BORDERS

# 2

## Constructing a Movement

*Sanctuary was a moment of Kairos, ... [an] invasion of time. If time is going on like this, suddenly, Kairos swoops in! It's the moment when everything comes together, the crisis. Suddenly Americans were saying, "Oh my goodness! All this slaughter has something to do with us!" And the Jews were saying, "[Such and such] airline is sending people back to the same kind of thing that Hitler was doing in the Holocaust!" I remember that during the [Tucson sanctuary] symposium, I went to the synagogue [where the symposium was being held], and I said to the rabbi, ... "Well, Rabbi, all your symbols are coming together." And they were! The Exodus, the holy candles burning in the temple—*
—Simon Portnoy, former pastor of a Tucson sanctuary church[1]

By 1986, when I first approached the manager of the East Bay Sanctuary Covenant office in Berkeley to inquire about volunteering, sanctuary workers were regularly bringing undocumented Central Americans into the United States, sending delegations of international observers to Honduran refugee camps, and organizing events attended by members of sanctuary congregations, covenants, and task forces from around the United States. However, only six years earlier, the praxis, philosophy, and networks that came to be known as "sanctuary" did not exist. This movement was produced through a complex interplay of historical circumstances, cultural processes, and individual choices. During the early 1980s, events led certain individuals and communities to devise a set of practices, meanings, and relationships that would counter U.S. policies on Central America and immigration. To do so, participants drew on and reformulated their cultural knowledge, personal experiences, and social networks. Once created, the resulting oppositional subculture was continually reproduced and reshaped as new volunteers joined, additional congregations declared, and sanctuary workers responded to and precipitated historical events and authorities' actions. By its very existence, the sanctuary movement altered the social and historical landscape out of which it emerged.

Because they regard social movements as analytically distinct from other kinds of action, the two currently dominant approaches in social movement theory—resource mobilization theory in the United States (McCarthy and Zald 1973; Tilly 1978; Gamson 1975; Oberschall 1973; McAdam 1982; Piven and Cloward 1977;

Jenkins 1983) and the new social movement literature in Europe (Melucci 1989; Touraine 1981; Pizzorno 1978; Castells 1983)—explain the emergence of social protest in terms that ignore or misconstrue the cultural changes wrought by this process. Because they believe that, despite the constancy of oppression, resistance is rare, resource mobilization theorists focus on the conditions that enable people to protest. These theorists reason that social movements arise when either the costs of action decrease or the benefits of action increase. Constructing a movement, then, consists of *mobilizing* the resources—people, money, meeting halls, institutions, organizations, persuasive symbols—that allow aggrieved groups to recruit participants, win public support, and confront authorities. Because they view mobilization as a rational process aimed toward achieving a particular end, resource mobilization theorists assume that the content of a social movement consists of strategies, such as holding sit-ins, organizing demonstrations, or calling for a boycott, designed to strengthen the movement and achieve its goals. Moreover, according to this perspective, organizing a movement is a first step toward the end goal of effecting social change (or, if one is, for example, opposing the construction of a nuclear power plant, the end goal of maintaining the status quo). By comparing movements' goals, strategies, and outcomes, resource mobilization theorists hope to determine the "laws" that govern the process and outcome of protest.

Though it effectively illuminates the strategic side of collective organizing, resource mobilization theory obscures the cultural innovation that takes place when individuals devise methods of protest. If resistance—which is not limited to organized movements—is an ongoing facet of social life, then explaining the emergence of social movements entails analyzing not only the *mobilization* of resources needed to protest but also the *improvisation* through which actors create the meanings, practices, and organizational forms that constitute a protest movement. These meanings, practices, and organizational forms cannot be reduced to strategies, because protestors not only pursue long-term goals but also seek to enact internally what they seek externally (Evans and Boyte 1986). By defining change as an end result rather than an ongoing process, resource mobilization theorists overlook the ways that protest reshapes the social and historical conditions in which it arises. Finally, abstracting movements from their social and historical contexts[2] obscures the ways that movements are continually renegotiated in relation to changing conditions.[3]

In contrast to resource mobilization theory, the new social movement literature paints a historically and culturally contextualized portrait of protest. Contending that movements flourish during particular historical periods, new social movement analysts address themselves to the forms of protest that have arisen in Western societies since the 1960s. Rather than treating movements as entities obeying universal principles of movement behavior, these researchers view protest as a response to particular social and historical developments. To understand the changes enacted by social protest, the new social movement literature examines not only movements' long-term strategies but also their efforts to embody what they seek. Such attention to the ways that social movements alter participants' relationships, activities, and lifestyles captures the cultural changes that occur in the process of protest. However, because they distinguish social movements from other kinds of social action, new social movement theorists fail to grasp the pervasive and ongoing nature of social change in society as a whole. For example, Alberto Melucci, one of the foremost new social movement theorists, has argued that unlike other social phenomena, "[movement] actions violate the boundaries or tolerance limits of a system, thereby pushing the system beyond the range of variations that it can tolerate without altering its structure" (1989:29). Melucci implies that social systems are generally unchanging and that they are only redefined when social movements arise. He writes, "Without the challenges posed by these movements, complex societies would be incapable of asking questions about meaning; they would entrap themselves in the apparently neutral logic of institutional procedures" (1989:11). This argument misrepresents the relationship between social movements and society by portraying the protest as a means of rejuvenating an otherwise static institutional structure.

In contrast to both resource mobilization theory and the new social movement literature, I regard protest not as a unique social phenomenon to be analyzed differently from other events but rather as a more organized and observable version of processes that are ongoing within society. If social action, both within and outside of organized protest, continually reconstructs and reproduces society (Bourdieu 1977; Foucault 1980a, 1980b; Giddens 1976), then examining the emergence and development of social movements is no different from analyzing other instances of cultural innovation and social reproduction. Actors protest by improvising on their cultural repertoires[4] in response to and in order to influence historical events. Creating a protest movement is, as resource mobilization theorists have noted, an instrumental process, as movements *are* designed to bring about change. In the course of pursuing long-term goals, however, movements also create social forms that carry out changes in the here and now. These social forms, which constitute the content of a movement, are shaped by unfolding events, the ways that activists encounter or experience a particular injustice (Thompson 1963; Nash 1979; Kaplan 1977), and participants' social positions, cultural knowledge, creativity, and notions of justice. The process of creating a movement continues as long as the movement exists, as the choices that people make in particular social and historical conditions alter those conditions and thus affect subsequent actions. Like all social action, creating a movement incrementally changes society and makes history.

## Founding a Movement

The paths through which the sanctuary movement was constructed are many, and here I will retrace only two: those of Berkeley, California, and Tucson, Arizona. These two paths have a common beginning. In March 1980 the Salvadoran Archbishop Oscar Romero was assassinated while giving Communion. The blood of the man who had promised to be the voice of the voiceless mingled with the blood of Christ, spilled from the chalice. The following December, four religious women from the United States were raped and murdered, allegedly by members of the Salvadoran National Guard. Suddenly, U.S. churches turned their attention to El Salvador, a country that most U.S. citizens could not place on a map. While newspapers in the United States filled with stories of death squad killings, missionaries stationed in Central America relayed tales of horror to their sponsoring congregations. U.S. church people began to learn about their counterparts in Central America. They learned that Archbishop Romero, who had been chosen for his conservative views, had undergone a conversion when one of his priests, Father Rutilio Grande, was killed for working with the poor. They learned that catechists in the Guatemalan highlands were being assassinated for organizing indigenous groups. They learned that the church in El Salvador was undergoing a radical transformation by identifying with the suffering of the poor, even unto death.

The transformation of the Central American church was located within the social movements of the 1960s. Vatican II (1963–1965) created broad changes in the Roman Catholic church, making Mass more accessible to believers and adopting a preferential option for the poor. In 1968, a bishops' conference in Medellín, Colombia, carried out the principles of Vatican II by advocating the formation of Christian base communities to discuss the political, human, doctrinal, and religious issues faced by Catholics. As a result of Medellín,

> Many priests and nuns at the local level changed dramatically. They had begun the seventies ministering to the poor and obeying the instructions of their bishops. They soon learned that neither their commitment to the campesinos nor the principles of Medellín could be carried out without political action. When peaceful attempts to obtain food, land, and other rights ended without change or in repression, the clerics moved to nonviolent opposition then to supporting violence. A religious commitment to ameliorate poverty could end in a political, even an armed, commitment to oppose the government (LaFeber 1984:222–223).

During the late 1970s and early 1980s, armed conflict and mounting human rights abuses in El Salvador and Guatemala produced an exodus to other Central American nations, Mexico, and the United States. Civil war made average people in El Salvador and Guatemala choose between persecution and exile. For example, Clemente Rivera, a young Salvadoran whom I met in Berkeley, told me that he fled El Salvador out of fear that both sides in the conflict would consider his political neutrality support for the enemy. An eighteen-year-old Salvadoran woman, whose testimony is quoted in Chapter 6, came to the United States after her father was brutally murdered and her neighbors began disappearing. Central

Americans whom I met while assisting political asylum applicants in Tucson often spoke of hiding from death squads or guerrillas by moving across the country
or sleeping at friends' homes. If discovered, these people had to flee abruptly, leaving children, siblings, and parents behind. Thousands came to the United States
in search of safety.

In the United States, Central Americans were to encounter individuals and
communities that, in diverse ways and to different extents, were heir to a tradition
of religious activism. For example, Virginia Quillen, a seventy-nine-year-old
Quaker who would become an EBSC office volunteer in 1987, had worked with
the Red Cross during World War II and then dedicated her life to pacifism. Anya
Fischer, who would raise the issue of sanctuary at her synagogue in 1985, had
spent the 1960s, "getting establishment white-folk types down to the South to
serve as a presence, to maybe help curtail the worst abuses, ... [to] visit the pris-
ons where the civil rights workers were being arrested and held, to at least cut
down on the brutality that was going on there." A Tucson minister credited with
being one of the founders of the sanctuary movement in 1982 had been "on the
streets when [Martin Luther] King was shot, and then from 1967 to 1970, [when]
the cities were on fire." Paul Dedona, who would become a member of First
Church's Sanctuary Committee in 1982, had, as a boy, gone door-to-door with his
minister father collecting money for a *New York Times* ad to protest the Christmas
bombings at Hanoi. During the late 1970s and early 1980s, religious volunteers
supported such causes as nuclear disarmament, farm workers' rights, Witness for
Peace, divestment, and aid for the homeless. The development of liberation theology in Latin America also influenced U.S. religious activism, creating a philosophy summarized in the slogan, "If you want peace, work for justice." Given this
background, it was but a small step for religious workers to apply their commitment to social justice to the situation of Central American refugees.

The paths leading to sanctuary in Berkeley and in Tucson diverged during the
summer of 1980, when a group of Salvadorans was found in an Arizona desert
where they had been abandoned by their *coyote*.[5] Half had perished. Several
church groups in Arizona set out to aid the survivors, only to find the U.S. Immigration and Naturalization Service preparing to deport them to El Salvador. Such
deportations were beyond the experience of church workers who had aided Cuban, Southeast Asian, Indonesian, and Chilean refugees with the *support* of the
U.S. government. Patty Sherwood, a religious worker who had initially assumed
that aiding Central Americans would be like previous church refugee work, recalled discovering

> the difference between a "refugee" and a "refugee." Before, I'd thought of a refugee
> as someone who is seeking shelter, but after working with the Central Americans, I
> became aware that it's a legal status. [Unlike Salvadorans and Guatemalans,] the
> Vietnamese and Laotians that we worked with were people that had been processed,
> and who had a stamp of approval from the U.S. government.

The Salvadorans abandoned in the desert, combined with the assassination of Archbishop Romero, alerted Tucson community groups to the emergency unfolding along the border. The Manzo Area Council—a community organization that had formed during the War on Poverty and had aided the abandoned Salvadorans—began noticing Central Americans among its undocumented clients. In spite of being under government scrutiny for helping "illegals," Manzo began to take on political asylum cases. At the same time, two Tucson clergy concerned about the violence in Central America organized weekly prayer vigils in front of the Tucson Federal Building and invited the congregations that made up the Tucson Ecumenical Council (TEC) to attend. Those who accepted this invitation eventually organized a Task Force on Central America with the TEC's sponsorship. A minister who was involved in these events described the relationship that developed between Manzo, these churches, and the INS: "In those days, the INS would let people out on O.R. [own recognizance] if they had a letter written on church stationery saying that the church would be responsible for people and would provide social services. So that was the relationship that we developed. Manzo would do the legal work, and the churches would provide social services."

Several months after Ronald Reagan's January 1981 inauguration, the INS ended its policy of releasing detainees who were backed by churches. At the same time, Manzo traced several clients to the El Centro detention center, only to discover some 200 Central Americans detained in deplorable conditions. Participants from Manzo, the vigils, and the Task Force met to address this situation. A minister present at the meeting related:

> TEC had decided to form a Task Force to deal with the situation of the Central Americans. … So, a crazy bunch of people at that meeting decided to mount an enormous effort to bond out the people who were in detention. Within a short period of time, we had raised something like $30,000 for bond money, and folks put up their homes for the bonds. … I think that we bonded out fourteen people in one day. … We found that we were responsible for a legal aid project, for raising bonds, and for social services for people who were bonded out.

Through their bail-bonding work, church workers acquired firsthand knowledge of Central American refugees' suffering and of the obstacles in the political asylum process. One overworked Tucson minister was reluctant to join the bail-bonding effort until he remembered how boatloads of Jews were returned to Nazi Germany. He decided to volunteer at El Centro: "I was working typing the English into the forms, and as I did it, I was getting the story of the people. … When I heard the personal stories of the Central Americans, I got hooked. And that's what happened to the other volunteers as well." A TEC member recalled that the bail-bonding process was accompanied by an amazing fund-raising effort that, using property as collateral, produced approximately $1 million for bonds within two weeks. The euphoria over such successes faded, however, when paralegals returned to El Centro the following week only to learn that 200 more Central Americans were in detention.[6]

During fall 1981, Tucson church workers met with other southwestern religious and legal groups and discovered that the obstacles in the political asylum process were widespread and systematic. This meeting revealed that the INS was separating families and telling one spouse that the other had signed deportation papers. Detained Central Americans were instructed to sign papers in English because "everyone does," only to find themselves on a plane headed for El Salvador the following day. Salvadorans and Guatemalans were consistently being denied political asylum around the nation. Bond increases—rising from $500 to $1,000 and then to $5,000—drained sources of bond money. Legal workers reported INS harassment during efforts to represent Salvadorans and Guatemalans. A minister who attended the regional meeting recalled, "It was helpful to know that we weren't crazy. We thought at first that what we were experiencing was a strange, isolated situation of some red-necked administrator, but we discovered that everyone had had the same experiences."

Even as this meeting concluded, events in Tucson were proceeding toward sanctuary on yet another front. In 1981, a Tucson Quaker who had tried to assist a detained Salvadoran hitchhiker had also encountered obstacles in the political asylum process. After bonding out a number of refugees, this Quaker concluded that the best service religious workers could offer Central Americans was to help them evade detention in the first place. This man explained his reasoning in a January 1982 statement: "The most urgent need of the vast majority of Salvadoran refugees is to avoid capture. Actively asserting the right to aid fugitives from terror means doing it—not just preaching at a government that is capturing and deporting them, not just urging legislation that might help future refugees" (Corbett 1986:29) . To carry out this work, the Quaker organized the Tucson refugee support group (Trsg) along with other Quakers and members of a goat-milking cooperative to which he belonged. During a 1988 interview, this man recalled his early refugee work:

> During that first summer that I was involved, I was simply going down to the border, meeting refugees, going to the prison with [a Mexican priest], and then, many of the refugees, until they had somewhere else to go, would stay in the apartment there at the [my] house. So, it was very much a catch-as-catch-can operation. The goat-milking cooperative ... tended to be a lot of the support system.

Out of these historical circumstances, prior activism, and preexisting networks, Tucson volunteers arrived at the idea of sanctuary. Confronted with Central Americans showing the marks of torture and telling horrific tales of persecution, religious workers along the U.S.-Mexico border concluded that these immigrants were clearly refugees entitled to safe haven in the United States, regardless of INS policy. Volunteers' sources of bond money were exhausted, yet detention centers continued to fill and Central Americans continued to be deported. The minister who had recalled the boatloads of Jews fleeing Nazism explained how he and others decided that what they were doing to aid Central Americans was insufficient:

> We did everything that we could think of to stop the deportations. Increasingly, people knew what the true story was, and they learned what was happening in these countries. We wondered what we could do to stem the flow. Because if a legal office ... is *all* that we do—and don't misunderstand me, I think that it's important—but if it's *all* that we do, then the conditions that cause people to flee from their country won't change. ...
>
> What we *were* doing wasn't getting anywhere. We realized that number one, when we had had firsthand experience with real live refugees, our own lives and our understandings had changed. Since that's how we'd been converted, we thought that it might work for others as well. ... They could always dismiss us as bleeding hearts, or naive, or liberals, or "Oh, they're just church people," or whatever. But they couldn't dismiss the refugees who told about their own experiences. ...
>
> The other thing was that we were a people with a history and a theology and so we turned to our religion as a source, and we discovered the very old idea of sanctuary.

Meanwhile, a group of clergy in Berkeley had independently made a similar discovery. The pastors of six congregations located near the University of California were holding a weekly Bible study on the lectionary readings that were the basis of their sermons. As they studied the Old Testament books of the Prophets, they became increasingly convinced that God calls his followers to do justice. Galvanized by the deaths of Archbishop Romero, the four nuns, and the Salvadorans abandoned in the desert, the Bible study group began to read about deportations and human rights violations. Bible verses such as the following leapt out at the participants:

> You must not molest the stranger or oppress him, for you lived as strangers in the land of Egypt (Exodus 22:21).

> When a stranger sojourns with you in your land, you shall do him no wrong. The stranger who sojourns with you shall be to you as the native among you, and you shall love him as yourself; for you were strangers in the land of Egypt; I am the Lord your God (Leviticus 19:33–34).

When the lectionary group asked itself how to respond to human rights abuses in Central America, members drew on their collective experiences. One minister reminded the group that during the Vietnam War, his church had declared itself a sanctuary for conscientious objectors who deserted the armed forces. Like Tucson congregations, Bay Area churches had resettled refugees from Argentina, South Africa, Hungary, and Vietnam. Members of First Church had housed transients during the 1960s, although this activity was not defined as sanctuary work. Rev. Henry Carson, a former pastor of First Church who was not part of the lectionary group, recalled his own experiences housing transients:

> You'd get a call at, say, six or seven at night, and [the caller would] say, "Can you house someone tonight?" And I'd say, "Sure, send them out." I would guess that my wife and I had someone in our home three or four nights a week. And then they had also what they called a special list, and that was those of us that, when we got a call and they said, "We have a special tonight," we didn't ask questions. And that was for our own protection. Because it could be an AWOL soldier or sailor; it could be an underage child who'd run away from home.

The lectionary group began to consider whether the tradition of sanctuary could be applied to Central American refugees. Shortly thereafter, a member of the lectionary group received a letter from Tucson.

In 1981, the Tucson Quaker had asked All Saints Church to consider housing undocumented Central Americans. Until this time, the Quaker and his colleagues had been bringing undocumented Central Americans across the border and housing them at his home, while TEC members were helping detainees apply for asylum, obtain bail-bond money, and, upon their release, secure food, shelter, and other social services. The Quaker's query posed a difficult dilemma because, unlike political asylum applicants, who were authorized to stay in the United States until their cases were adjudicated, the Central Americans whom the Quaker had aided lacked legal status. For this reason, extending its services to Central Americans who had not applied for asylum would involve All Saints in activities that the U.S. government defined as illegal. All Saints' pastor described his congregation's response:

> I had to confront the question, "Is this a correct ethical response to the situation?" Because I knew that if I was going to present it to the [church's administrative body], I would have to make up my own mind about it. And because I knew the dilemma of the refugees, their suffering, their fear, and what INS policy was, I decided that what he was doing was good Christian work, and the [administrative body] agreed. Their reasoning was based on Christian hospitality. We decided that we had always helped people before on the basis of human need, and that we'd never asked anyone for their I.D.'s, or green cards.

Shortly after All Saints agreed to the Quaker's request, several Tucson clergy learned that the INS planned to indict them if they continued to cross and house undocumented Central Americans. Wanting neither to stop nor to be arrested, the clergy decided to seek public support. All Saints once more faced a difficult decision, as its pastor related:

> A group of people from TEC and Manzo met here to talk about the message and to decide how to respond. ... We had gotten a letter from a Lutheran pastor in L.A.

who'd had a Salvadoran run into his church, and then be dragged out in handcuffs. We saw that maybe sanctuary was the appropriate tradition for what we were already doing, and decided that one church ought to declare itself a public sanctuary. We then thought, "Now, which one?" and I found everyone in the room looking at me.

All Saints voted overwhelmingly in favor of public sanctuary and, using the mailing list from the 1981 gathering of southwestern legal and religious groups, invited other congregations working with Central American refugees to do likewise. On March 24, 1982, the second anniversary of the assassination of Archbishop Romero, All Saints, five of the East Bay congregations, and a number of other churches in the United States declared themselves sanctuaries for Central American refugees. A Catholic layworker described the Tucson declaration:

I remember a very cold day, being there ... in front of the church at the time the news media wanted to be there for the declaration. The front of the church had a table out front where the media had microphones. ... There were different things said by different people, and some of them included scripture, but not a real prayer service. It was really an announcement. There was an undocumented person there in a bandanna that was with us so he couldn't be recognized.

Like All Saints, the five East Bay churches that declared sanctuary underwent a process of study and reflection before making their decision. Unlike All Saints, however, they immediately formed a covenant to support the two churches among them that actually received refugees—including one of the survivors of the Arizona desert tragedy—into church protection. The five congregations declared sanctuary by publicly affirming a written covenant statement and holding a worship service, a procession, and a celebration. A minister whose church received refugees described the proceedings:

We decided that we should establish some achievable goals. ... We said that they [the refugees] would stay in the church building for five days, from Wednesday until Sunday. And during those five days we would try to do certain things. We would try to get 500 letters written to Ronald Reagan. We would try to get 100 volunteers to go over and monitor asylum hearings in San Francisco. We would try to get ... twenty people who would be trained to do paralegal work and help in filling out asylum applications, and I think it was $5,000 we wanted to raise. And we did all of those things in those five days. We did everything.

And then we had a procession after church of all of the five churches ... and we celebrated that we were doing this; we were involved in this together.

With the March 1982 declarations, sanctuary—which was not yet a movement—was created. Through a specific set of historical circumstances, religious volunteers had improvised on preexisting practices (such as refugee resettlement), knowledge (such as liberation theology), and institutions (such as the lec-tionary Bible study group), first to provide legal and social services to detained Central Americans, then to aid undocumented refugees, and finally to declare their congregations sanctuaries for Central American refugees. Though partici-pants did mobilize preexisting practices, knowledge, and institutions in order to oppose the deportation of Central Americans, they also reshaped these forms to create new actions, meanings, and structures. A close look at the resulting con-structs reveals that these products of history were also history in the making.

## Covenant and Community

When they organized the sanctuary movement, religious volunteers were re-sponding to the social and historical conditions in which they were positioned. At the same time, producing the movement *re*positioned participants and thus al-tered these conditions. As a result, the forms that participants created were simul-taneously products of and departures from the movement's context. In the East Bay, members of the lectionary Bible study created a covenant that embodied their sense of functional legitimacy, congregational authority, and organizational identity. In Tucson, the individuals involved in border crossings formed a com-munity in which personal networks and the urgency of saving Central Americans' lives took precedence over institutional arrangements. While covenant and com-munity were both vehicles for ending human rights abuses in Central America and in the United States, each also constituted a unique cultural construct that deserves attention in its own right. For, by creating the practices, meanings, and relationships that made up each of these constructs, volunteers reshaped the so-cial and historical circumstances out of which the movement arose.

After the public sanctuary declarations, the five congregations that comprised EBSC formed a Steering Committee that met monthly for a potluck dinner, dis-cussion, and report. Almost immediately, EBSC took on a new project. In order to protect Central American refugees living in UN-sponsored camps in Honduras from incursions by Salvadoran and Honduran armed forces, Bay Area religious workers agreed to maintain a continuous international presence in the camps.[7] Every two weeks, a new delegation replaced its predecessor. Meanwhile, in the United States, each monthly meeting of the EBSC Steering Committee featured the latest delegation's slide show and report, which served as an orientation for the upcoming delegation. In this way, numerous sanctuary workers traveled to the camps, and EBSC congregations were continually informed about conditions in Central America. Moreover, delegation members gave presentations to a vari-ety of groups and congregations in the Bay Area, which resulted in new sanctuary declarations. By the time I began fieldwork, EBSC had grown from the five origi-nal churches to twenty-six congregations and groups, and the Steering Commit-tee had elected officers, created subcommittees, and opened an office run by five staff people and some twenty to thirty volunteers.

As EBSC grew, the covenant established by the original five sanctuary congregations remained EBSC's organizational structure. Following their predecessors' examples, congregations that wished to join the movement publicly affirmed a written covenant to provide sanctuary to Central American refugees. Congregations that wished to declare themselves sanctuaries but objected to the original statement's wording were invited to write their own versions. These covenant statements created and defined EBSC in a legal sense. Steering Committee representatives located authority in member congregations rather than in EBSC by limiting themselves to actions implied by their covenant. One Congregation Aron Kodesh member explained:

> We're each representatives of a congregation, and there's no authority over the congregation. The congregation is the top. In a sense, I am on the same authority as [the EBSC director]—even though she does a lot more work and gets into it more deeply—because structurally, the congregation is the unit of operation. So we're all independent of one another, and no one has any authority over anyone else.

Because EBSC was a covenant of *congregations,* sanctuary committees at undeclared congregations participated in EBSC as affiliate rather than full members (a distinction with little practical but much philosophical significance). Similarly, in order to preserve the religious implications of being a covenant, a participating refugee organization and a student sanctuary coalition were also made affiliate rather than full members.

By affirming a shared commitment to Central American refugees while permitting religious diversity, EBSC's covenant structure was able to incorporate synagogues into what had originally been a body of Protestant and Catholic churches. The impetus for East Bay synagogues to join the movement originated in Tucson in 1984 when All Saints' pastor began to encourage local congregations, including one synagogue, to declare themselves sanctuaries. The Tucson synagogue initially refused, but its rabbi raised the issue a second time. The rabbi related:

> I decided that this was the most important issue that everything else depended on, and I prayed to God, I prayed to please let it go through. And I decided that if it didn't pass [the second time], I would give up my rabbinate. So, when Yom Kippur came around, which is one of the most important Jewish holidays, I didn't write a normal sermon, and I didn't speak from notes. I walked away from the pulpit and I preached a sermon facing the congregation eye-to-eye. And the president of the congregation walked out halfway through the sermon. But afterwards, a man came up to me with tears in his eyes, and he said, "Now I know why I belong to a synagogue."

On the second vote, the sanctuary declaration passed by a two-to-one margin.

Several months after the Tucson synagogue declared, Bay Area Jewish activists invited its rabbi to come and speak about his congregation's experience. Karen Hirsch, who attended one of his talks, recalled:

> There was a rabbi from Arizona who came out to speak at a Jewish Community Center near here to over 100 people—it was packed. And there was some refugee who gave testimony. And it was the most *moving* thing. And after that they said, "Whoever wants to help get Jews involved in sanctuary, please come up to the front." So I went. I mean, I was crying, that's how moving it was. He related it all to the Holocaust, and he was a brilliant speaker.

As a result of this rabbi's visit, Jewish sanctuary coalitions formed in San Francisco and in the East Bay. The San Francisco Jewish Sanctuary coalition has continued to exist, whereas the East Bay group disbanded after member synagogues began to join EBSC. Yosef Meyer, an East Bay attorney and activist, helped draft a Jewish Covenant Statement (quoted in the Appendix) that "came out of a place of Jewish consensus; that is to say, that it was something that could be agreed to by all Jews who supported sanctuary, whether or not they were Orthodox, Conservative, Reformed, or *even* if they were secular Jews." By the time Jews joined the movement, EBSC members had renamed themselves the East Bay Sanctuary *Churches,* believing, as a Jewish participant explained, that "it was not a correct term to call a group of people a covenant." However, in 1985, to include its new members, EBSC reverted to its original name, the East Bay Sanctuary Covenant.

The organizational structures created by Tucson activists differed from EBSC in form, philosophy, and focus. Following the 1982 declarations, Tucson sanctuary work continued to center on border crossings and social services for newly arrived refugees. Along with colleagues in other states and nations, Tucson sanctuary workers developed an underground railroad that brought threatened Salvadorans and Guatemalans from Central America through Mexico and into the United States and Canada. A core group of individuals from the Task Force and from the groups that had participated in the Central America vigils and the bail-bonding effort took responsibility for Tucson's portion of the railroad. Though they would eventually conclude that their work enforced U.S. laws granting safe haven to the persecuted, these volunteers initially construed crossings as civil disobedience along the lines of 1960s protest activities. According to one participant, the urgency of early border work precluded the kind of analysis that would enable border workers to conclude that crossing and sheltering undocumented refugees was legal:

> We were living in the midst of a crisis then. There was no planning, and we had no time for reflection about what we were doing. It was literally a moment-to-moment, life-and-death crisis for us. We were *overwhelmed* by the critical situation that people were in and by the numbers of folk that needed our help. ... We would set off each time, lighting a candle and saying a prayer, and thinking that this would be it,

this would be the time when we'd be picked up. Then you'd laugh when you did make it. It's still a source of amazement to me that we were able to do what we did.

Like EBSC, the organizational structures devised by Tucson sanctuary workers were rooted in the history of the local movement. At the time of the 1982 declarations, while East Bay churches were forming a covenant, Tucson sanctuary workers decided that only All Saints would publicly declare itself a sanctuary congregation. That way, they reasoned, if All Saints members were arrested, volunteers from other congregations would still be available to do border work. Responsibility for border crossings fell to the Task Force rather than a congregational body like EBSC. However, early in 1982, the Tucson Ecumenical Council, comprising some forty mainstream congregations, officially endorsed the sanctuary work already being performed by Task Force members, thus granting Tucson sanctuary workers, like their East Bay counterparts, the legitimacy of congregational backing. In addition to the Task Force, other community groups performed sanctuary-related work. Though its services in some ways duplicated those of the Task Force, the Tucson refugee support group (Trsg) continued to exist. The Manzo Area Council handled Central Americans' asylum applications until 1984, when it dissolved owing to lack of funding. Manzo was later replaced by Tucson Ecumenical Council Legal Assistance (TECLA). TECHO, a group that branched off from the Task Force, developed Central American cultural and educational programs. And in 1984, with the encouragement of All Saints' pastor, approximately one dozen Tucson congregations (including the previously mentioned synagogue) declared themselves sanctuaries and organized the Covenant Communities. However, this group, which was meant to follow an organizational model similar to EBSC, was destined to be sidelined: In January 1985, before the group had even defined its purpose, the U.S. government indicted fourteen members of the local movement.

Despite this plethora of organizations, the networks that performed Tucson sanctuary work only partially coincided with this structure. Connections between All Saints' pastor, the priest in charge of the vigils, the Tucson Quaker, and other participants involved in the bail-bonding effort *predated* the organizational structures that eventually developed. From the movement's early days, border work spilled over the bounds of its institutional framework. One Task Force member recalled that at the time of the original declarations:

There were twelve to fifteen of us ... who were going to the Task Force meetings. [Four of us] formed sort of an executive committee, because things were so dynamic that we couldn't wait for the weekly meetings. ... In those days we had no money and there was no staff. ... And when we took actions in between the meetings, we would always report back to the group as a whole and we were held accountable to them.

By the time I began fieldwork in 1987, this informal "executive committee" had ceased to operate, but sanctuary work was still being carried out through personal networks in addition to formal organizations. In Tucson, I found it impossible to neatly categorize participants according to their positions within the movement. Some individuals held multiple positions, a few extremely active volunteers did not participate in any formal group, and key movement figures consulted each other regarding important events, regardless of their formal positions. To arrange interviews, I usually had to work through these personal networks, constructing my identity by naming the movement members who were personal contacts.

These linkages between organizational principles and the contexts in which they were formed suggest that, rather than obeying universal laws, social movements are historically and socially particular. The structures that movement participants create are not only strategies but also products of the events, relationships, and principles that bring them into existence. That constructing a movement is a historical process was further demonstrated in 1985–1986, when eleven sanctuary workers were prosecuted in Tucson, Arizona.

## The Tucson Sanctuary Trial

The January 1985 indictments were the federal government's response to sanctuary work and, in participants' eyes, constituted an effort to repress the movement. When the indictments were issued, sanctuary communities in Tucson, Phoenix, and Nogales discovered that two volunteers who had joined the movement ten months earlier were actually government infiltrators who had used body bugs to secretly record participants' meetings and conversations. Based on information provided by undercover agents, the government brought charges of conspiracy and alien-smuggling against two priests, three nuns, a minister, eight layworkers, and two individuals who were not connected to the movement. Additionally, fifty-eight undocumented Central Americans being assisted by the movement were detained around the country and approximately a hundred citizen and alien unindicted coconspirators were named in the indictment.

The trial, which began in November 1985 and ended in May 1986 with the conviction of eight of the eleven defendants who actually stood trial,[8] had an enormous impact on the Tucson sanctuary community. Local sanctuary supporters threw themselves into defense work. Volunteers attended the trial, housed Central American witnesses subpoenaed by the government, checked the transcripts of the undercover tape recordings for inaccuracies, and organized fund-raising and trial-related events. Congregations took turns hosting weekly ecumenical prayer services and providing lunch for the defendants and their attorneys. Sanctuary workers took advantage of the news media's interest in the trial by organizing press conferences, publishing weekly bulletins containing participants' analyses of the trial, and traveling around the nation to speak about their work. Such publicity attracted new volunteers to the movement. A Phoenix minister whose church had been infiltrated recalled, "Before the indictments, there were two or three of the people on each of the [sanctuary-related] committees, and then when the indictments came, a whole church full of people showed up to do the work."

The trial and the undercover investigation forced Tucson sanctuary workers to rethink their organizational structure and border-crossing procedures. At a 1985 retreat, volunteers reorganized their work in order to protect Central Americans from the kinds of detentions that had taken place at the time of the indictments. Responsibility for the border crossings was transferred from the Task Force, which had been infiltrated, to Trsg. (Eventually, personality and philosophical differences would lead several former Trsg members to form a separate border-crossing group. Due to animosity between the two groups, I chose to work primarily with Task Force and Trsg members, though I did interview several members of the newer group.) Since many of the original border workers had been identified, they had to be replaced by the new volunteers brought in by the trial. A Trsg member observed that, in contrast to the improvised nature of early border crossings, "we now have screening [materials], counseling materials, all sorts of written material to orient people and integrate newcomers, very specific procedures that we go through as we deal with arriving refugees." Another Trsg member reported that, after the indictments, border workers adopted a more restrictive definition of "refugee." She explained, "With the trial, ... we had to look closely at the justification for what we were doing, and we realized that just about the only defense that would work was the notion of the necessity defense." By documenting the desperate straits of those they assisted, border workers hoped to prove that they had had no choice but to aid Central Americans.

Like other sanctuary communities around the United States, EBSC supported the Tucson defendants. On the opening day of the trial, sanctuary workers held a prayer service and took refugees into sanctuary. During the trial, EBSC volunteers held fund-raisers to benefit the National Sanctuary Defense Fund, a group that solicited money for indicted sanctuary workers' legal expenses. Following the verdicts, EBSC members organized a vigil at the local INS office, a reaffirmation service, and a caravan of sanctuary workers driving undocumented Central Americans between San Francisco and Berkeley.[9] The trial and the undercover investigation affected East Bay sanctuary communities, but not as deeply as it had affected the Tucson groups. One EBSC staff member reported that the trial "was the best media push we've ever had. It got a lot more people interested in us. It was a great fund-raising gimmick." Another EBSC member contended that the verdicts had a negative impact on the movement because they undermined the claim that sanctuary work was legal. EBSC was not untouched by the undercover investigation: The office suffered two mysterious break-ins in which thieves disturbed files but ignored valuable office equipment. Lacking arrests, hard evidence of surveillance, and the legal risks of border crossings, however, East Bay participants felt relatively safe from prosecution. During an interview, an EBSC staff member told me, "At first we started to wonder,'Who's an infiltrator among our volunteers?' We wondered about you! You came asking questions. ... And then we thought, 'Well, what have we got to hide?'"

After convicted sanctuary workers were sentenced to probation, participants around the nation reassessed the movement and found that, after four and a half years of work, most Salvadorans and Guatemalans still lacked refugee status in the United States, war and human rights violations continued in El Salvador and Guatemala, and the U.S. government still supported the Salvadoran and Guatemalan governments. After the excitement of the trial, the struggle to change these conditions seemed particularly daunting. Public interest in sanctuary had waned, press coverage had decreased, the movement's focus had became unclear, and growth had slackened. In meeting after meeting, I heard sanctuary workers ask themselves, "What should we do now?" As participants addressed this "lull" in their work, the process of constructing the movement continued. Some sanctuary workers attributed the movement's loss of momentum to increasing institutionalization and therefore sought to reinforce the grass-roots nature of the movement. Others, arguing that it was the *lack* of centralized structures that was preventing the movement from moving forward, proposed organizing the movement on a national level. Throughout this debate, Tucson and East Bay activists adhered to the notions of covenant and community that they had developed early in the movement.

## Institutionalization

Because of local movement history, most sanctuary workers in both Tucson and the East Bay considered institutionalization inimical to grass-roots organizing. In the East Bay, sanctuary workers conceived of themselves as a covenant made up of autonomous congregations that had authorized their members to do sanctuary work. Many East Bay participants feared that institutionalization was divorcing sanctuary work from this congregational base, thus transforming EBSC from a covenant body into a separate organization. By 1987, some of EBSC's publicly declared sanctuary congregations had stopped sending representatives to meetings and, in fact, seemed to participate in the sanctuary movement solely by lending their names to EBSC stationery. Volunteer work had become structured to such a degree that the EBSC office increasingly performed tasks previously done by sanctuary congregations.[10] Moreover, in contrast to media images of sanctuary volunteers housing, transporting, and otherwise providing direct assistance to Central Americans, congregation members, office volunteers, and even EBSC staff members complained during interviews that they lacked direct contact with the refugees they were trying to help. Because Central Americans in the Bay Area numbered, at the time of my research, between 60,000 and 80,000 individuals, the original model of a congregation sheltering a single refugee or family had proven inadequate as a means of social assistance. Instead, congregations donated food, clothing, housing, job opportunities, and money to refugee organizations and social service programs. To reestablish the kind of direct yet oppositional interaction typical of the original sanctuary relationships, East Bay congregations were increasingly turning to accompaniment—strategies for supporting the struggles of Central Americans who had not yet fled their countries. These strategies included opposing U.S. aid to El Salvador, adopting sister parishes in Central America, and accompanying refugees and displaced persons who sought to repatriate or repopulate their lands.

In Tucson, the somewhat chaotic nature of border work, the personal networks through which it was performed, and the local movement's Quaker roots infused the Tucson sanctuary community with a strong antibureaucratic tendency. Nevertheless, like their East Bay colleagues, Tucson sanctuary workers found their movement becoming more institutionalized. As All Saints' pastor explained:

> The primary struggle has been to … find a balance between overorganizing, [between] developing criteria that are almost too bureaucratic, and to keep at the same time the same sense of spiritual ground that we were working from [originally]. … It's a far cry from when we were just dealing with individuals, and folks were living in the backs of cars and in people's backyards.

Despite these concerns, Tucson sanctuary workers prided themselves on being less institutionalized than other segments of the movement. One priest told me succinctly, "Sanctuary leaves bureaucracies in the dust!" and a minister commented, "Institutionalization is at its minimum in those closest to the flow of refugees on a day-to-day basis; [among] the people bringing them across the border, transporting them, seeing to their immediate physical and psychological needs." These antibureaucratic values were manifested in a work mode that one frustrated volunteer termed "a lifestyle more than an office." In contrast to EBSC, where businesslike agendas, motions, schedules, and minute-taking were typical, Task Force meetings usually began when someone pulled out a notepad and said, "Let's see, what will our agenda be?" In November 1987, while gathering for a meeting, Task Force members laughingly accused one women who was writing out a grocery list of "planning in advance." The nature of Tucson sanctuary work often made planning impossible. For example, during a Trsg meeting that I attended, an All Saints congregant called to say that a group of refugees who had spent five days crossing the desert had walked into church during evening choir practice and requested sanctuary. Misunderstandings and delays were so common to border work that one Tucson minister developed a recipe he called "refugee stew" because it could be reheated several times and would still taste good.

Following the 1985–1986 Tucson sanctuary trial, such attitudes toward institutionalization became part of a divisive movement-wide controversy about whether and how to organize the movement on a national level. In the East Bay, proposals for creating a national sanctuary structure produced wrenching debates about how to maximize effectiveness without sacrificing organizational integrity and congregational autonomy. One East Bay volunteer summarized the dilemma: "I think that the real strength of sanctuary is in its grass-roots nature. To lose that is to lose its character. On the other hand, it's hard to translate grass-roots pressures into any real action without any kind of real structure." By 1986, EBSC had joined the South Bay Sanctuary Covenant, the San Francisco Sanctuary Covenant, and other northern California groups in a regional association called the Northern California Sanctuary Covenant (NCSC). In January 1987, NCSC members met to formulate a position on national organizing. An EBSC staff member related the history of this controversy to those present. According to the speaker, Tucson sanctuary work met the immediate needs of refugees-in-transit, while Bay Area sanctuary work helped refugees settle and tell their stories. In Chicago, she added, the movement began before Central Americans arrived in the region, so publicly declared sanctuary congregations had remained without refugees for long periods. The speaker noted that relations between Tucson and Chicago were strained because Chicago had at one time tried to become a national clearinghouse for refugees. Since then, the speaker said, Tucson sanctuary workers had distrusted national organizing.[11] The speaker told the group that a National Sanctuary Communications Council (NSCC), made up of regional delegates, had met since 1985, but that this body had not had decision-making power. She concluded by announcing that in preparation for the next NSCC meeting, the northern California region would have to select five delegates—three North Americans, one Salvadoran, and one Guatemalan.

At this and other meetings and during interviews in the Bay Area and Tucson, I heard impassioned opinions about the pros and cons of creating a national structure. Proponents—who at the time of my research were in the minority in both Tucson and the East Bay—argued that a national structure would enable the movement to take unified action on the political causes that produced refugees in Central America. For example, a Tucson Salvadoran whom I interviewed enthusiastically pointed out that discussion of a moratorium on military aid to El Salvador was slated for an upcoming national sanctuary meeting. At the January 1987 northern California sanctuary meeting, several participants argued that infiltrations, surveillance, and indictments constituted national action *against* the movement, and that sanctuary workers could best fight back with their *own* national actions. Some northern California sanctuary workers were swayed when told that sanctuary communities in other parts of the United States saw national structure as a way of combating their own isolation. Finally, some participants, such as Gloria Murdock of Tucson, argued that refugees were frustrated with North Americans' reluctance to take political action, and that a national structure could respond to such frustrations.

In contrast, proponents of decentralization argued that rather than increasing effectiveness, a national structure would be the nail in the coffin of the sanctuary movement. Many feared that creating a national office, a spokesperson, and a policy-setting national body would undermine the spontaneous, grass-roots, populist character of the movement. Claude Grimshaw, a member of First Church's Sanctuary Committee, wondered if a national structure would transform sanctuary into a public policy pressure group alienated from small groups that formulated their own policies. At a Tucson sanctuary meeting, participants belittled the idea of putting money and energy into maintaining institutional structures rather than meeting refugees' needs. Taking the Tucson sanctuary trial as a lesson, proponents of decentralization argued that creating a national structure would play into the government's hands by giving it an easy target. Finally, just as advocates of national organizing claimed that refugees wanted such structures, critics of further institutionalization argued that Central Americans favored decentralization. A Tucson pastor who deeply opposed national organizing told me, "Another effect of the base community movement has been the grass-roots effort to keep sanctuary at the base and not to organize it nationally in North American style."

Advocates and opponents of national organizing created an impasse at national meetings until both extremes dropped out, and thereafter the process changed drastically. At the January 1987 meeting described above, the northern California region decided that to maintain grass-roots integrity, its delegates would oppose such centralization as a national office and spokespeople but would support an increase in national coordination. EBSC members were willing to participate in regional and national groups as long as these were not policy-setting bodies that would remove authority from the congregations that had covenanted to do sanctuary work together. Other questions also underlaid northern California's opposition to centralization: What about Tucson? Would a national structure create a schism between Tucson and other regions? In April, when northern California's delegates reported on the March NSCC meeting, a delegate told the EBSC Steering Committee, "Basically, the North and East of the United States wanted a strong national structure, and the rest of the country didn't. It's ironic, because we went down there with more negative ideas than positive ones, and we ended up being identified with Tucson." This delegate and others reported that despite an extremely frustrating process during which participants' differing definitions of sanctuary had inhibited communication, the NSCC had decided to form a National Steering Committee made up of three members from each region. News of this form of regional representation spawned a months-long local debate about whether northern California—which had eighty sanctuary congregations, one-sixth of all sanctuary congregations nationwide—should divide into several regions in order to obtain more than three delegates. As one delegate phrased it, should the NSCC be a House of Representatives or a Senate?

This debate was cut short when northern Californians learned that a group of individual sanctuary workers from around the nation had grown frustrated with the NSCC's impotence and had distributed a Call to Sanctuary, which invited those interested in increasing sanctuary's political advocacy to meet in Chicago in July 1987.[12] This meeting—which became known as the Call—abandoned the process of electing regional delegates—a move that the Northern California Sanctuary Covenant Steering Committee feared would violate the principal that sanctuary was the action of communities rather than individuals. At the Call meeting (which I attended), some 150 participants from around the nation spent two days discussing strategies, tactics, and political reality and then almost unanimously voted to create a national organization that would challenge U.S. immigration law, promote accompaniment, create communities of resistance, and form alliances with solidarity groups. Throughout this process, participants celebrated, in the words of one speaker, that "the sanctuary movement *can* make decisions." The Call meeting deliberately avoided the debates that had plagued NSCC meetings—debates over humanitarian versus political action, religious versus secular participation, symptoms versus root causes, consensus versus majority decision making, and diversity versus unity. However, left unclear were the relationships between the Call, the NSCC (several members of which attended the meeting), and well-known Tucson sanctuary workers, conspicuous by their absence.[13]

Two weeks after the Call meeting, I left the East Bay for Tucson, eager to learn the answer to the question, "What about Tucson?" This answer took months in arriving. At a time when East Bay sanctuary leaders were deeply concerned about the future of the NSCC and its relationship to the Call, I was surprised to hear next to nothing about this debate in Tucson. For example, during an interview, a prominent Tucson sanctuary pastor denied that a national organization existed, saying, "The nature of sanctuary has confounded attempts to organize it." Trsg members scoffed at national organizers for wasting money to fly around the United States and for having so little to do that they spent their time organizing meetings. Although a minority supported organizing nationally, most Tucson sanctuary workers whom I interviewed did not. During a presentation on sanctuary, one rabbi made this comment about the Tucson/Chicago split: "When you've brushed the dust off people and learned their names and hugged them in the middle of the desert, it's different from sitting in an office in Illinois discussing the theory of sanctuary." Similarly, a Tucson minister told me, "In Chicago, they've put so much energy into institutionalizing the movement that they're taking steps that have to come from the people themselves. ... If you asked me who is doing the work of the gospel, I'd have to stand with my brothers and sisters in Tucson who are crossing the border to help refugees in need."

When I completed fieldwork in March 1988, questions about national organizing were still very much alive. After leaving Tucson, I learned that at the October 1987 NSCC meeting, the NSCC had merged with the Call group to form an Alliance of Sanctuary Communities (ASC). The Task Force and Trsg were not participating in the ASC, as were EBSC and members of the rival Tucson border group. The histories of sanctuary in Tucson and in the East Bay had produced communities with different organizational philosophies, structures, and work styles but that nonetheless shared dilemmas born of a common moment within the movement's development. Each sought to maintain the grass-roots character of the movement, to transform short-term response into long-term struggle, and to rekindle the enthusiasm, excitement, and vision that had originally inspired the movement. The choices made by sanctuary workers in 1987 and 1988, like the initial border crossings and sanctuary declarations, continued to construct and reconstruct the movement.

## Conclusion

The ways that religious volunteers constructed the sanctuary movement demonstrate that the content of protest is intricately linked to the historical and social context that produces it. Developments within the Central American church mobilized U.S. religious groups to respond to the plight of Central American refugees. Preexisting organizations, including legal agencies, religious associations, Bible study groups, and even a goat-milking cooperative, were reconstituted to form a network that would aid and advocate for Salvadoran and Guatemalan immigrants. To arrive at the idea of declaring their congregations sanctuaries for Central American refugees, volunteers improvised on their knowledge of religious activism, following models provided by church efforts to resettle refugees and to aid conscientious objectors during the Vietnam War. Their early work, bonding Central Americans out of detention, fomented a disillusionment with the Immigration and Naturalization Service and gave participants the expertise to incorporate legal procedures into their oppositional practices—a subject that will be addressed in greater detail in Part Two. Differences between the Tucson and the East Bay segments of the sanctuary movement can be attributed to differing histories and social contexts. Tucson's proximity to the border and participants' early contacts with the Salvadorans abandoned in the desert led Tucson sanctuary workers to concentrate on border work and social services. East Bay sanctuary workers' early opportunities to visit Central American refugee camps led them to focus on delegations and accompaniment. Because of their roots in the lectionary Bible study group, East Bay activists formed a covenant, whereas in Tucson, the risk of arrest led participants to limit the number of publicly declared sanctuary congregations. In both Tucson and the East Bay, a commitment to community autonomy fostered a dislike of institutionalization. EBSC's organizational structure permitted it to participate in national associations, but the Tucson sanctuary community opposed national organizing.

The histories of the Tucson and East Bay branches of the sanctuary movement also reveal that the process of creating a movement is ongoing. Participants continually reshaped the movement in response to and to precipitate events. As a result of human rights abuses and the influx of Central American refugees, religious volunteers along the U.S.-Mexico border organized legal and social services. When these didn't achieve the desired results, participants resorted to actions that the U.S. government considered illegal. The public sanctuary declarations that marked the initiation of the movement were a response to threats of indictments. As the movement grew and became increasingly diverse, participants developed methods of incorporating new volunteers. In the East Bay, these methods took the form of sanctuary declarations and covenant statements, whereas in Tucson, in addition to the sanctuary declarations in 1984–1985, new volunteers simply joined in the work already being performed by sanctuary groups. With growth came structural elaboration. EBSC formed subcommittees, while Tucson groups created new agencies, such as TECHO, TECLA, and the Covenant Communities. The 1985–1986 sanctuary trial, a result of the movement's practices, reshaped sanctuary work in Tucson and attracted new volunteers to the movement. Sanctuary workers' decisions about participating in national organizing efforts redefined local groups as being either part of or apart from national associations. Finally, when EBSC members turned to accompaniment, they reinterpreted the nature of their commitments to Central American refugees.

Regardless of the ultimate success or failure of the movement, the structures, practices, and discourses devised by sanctuary activists constituted social change. The covenant created by East Bay participants created new relationships between members of diverse religious groups. Similarly, in Tucson, All Saints, the Task Force, Trsg, and other sanctuary-related groups formed a community of religious folk concerned about Central American immigrants and issues. The practices devised by sanctuary covenants and communities thus not only enabled participants to pursue long-term strategies, they also enacted new understandings of religion, culture, and the law. Among these innovations were the border crossings that brought sanctuary workers to Central America or Salvadorans and Guatemalans to the United States. Through such crossings, the movement reproduced itself over time.

## Notes

1. In order to differentiate places where I've omitted part of a quotation from places where a speaker trails off or leaves a sentence incomplete, I've used ellipses to designate the former and dashes to indicate the latter.

2. Resource mobilization theorists do examine movements' bases in preexisting social groups. See Oberschall 1973 and Klandermans 1984.

3. Tilly (1984) pointed out that the phenomenon known as a social movement developed in the nineteenth century in Western countries and therefore is not universal, as most definitions of "social movement" imply. Tilly argued that there are cycles of protest and that the collective action repertoires available to actors change from era to era. To this argument, I would add that the culture of a given movement is linked to the particular conditions and events through which it is produced (Thompson 1963).

4. Tilly (1984) noted that to construct social movements, individuals rely on "collective action repertoires." I borrow and expand this notion of "repertoire" to include cultural knowledge in general (e.g., concepts of work, faith, commitment, ritual, social praxis, and so on).

5. A "coyote" is a person who, for a fee, smuggles immigrants across the border and into the United States.

6. Another TEC member provided more details of this early bail-bonding effort:

TEC, in partnership with Manzo, did two mass bond-outs at El Centro, one in July 1981 and the other in August of 1981. Because of the costliness of this bonding operation, with the obvious difficulties in raising bond cash and collateral, further mass bond-outs were impossible. Following the two mass bond-outs, the TEC Task Force on Central America pledged to financially support an ongoing presence of Manzo to represent Central American refugees detained in the El Centro facility. We further pledged to raise bond cash or collateral for at least five refugees each week at El Centro (the ones imprisoned the longest). In practice, we often bonded out more each week, from September 1981 until May 1982.

Eventually, a San Diego office took responsibility for representing Central Americans detained at El Centro.

7. Due to a complex situation that developed among those aiding camp residents, these delegations were discontinued after two and a half years. In 1986–1987, delegations resumed, focusing on (1) Salvadorans who had been displaced by bombings and conflict but who had remained in El Salvador and wished to repopulate their land and (2) Salvadoran refugees in Honduras who wished to return to El Salvador.

8. The government dropped charges against two of the nuns because of their ill health. One sanctuary worker and the two individuals who were not connected to the movement chose to plea-bargain.

9. Transporting illegal aliens was one of the acts for which the Tucson defendants had been indicted and convicted.

10. In the EBSC office, volunteers put in three-to-five-hour shifts weekly, found tasks in a well-organized Task Book, kept logs of all phone calls received, used forms to take down information about a job offer or a speaking engagement, and accounted for their hours on a volunteer sign-up sheet.

11. For a description of the tensions between Chicago and Tucson, see Bau 1985 and Lorentzen 1991.

12. This call was only sent to certain individuals, a fact that led East Bay sanctuary workers to speculate that they had deliberately been excluded. In response, EBSC members simply photocopied one of the invitations and distributed it to all local sanctuary congregations.

13. Several members of the Tucson border group that had split off from Trsg attended the Call meeting, but no one from Trsg or the Task Force participated.

# 3

# The Meaning of Crossing Borders

*Accompaniment for me is a way of saying, "We will be with you." And that means "with you"! That doesn't mean "above you" or "bring our goodies to give to you." That means "We will somehow join you in the struggle. ... Join you in your life situation and put our lot with yours." Which is what Jesus did with the poor. Which is what the prophets did with the oppressed. It's a very faithful thing to do, it seems to me.*
—Linda Allen, an EBSC staff member and minister

The cultural forms that are created when protestors reinterpret preexisting notions, practices, and institutions in light of particular social, political, and historical conditions must, as every activist knows, be recreated if a particular act of protest is to be more than an isolated incident. At the same time, because movement culture must adapt to changing historical circumstances, reproducing social movements entails altering, as well as simply recreating, forms of protest. Therefore, the reproduction of social movements, like the reproduction of society (Bourdieu 1977; Giddens 1976), is a *dialectical* process. This process begins when a particular interpretation of reality leads individuals to devise practices that seek to reshape that reality. As they engage in these practices, participants construct a discourse that makes sense of their experiences (Gusfield 1970).[1] Accepting the validity of this discourse encourages actors to perform additional practices, which are then interpreted in light of the previously created discourse, and so on. Because this dialectic unfolds over time, experiences and interpretations are never recreated identically (Sahlins 1981, 1985). Rather, they shift, either dramatically or moderately, in relation to changing conditions.

Though a variety of sanctuary practices served to reproduce the movement, my analysis focuses on border crossings, a motif and practice that informed most of the other activities in which sanctuary workers engaged. In Tucson, sanctuary workers brought undocumented Salvadorans and Guatemalans from Mexico into the United States, and in the East Bay, movement members sent delegations to Central America to provide an international presence in communities threatened with violence. Meeting torture victims in a Honduran refugee camp, helping undocumented immigrants hide from surveillance aircraft in an Arizona desert, and being questioned by Salvadoran military authorities gave participants the shared knowledge and experiences out of which to construct the movement's vision of reality—a vision that, in turn, informed crossers' interpretations of their experiences. Even sanctuary workers who did not travel to Central America or bring immigrants into the United States partook of border crossings. When a church committee collected money for a refugee family's rent or when an office volunteer arranged for a Salvadoran catechist to give testimony at a local synagogue, barriers between citizen and undocumented, U.S. and Central American, and First and Third World were being broken. One East Bay sanctuary worker observed of participants, "If they haven't gone down to El Salvador, at least they feel like they have."

An additional reason to focus on border crossings is that crossers often told stories about their experiences, and as ethnographer Renato Rosaldo has noted, "Listening to storytellers as they depict their own lives" reveals the significance of social action (1986b:98). In the early years of EBSC's existence, when members were sending regular delegations to Honduran refugee camps, returning delegates were required to give presentations at the next EBSC meeting. Similarly, in Tucson, every crossing that brought Central Americans into the country was followed by a report to crossers' colleagues. Crossing tales were also told during social gatherings, conversations, sermons, public presentations, and interviews. These tales shed light on how movement discourse both informed and was itself generated by crossings.

### Crossing Tales

Within the sanctuary movement, there were two types of border crossings and hence two types of crossing tales. The first kind of crossing occurred along the U.S.-Mexico border as part of the "underground railroad"—a term coined by the news media to describe the network through which sanctuary workers brought undocumented Central Americans into the United States.[2] Underground railroad crossings were motivated by sanctuary workers' belief that war and human rights violations endangered Salvadorans' and Guatemalans' lives in their home countries and that insecurity, government policy, and abuses of authority in Mexico made it difficult for Central Americans to seek refuge there. Concluding that the United States and Canada represented Central Americans' best hope of safety, sanctuary workers denounced the failure of U.S. Immigration authorities to create a mechanism for Central Americans to enter the country. [Immigration authorities contended that refugees could apply for asylum at U.S. embassies in their home countries or seek refuge at UN-operated camps in Mexico and Honduras (Subcommittee on Immigration and Refugee Policy, Committee on the Judiciary, United States Senate 1984).] Sanctuary workers argued that, as people of faith, they were both religiously and legally required to bring Central Americans into the United States regardless of the sanctions—including stiff fines and imprisonment—that they might face.

The second type of border crossing occurred when North American religious workers traveled to Central America to accompany the oppressed. Because the Salvadoran government depended on U.S. aid, sanctuary workers reasoned, the presence of U.S. citizens (who had access to members of Congress and the international press) could prevent military and paramilitary units from committing abuses that, if publicized, might jeopardize their funding. The rationale connecting "accompaniment" to the underground railroad was that accompaniment extended sanctuary to those who had not yet fled. From 1982–1985, East Bay sanctuary workers sent regular delegations to refugee camps in Honduras, and in 1987–1988, movement members began accompanying internally displaced Salvadorans as they repopulated their villages as well as Salvadoran refugees as they left Honduran camps for El Salvador. Though it avoided the legal risks of the underground railroad, accompaniment exposed North Americans to the physical dangers of traveling through areas of armed conflict, spending time in persecuted communities, and taking political action in countries noted for human rights abuses. When the American relief worker Benjamin Linder was killed by the Contras in Nicaragua in 1987, an EBSC Steering Committee representative soberly reminded his colleagues, "It could have been any of us who this happened to."

Because of the underground railroad's legal implications, accounts of bringing Central Americans into the country risked defining both speaker and listener as participants in an alien-smuggling conspiracy. The danger of telling such stories was shown by Tucson border workers' use of euphemisms, such as "hiking" or "going on a run" when discussing crossings. When I asked one Tucson minister to tell me anecdotes about border crossings, he prefaced his remarks, "It's a lot easier to talk about those in terms of 'for instances.'" Similarly, one of the few Tucson border workers whose interview I tape-recorded told me carefully, "I've had phone calls, 'Will you take so-and-so somewhere?'" Because mere knowledge of border crossings could be used as evidence of conspiracy, accounts of bringing Central Americans into the United States endangered listeners as well as speakers. Marcia Dalton, an immigration attorney sympathetic to sanctuary, told me that to avoid being implicated in alien smuggling, she "was always insistent about never knowing about the actual crossings. I knew that they did it, but I didn't know when or who. And I never asked my [Central American] clients how they'd gotten here, or who had helped them. " According to one border worker, simply attending meetings at which crossings were planned and evaluated would define one as a coconspirator.

Unlike stories about bringing Central Americans into the United States, tales of accompaniment endangered neither speaker nor listener. Accompaniment entailed no legal risks and the physical danger of traveling in Central America evaporated with the traveler's return. Because accompaniment exposed dissidents to U.S. and Central American authorities, however, stories sometimes did convey speakers' uneasy suspicion that they, like Tucson border workers, were under surveillance. Arthur Theede, a San Francisco sanctuary worker who served as his delegation's spokesperson during a trip to El Salvador, reported:

> When I got to Customs coming back [to the United States], ... they said, "Professor Theede!" And called me back. Over a loudspeaker! [They said,] "Not that line, this other line." And in this other line, all this stuff was gone through, and I was bodily searched. ... I don't know that they had looked at my passport. In fact, I don't know that it says "professor" [on my passport]. ... Anyway, I think I'm on their computer.

These risks shaped the way that I encountered and listened to the tales reproduced here. I had no qualms about asking Bay Area sanctuary workers to describe their trips to Central America, so many of the accompaniment stories that I quote were elicited by direct interview questions. In contrast, determined not to record information that could endanger speakers, and not wanting to be mistaken for a government infiltrator, I generally did not ask Tucson sanctuary workers for detailed accounts of crossings. Therefore, with few exceptions, the border-crossing stories that I heard in Tucson either were volunteered during an interview or arose naturally in conversations or presentations at which I happened to be present. As I recorded these stories, I could not occupy the position of a detached observer. Rather like the French ethnographer Favret-Saada (1980), who became enmeshed in the witchcraft discourse she was studying, I found it impossible to escape the force of these stories. When one of the sanctuary workers who stood trial in 1985–1986 recounted a series of crossing anecdotes during an interview, I was uncomfortably aware that my tape recorder was capturing potentially incriminating words. On another occasion, when I met a Tucson border worker at her home for lunch and an interview, I was disturbed to hear that upon learning of my impending visit, the border worker's roommate had left the house. When I asked why, the border worker answered, "She didn't want to be a conspirator." Naively, I protested, "I didn't know that eating lunch together was a conspiracy." The border worker replied more astutely, "Well, I didn't know what kind of questions you would be asking me, and I thought that maybe—" As her voice trailed off, I was reminded that I could not avoid being defined within the discourses that I was analyzing. Acquiring knowledge of activities the government defined as illegal defined me, willingly or no, as a "co-conspirator."

The way that sanctuary workers structured crossing stories conveyed participants' understandings of border crossings. To some extent, the narrative structure of crossing stories was predetermined by cultural conventions of storytelling. According to sociolinguist William Labov (1972), tales told in the United States usually begin with an *abstract* summarizing the point of the story. Next comes an *orientation* that provides background information about the story's setting and participants. The plot of the story is told through a series of *complicating actions*, which are settled in the *resolution* of the story. Interspersed throughout are *evaluations*, which furnish a commentary about the tale. For example, in the course of the story, the teller may say, "It was scary," or "I felt terrified." Stories conclude with a *coda*, which restates the abstract or otherwise indicates that the action in the story has ended (Pratt 1977:3–37). By utilizing these elements in their stories, sanctuary workers who told crossing tales observed their own cultural norms. Because some of the stories that I quote were excerpted from longer narratives, however, the codas—which were often deferred until the end of the entire narrative—are not always included. Also, when talking to insiders or stringing together a series of anecdotes, storytellers sometimes omitted the orientations.

While the narrative structure of crossing stories derived from tellers' cultural knowledge, the types of complicating actions that storytellers chose to emphasize, the ways that these were resolved, the nature of evaluative statements, and the points of the stories' abstracts all expressed speakers' interpretations of their border-crossing experiences. These tales should not be read as accounts of "typical" border crossings because, as Renato Rosaldo (1986b) noted, good stories describe the unexpected rather than the conventional. The complicating actions featured in these stories usually consisted of mishaps that risked exposing protagonists to authorities. Protagonists escaped their predicaments through luck or another individual's intervention rather than through their own cleverness. Evaluations and abstracts emphasized the riskiness of crossings, the crossers' inexpertness, and the humorous or frightening nature of the situations they encountered. By choosing to highlight these facets of their experiences, crossers constructed images of themselves, their enterprise, and their destinations. These representations in turn shaped the way that crossers experienced crossings.

Telling stories was not, of course, the only way that participants made sense of crossings and other movement activities. Participants also constructed movement discourse by drawing on preexisting cultural discourses (such as liberation theology), conversing with other participants, hearing and making public pronouncements, listening to other narratives, reflecting privately on the significance of events, and countering competing interpretations, such as the government's contention that the underground railroad constituted alien smuggling. It would be useful to know what first prompted sanctuary workers to narrate their crossing experiences, how stories were initially constructed, how they changed during subsequent retellings, and so forth, but in most cases, I only have one version of each crossing tale. It would also be helpful to have heard the conversations that took place during crossings, the presentations that Salvadoran priests and others made to delegations of sanctuary workers, and the comments that Central Americans made as sanctuary workers helped them over fences or drove them through checkpoints, but again, I did not go on the crossings that are rendered here in story form. Therefore, in using narrative to analyze individuals' interpretations of their experiences, it is important to acknowledge that these stories are the evolving products of many influences. The meanings that are embedded in crossing stories are the distillation of a process that began before the movement itself.

## A Dangerous and Unfamiliar Realm

Analyzing the abstracts, complicating actions, resolutions, evaluations, and codas that occur in crossing tales reveals that crossers experienced these trips as journeys into a dangerous and unfamiliar realm. The underground railroad stories I heard from two Tucson ministers and a layworker provide an entree into this domain. The first two stories were told by a well-known pastor who had been involved in border crossings before public sanctuary declarations were issued. Toward the end of an hour-long tape-recorded interview, after he had sadly recounted meeting church workers in Central America who knew they would soon be tortured and killed, I asked this pastor if he could tell me any stories about his sanctuary work in Tucson. The pastor initially continued on a melancholy tone, describing the emotional discord of aiding torture victims while living amidst Tucsonans who knew nothing of torture. He then changed moods, beginning a story:

> There's lots of funny times. One time Joe [a border worker] was going down to Nogales to pick up a family, and the car broke down, and the border patrol came along and jump-started them and got him going, and he went on down to pick the family up, thanks to the border patrol.
>
> Another time we went to Douglas to pick up three or four folks who were going to hop the fence. And we didn't have anyplace for them to go in Douglas, so they just had to wait for them [us]. It was pretty dicey. But, before they got to the car, the border patrol picked them up. There were three of them—three or four. One of them had run down an alley, so the border patrol put the other three guys in the back of the border patrol van and went chasing off after the other guy. At one point, they slowed down or stopped, and these guys discovered that they had forgotten to lock the back of the border patrol van, so they just opened the door and slipped out. And, I don't know what the border patrol did, but they made it back to the car.
>
> And just other kinds of things. We were extraordinarily lucky, that's all.

Additional crossing anecdotes were recounted by a second Tucson minister as I interviewed him in his church office. This minister had been involved in crossings in the early years of the movement when he lived in a border town. As our interview (which was not tape-recorded) concluded, I told the minister, "I think that that's all of my questions. Do you think that there's any issue that I forgot, or that's important to talk about?" The minister answered:

> *Minister:* No. The only other thing that I'd like to say is that it's been fun. Through all the pains, the agonies, and the disagreements, it's provided joy. There's just a lot of things to laugh at!
>
> *Susan:* Really? Like what?
>
> *Minister:* Oh, there was the time that two cars went on a run, and they met the people doing the drop-off, and they quickly got everyone into the cars, and they sped

off, and then, Robin and—Carol [two border workers]—they were the ones. They looked at each other, and they said, "I think we've been left."

*Susan:* Oh, no! Didn't anyone realize?

*Minister:* No. So, I think they had a roll of toilet paper. And so they spent the next six or seven hours until someone came to get them sitting there writing a long, nasty letter on the toilet paper! They were so angry! And they were really out in the boonies. Finally, the car came back with all the refugees, making it doubly dangerous.

And then there was the time that Robin got her van stuck in the mud out on some dirt road, and she knew that she had to be someplace at a certain time to pick people up, and she was worried, because if the border patrol came along, how could she explain being there on this road? So she dug the truck out of the mud with her bare hands. ...

And then, there was another time, and this was just plain stupidity. Not ignorance, but stupidity. Robin had gone down in a little Toyota, and she was going to pick up thirteen people. Thirteen people in that little car! And we decided to do it right through town, and we knew that they had set up sensors, that they would know someone had crossed. So I was supposed to sit in front, and if I saw the border patrol, I was going to pull out into the road and flash my signal lights. So I was there waiting, and sure enough, there came a border patrol car, and I was about to pull onto the road and flash my lights, when I realized that if I did that, I might as well flag him down and tell him what she was doing. So I just quietly drove away, and I figured that that was it, this was the first arrest. It was just a one-lane road. I went home, and I called a few people, and I was planning on going to get her bailed out, but then she drove up. She said that the border patrol had driven right past her, and she'd waved at him, and he hadn't seen that mass of humanity in the car.

Finally, Randy Silbert, a Tucson border worker, told the following story during an interview (which was not tape-recorded). When Randy told me that going on crossings had taught him how to deal with fear, I asked him, "I was wondering if you could tell me how it feels to go on a crossing?" He responded by telling two crossing stories. The first described running into an army roadblock in Mexico while he was carrying documents that could identify him as a sanctuary worker. The second went as follows:

There was another time when I was stopped [in Mexico] with a deserter from the Salvadoran guerrillas. He was in terrible trouble, because the guerrillas were against him, and as a former guerrilla, he could be taken away by the government as soon as he got there. ... It was the *Federales* [Federal police] who stopped us. I was terrified, because those *Federales,* they're crazy, they're *nuts!* But luckily, the Salvadoran talked his way out of it. He said that he was from Mexico and that I was taking him to be an actor in a play I was doing. My jaw was just going, and I literally couldn't speak out of fear. I think they liked that. They liked being able to intimidate a *gringo.*

So, there are moments of stark terror.

The stories recounted by these three sanctuary workers portrayed border crossings as an exciting, terrifying, and sometimes comical enterprise carried out by inexperienced individuals. Whether driving through town, out in the boonies, or in Mexico, the protagonists in these tales were in an unfamiliar arena where they had to elude authorities by concealing their true purposes and identities. The complicating actions that created adventure within these stories were of the protagonists' own making. Border workers left their colleagues behind in the desert, drove cars that broke down, used impassable roads, and planned lookout systems that alerted the border patrol to their activities. The protagonists in these tales resolved their difficulties through luck, sheer perseverance, a Central American's cleverness, and ironically, border patrol agents' unwitting assistance. Rather than glorifying protagonists, such resolutions highlighted crossers' inexperience. For example, Randy Silbert chose to describe how, while his Salvadoran passenger talked their way out of danger, he had been muted by fear. Evaluations such as "It was pretty dicey," "I figured that was it," and "There are moments of stark terror" emphasized the danger of going on crossings, while references to border workers' ineptitude reinforced the movement's claim that, far from being professional alien-smugglers, sanctuary workers were ordinary folk unaccustomed to bringing undocumented refugees across U.S. borders.

Like stories about bringing Central Americans into the United States, tales of accompaniment conveyed the travelers' senses of entering an unknown and hazardous realm. The following two accompaniment stories describe such journeys. The first was told by Paul Dedona, a young First Church Sanctuary Committee member. During an interview at a crowded Berkeley cafe, I asked Paul to tell me about the two trips he had made to Central America. Paul explained that in 1982, he had visited the Mesa Grande refugee camp in Honduras then in 1986 had gone to El Salvador to accompany a caravan of displaced Salvadorans. After noting that he had enjoyed his second trip, Paul began a story about his earlier journey. He related:

> The time I went to Mesa Grande was quite stressful for me. It was with a larger group of people, and there were about six of us, and a lot of the people had brought two little bags or things. And we had ten bags that were luggage, and we had another ten bags that were full of clothes and supplies for the volunteers in the camps. We had confusion at the airport where we had left the bags. We had to go back early the next morning before leaving and find them there. So that was kind of bizarre, after going through this intense thing about being afraid about whether we would get in through customs, because we were taking quite a bit of medicine and things for the camps. ...
>
> But we had no trouble getting through customs, although we had to wait for a long time, because the custom guy was—people were coming back from Miami with a lot of luggage that was basically imported things, and so the customs people were taking a duty in kind. They were counting out shirts, and counting out ten and taking one. Counting ten Waring blenders and taking one. This went on for a long time.

We had—we were told not to say we were going to refugee camps or anything like that, to say that we were tourists going to the Caribbean Islands, but then we had this big suitcase full of pills and a suitcase full of eyeglasses and stuff. When the customs guy started looking at this one thing full of eyeglasses, he asked us, "What's in it?" And we kind of pretended that we didn't speak Spanish, and I think maybe we had so much luggage that we didn't know what exactly was in it. It was in this big Tide box. So we said, "Soap," or something like that. There were all these military CIA types around who had brown U.S. passports, and there were a lot of tourists going into Honduras in those days. So one of these guys took the trouble to translate for us.

So we finally got to the hotel and everything, and we got to the train station early the next morning and discovered luggage missing. And because there were a lot of personal things for the camp volunteers, and letters and things, we felt real bad, so we went back after trying to be discreet and move through there quickly and everything. [We had been discreet] because they interrogate people there. We went back and said, "Where's our luggage?" We got there at six o'clock, and nothing had opened. Finally we got it back, and it was all in a little room.

I think when I finally got up into the refugee camp at the end of the day, I almost felt like a refugee myself. And I didn't make as much of the two weeks there, as far as trying to meet people and talk to the refugees. I was quite stressed.

The second accompaniment story was related by Ruth Moss, an EBSC staff member whom I interviewed at my apartment after we had eaten dinner together. Like the previous speaker, Ruth had visited a Honduran refugee camp during the early years of the sanctuary movement. When I asked her to describe her trip to Central America, Ruth explained that upon reaching the Honduran capital, she and her companion had learned that shortly before their arrival, a Guatemalan doctor had been killed, a North American woman had been raped, two North Americans had been placed under house arrest for five days while bombs fell around them, and a North American woman had been detained along with three Salvadorans. The storyteller then began her tale:

*Ruth:* So, anyway, we didn't know what would happen. But we figured everything had already happened. So we—and we left [the capital] too late because of hearing all these stories—we were supposed to try to travel before dark, and we were traveling after dark. And we were in a head-on collision with this big truck.

*Susan:* That's terrible! But you guys were all right?

*Ruth:* We were [all right]. ... We got out of the truck and realized that we were all okay, and then the woman that I had gone down with lost her memory. [She] didn't forget who I was—I'd known her before—but didn't know where we were, what we were doing there, why all the soldiers [were] needed in here.

*Susan:* That's terrible! I can't believe that!

*Ruth:* It was amazing. It was very scary. But she really needed help, and she never forgot me, and so she continually asked me the same questions over and over. Did her boyfriend know she was here? Did her parents know? Did they feel it was okay? The same questions over and over. Where are we? Who are these guys?

So, I just tried to take care of her. Plus, we were concerned. We were on our way to the camps. We were taking medicine. ... We also had mail, including a letter from somebody who was in Cuba. ...

Some Mennonite volunteers happened to be coming by, because all traffic was stopped on this road. Anyway, they stopped, and they took the person I'd gone down with and myself on. ...

Traveling with them, we hit, I think, three roadblocks on the way to the camps. ... At one of them, the men that stopped us were ... not in uniform, and they had ski masks over their head[s], and we later learned they were the Honduran secret police. And they separated us from our luggage. ... At this point, the person I was traveling with, her memory was coming back, and she was giddy, and she was just talking. And I was really scared she was going to start talking about what we were doing. I guess she was in another phase of shock.

Anyway, they [the secret police] came across digital watches, and got totally wrapped up in these digital watches, and stole some, and bought some. These were the Mennonites that were bringing the digital watches. So they just got totally sidetracked with these watches.

The abstracts of these two stories stated, in the first case, that the trip was stressful, and in the second, that the protagonist did not know what would happen on the trip. These two abstracts emphasized the danger and uncertainty of accompaniment. In both stories, the protagonists were in a predicament, in that they had to be inspected by authorities without revealing their true identities. This predicament was stated explicitly in the first story: The protagonist initially described himself as a North American traveling to a refugee camp, then pretended to be a tourist, and finally, "felt like a refugee." In each story, the protagonists faced a series of complicating factors, such as the forgotten luggage and the head-on collision, that created suspense by threatening to expose protagonists' true purposes. These complications were brought on by the protagonists' own oversights. The first speaker's delegation left part of its baggage behind, and the second speaker ignored a warning not to travel after dark. In both stories, evaluative statements, such as "That was kind of bizarre" and "I was really scared," further conveyed the uncertainty and danger of the protagonists' predicaments. Rather than glorifying participants, these stories portrayed protagonists as vulnerable and insecure. Like their counterparts along the U.S.-Mexico border, these crossers did not escape their predicaments through their own skill. The first story did not reveal how the protagonist's difficulty was resolved, except that the crossers' attempt to feign monolingualism was foiled by overeager translators. In the second story, the protagonists' predicament was resolved by the secret police's fascination with the Mennonites' digital watches.

The realm that sanctuary workers traversed during these crossings can be located by contrasting the above stories with sanctuary workers' accounts of their earlier travels as tourists. Far from entering a dangerous and unfamiliar realm, the protagonists in tourist tales traveled without leaving their own world behind. For example, consider the following two stories. The first was told during an interview with Judith Bromberg, a member of Congregation Aron Kodesh's Sanctuary Committee. When I asked her whether she planned to visit Central America, Judith answered:

[If I travel to Central America,] I just have to feel as if I have something to offer. ... I went to Mexico City on a co-op charter about ten years ago, just because I wanted to take a week off. Strictly rest and recreation. And I stayed at this first-class hotel; it was part of the deal. It was a package deal. It was with a bunch of Berkeleyans. I was absolutely appalled at the contrast between richness and poverty that you saw on the street. It wasn't as if the poor were off in a tent city someplace and we-guys were in this hotel. The poor were walking barefoot in the streets selling peanuts or oranges or sitting on a piece of sidewalk, just like that. With a blanket. And on the blanket were twenty oranges, and that was their source of income. Or [they were selling] lottery tickets. And here we were sitting in the cocktail lounge of our hotel, looking out at these people selling their twenty oranges, with three babies. [And what we saw was] a woman who was probably thirty-six years old, and who looked seventy-five. In this country, unless you're in someplace like Mississippi, you don't see such contrasts. The poor aren't—

And so, if I went to a place like El Salvador, I wouldn't be in that position, because I wouldn't be staying at a first-class hotel, so that part, I wouldn't have that problem. I just want to be able to be of service.

A similar anecdote was told by Timothy Planchon, a Catholic EBSC member. When I asked Timothy how his background had led him to sanctuary work, he related:

In terms of having my consciousness raised, I remember vividly one trip I took to Mexico, where we came into Acapulco by bus from the interior, and what I remember about that was coming from the interior to the east side of the hills. And on the east side of the hills are where the squatters live, the poorest of the poor. Literally cardboard and tin shacks. Terrible squalor. And then you cross over the hills, and you see this beautiful bay, with all these skyscrapers, and hotels and things. And that really in a sense ruined Acapulco for me. I could not enjoy the luxury and the glitter of the hotels, knowing that on the other side of the hills was this terrible squalor.

The contrast between these two tourist tales and the border-crossing stories quoted above reveals that the domain that sanctuary workers entered during crossings was none other than the reality of the Central American poor. In the two tourist tales, the tellers traveled *without* crossing the border between First and Third World. The protagonists' predicaments arose not from entering a dangerous and unfamiliar territory but from *failing* to do so. In each of these stories, the glaring contrast between affluence and poverty made the protagonists critically

conscious of their own relative wealth and security. This predicament was compli-
cated by encounters with prematurely aged women selling oranges and tin shacks
surrounded by squalor. Speakers used evaluations such as "I was appalled" and
"terrible squalor" to emphasize their discomfort with the disparity between rich
and poor. The first storyteller escaped her predicament by resolving not to stay at
first-class hotels but rather to be of service to the poor. The second speaker did
not explain how he resolved his dilemma, but it can be inferred that his increased
awareness of poverty affected his political outlook and his future travel plans.

Having identified the realm in which crossers journeyed, it is now possible to
decipher other elements of crossing stories. In emphasizing protagonists' inexperience, storytellers indicated how far crossers had traveled from their own reality,
where they presumably were far from inept, into that of the Central American
poor. Moreover, highlighting protagonists' unfamiliarity with social norms
placed crossers in a position analogous to Central American immigrants who had
to confront the perplexities of North American culture. By depicting protagonists
as inept rather than clever and capable, tellers countered the "know-it-all" arro-
gance that many sanctuary workers believed typified their compatriots' attitudes
toward Central Americans.[3] Centering the tales' complicating actions around the
risk of discovery gave crossers complex identities. During complicating actions,
protagonists were middle-class North Americans who, by entering the reality of
the Central American poor, had temporarily become like impoverished Central
Americans but, to conceal this transformation, had to pretend to be who they in
fact were—namely, middle-class North Americans. By emphasizing the danger of
crossings, storytellers indicated that such journeys brought the protagonists into
Central American reality.

These images of crossings, crossers, and the land in which crossers journeyed
not only were an effort to *make sense of* prior experiences, they also *shaped*
crossings, encouraging new and former sanctuary workers to cross.

## Becoming One with the Oppressed

So far, I have used narratives to analyze the images of crossings that sanctuary
workers constructed. Now I propose to use crossing stories to discuss how movement discourse influenced crossers' experiences of traveling to Central America
and bringing undocumented refugees into the United States. As representations
of events, narratives not only reveal the interpretations that participants invoke
and create to define the significance of incidents that have already occurred; they
also relate the meanings that shape a particular action and the way that it is experienced in the first place. There is no such thing as raw, unmediated experience:
Even as actions occur, the individuals involved perceive events through lenses
provided by cultural discourses. Moreover, actions are themselves constructed
with particular goals, principles, and understandings in mind. Therefore, when
individuals narrate an experience, they simultaneously interpret its significance

and relate the discourse through which the event was constructed. The ways that border-crossing discourse shaped crossings can be uncovered by perusing crossing stories for tellers' rationales for entering the reality of the poor. Though I could reexamine the stories already presented, I will instead introduce three additional tales—tales that describe a moment when the protagonist confronted death.[4]

Before I turn to the stories themselves, it is important to reiterate that temporarily placing middle-class North Americans within the reality of the Central American poor was a strategy for preventing human rights violations. Participants reasoned that because U.S. citizens had access to the U.S. news media and the members of Congress who authorized aid to Central American governments, military and paramilitary units would avoid committing abuses when U.S. citizens were present. Paul Dedona, whose journey to the Mesa Grande refugee camp is described above, explained:

> The importance of having international observers there [in Honduran refugee camps] was brought home by the story of [an East Bay participant]. When she was visiting La Virtud [a refugee camp], ... the death squads from El Salvador had come across into the camp and gathered up a bunch of people and started taking them across the border. ... A group of journalists that she was with followed the people out and were taking pictures and were shouting, "We're going to notify the international press!" So they let the people go.

As the following three accompaniment stories show, however, entering the reality of the Central American poor was not only a means of preventing human rights abuses but also an encounter with truth. The first story was told by Paul Dedona. After recounting the tale of the forgotten luggage, Paul described an incident that had occurred after he reached the Mesa Grande refugee camp:

> The second night when we came back from cutting wood, it was quite tense because it was getting dark, and one of the officers—an older, mean-looking officer—and one of the relief workers said he was from the Salvadoran army and that he was there because he knew a lot of the refugees and stuff, or knew some of the people. But there were some people that somehow, what they did was they made a list of all the names of the people on the truck, and then the soldier would call out names, and the people would identify themselves and show their papers. And somehow in the dark, they had gotten to the end of the list, and there were still five people standing there. So, they asked the people their names and looked at the list to try to find where the name was crossed off. And there was this real young guy, who looked like he was about fifteen, who—either he was too frightened, or he was deaf, because he couldn't talk when they asked him his name. He was just kind of choking. So the other people were saying, "Oh, he's just too frightened." But it was just a real, for me, frightening experience, and the feeling I had was like, this is bizarre, this is like being in a movie. What am I doing here seeing this? It can't really be happening—to be around these perfectly mature adult men who moments before seemed real calm

and relatively happy and concerned about cutting wood, and now [they] were totally frightened. So somehow I wasn't feeling quite psyched.

The second story was related by Leanna Vance, an East Bay sanctuary worker
who had traveled to El Salvador to aid bombing victims in the town of Guazapa.
During an interview at her home, she told me:

> While we were there [in El Salvador], we had a very scary experience with a com-
> mander of the Orden[5] division, which was supposed to be outlawed, we had
> thought. But it definitely was Orden, we knew that. And one of the men who was
> with us was a former Jesuit priest who was bilingual, and so he was the one telling us
> things. Because most of us couldn't speak Spanish. I had a little bit. But it was kind
> of like, some of us felt it was better we didn't, [because by] kind of stumbling our
> way through things, we were making soldiers laugh. It was just the way the situation
> was. If we had been much more serious, and could speak the Spanish, we might have
> been in a lot more trouble.
>
> We had a bad experience with this Orden captain, who took us down to a se-
> cluded area near the lake, and I think it was that he was fascinated. I think it was
> that. Other people think it was very intentional, that he was trying to intimidate us.
> He was either drunk or stoned, and he—stared. It was intimidating the way that he
> stared at the women. It was toward the women. And he wanted to trade. For exam-
> ple, he wanted my scarf, and he wanted me to take his hat. While we were out there.
> It was very, very, very scary. Because he had an armed soldier with him with a ma-
> chine gun. And we didn't know what was going to happen. When he said, "Get in
> the car." Our own car. And he takes us out to this place. It was like, I was flashing
> back to *Choices of the Heart.* Anyway, I had these flashbacks to the four [North
> American] nuns [who had been killed by death squads], and how they must have
> felt when they were trapped.

The third story was told by Gail Stewart, an East Bay sanctuary worker. During
an interview at her college campus, I asked Gail to describe an experience that
represented the reason she was involved in sanctuary work. She said:

> The most important thing [about sanctuary work] is just learning to identify with
> them [the refugees], I think. Because their values are so strong and so true, when
> you learn to identify with them more, the more you do it, the more sure you are of
> yourself in life and of your own values. The reality comes in on you and the other
> stuff gets pushed aside as not as important as you thought it once was.
>
> And I guess the experience, of course, that brought all that home the most was
> our experience in Aguacayo last summer when a group of us ... went down to ac-
> company a group of displaced people who were repopulating a zone in Cuzcatlan.
> And the city was called Aguacayo. And the cooperative was called El Barrillo. And
> we were with them in the zone of conflict. ... The soldiers let us right through. We
> to this day wonder if it wasn't a mistake and if they didn't think it was a government
> repopulation effort. Maybe that's why they let us in. But anyway, once they let us in,
> they didn't like the idea that there were Internationals in this area accompanying the

refugees, and they didn't particularly want the refugees there, and the national police came in and told us to get out, and we refused to get out and sat down in the middle of the ground between the refugees and the army, and they came at us and we didn't know if we were going to live or die, and then they threw down their guns and dragged us away in the trucks, and we were eventually handed over to the Hacienda police, who are known for their brutality. And we were scared, we were really scared. And the refugees were scared for us, and we were scared for them, and it was horrible. It was just pure shit that whole time.

Well, eventually we were deported to Guatemala and we were sent back to the States from Guatemala. We weren't deported from Guatemala, but we just flew home.

And that experience, the moment when we sat down, and the few moments before they threw down their guns and dragged us away, was kind of a central experience in my life, because I really did feel that there was a fate that put me there, that God had put me there.

These three stories reveal that the movement's construction of the crossing experience led crossers to place themselves as fully as possible in the positions of persecuted Central Americans.[6] Implicitly drawing on liberation theology and the social gospel's tenet that the poor are closer to God than are the rich, Gail Stewart explained that "when you learn to identify with them [refugees], ... the reality comes in on you." Gail's comment suggests that participants considered the domain of the Central American poor more authentic than their own lives.[7] In other words, to participants, the reality experienced in Central America *was* reality. Moreover, this reality had a nonordinary quality. In Paul Dedona's and Leanna Vance's crossing stories, the protagonists had difficulty accepting the veracity of events. In the first story, Paul asked himself, "What am I doing here seeing this?" and said, "It can't really be happening," and in both tales, the protagonists felt as though they were in movies. Leanna Vance's comparison between herself and the four North American nuns and Gail Stewart's conclusion that God had placed her between refugees and the Salvadoran national police indicated that this unreal reality had religious overtones. To enter the quasi-sacred reality of the Central American poor, crossers had to put themselves in situations governed by unfamiliar norms. Paul did not know the identity of the interrogating soldiers any more than Leanna knew the Orden captain's motives or Gail knew why International visitors had been allowed to enter the repopulated village. Significantly, Paul's, Leanna's, and Gail's reconstructions of their crossing experiences dwelled on danger rather than on the unfolding plot. Paul failed to mention how the tongue-tied young man escaped from his predicament, and Gail quickly summarized her detention and deportation almost as an afterthought. Both Gail and Leanna returned at the end of their stories to focus once more on that moment when they confronted death. In this clarifying moment, this moment of truth, the protagonists truly became one with the persecuted. Yet, after this moment of coalescence passed, the protagonists reverted to being North Americans who would leave Central America and return to the United States.

This analysis of crossing stories has indicated how crossings both generated and were informed by a discourse that, though it drew on liberation theology and the social gospel, was unique to the sanctuary movement. Crossers made sense of their experiences by defining them as journeys into the reality of the Central American poor—journeys with the potential to transform North American sanctuary workers, albeit temporarily and incompletely, into impoverished Central Americans. This construction of events motivated individuals who believed that the oppressed were closer to God to go on crossings. Because they strove to occupy the positions of oppressed Central Americans, crossers took risks, left the familiar behind, and even confronted death. Lacking access to crossing tales recounted at earlier points in the sanctuary movement, it is difficult for me to analyze how the dialectic between meaning and experience changed crossings and their images over time. I *can*, however, examine the ways that sanctuary workers used crossing discourse to redefine other social practices. These redefinitions took place because, just as crossers could not completely leave the First World behind, neither could they, after entering the reality of the poor, completely return.

### Being Between Borders

Border crossings problematized crossers' identities, both in a practical and a political sense. Close to the surface of crossings, pretending to be innocuous hikers or tourists produced tension between protagonists' true and feigned identities. To prevent the border patrol from stopping their cars in search of illegal aliens, border workers and Central Americans tried to look like typical U.S. citizens on an outing. (After learning of large numbers of Central Americans waiting across the border, participants in one Task Force meeting joked about crossing them all at once, disguised as an orchestra or a new order of nuns.) Sanctuary workers who accompanied the oppressed in Central America tried to avoid problems with authorities by passing themselves off as tourists rather than political dissidents. However, on a deeper level, the border-crossing experience problematized "being American"[8] by making border crossers increasingly conscious of hierarchical and militaristic relationships between the United States and Central America. For example, during a slide show presentation at a Northern California Sanctuary Covenant meeting, one former delegate told his audience about a Mass he had attended in El Salvador:

> The statements that were made ... by that Dominican priest really hit home to me. He was very open about saying to them [the Salvadorans], "Yes, these are people from North America." He was acknowledging feelings that the Salvadoran community probably had, having among them people who, whether we like it or not, represent the North American state, a government that is supplying military aid that in many cases buys the bombs that destroyed villages where their relatives lived. And at the same time, he was saying, "See how much this says about the depth of feeling in these people that they make the effort to come down all this way to be with you here

in San Salvador and to learn about your story?" It was a very schizophrenic kind of experience in a way.

The problematic nature of being American led some sanctuary workers to re-define themselves as "North Americans" or, less frequently, "Internationals." Peter Lockhart, an EBSC volunteer, argued that it was arrogant to call oneself simply "American." Peter noted, "When we say 'American,' ... we don't think of Cana-dian, or Central American, or South American. We think of Yankees from the United States." Within the sanctuary movement, the term "North American" was employed as a substitute for "American," while "International" was reserved for non–Central Americans participating in a delegation to Central America (as in the following quotation from Gail Stewart's account of being detained and deported: "They didn't like the idea that there were Internationals in this area ac-companying the refugees"). Sanctuary workers who were still becoming accus-tomed to this new terminology sometimes corrected themselves while speaking. For example, Judith Bromberg, who related one of the two tourist tales quoted above, told me, "Not all Americans—North Americans—are like Ronald Reagan," and Randy Silbert, the Tucson border worker who had been stopped by the Mexican police, said that a Salvadoran acquaintance had "learned that Ameri-cans—North Americans—have little control over our government." Both of the alternative designations gave their bearers international rather than national identities: The expression "North American" defined individuals in relation to South, Central, and Latin America, while the term "International" implied that those so designated had ties to more than one nation.

Such redefinitions placed sanctuary workers between borders, enabling them to use the truth encountered during crossings to reevaluate their own practices. For example, while I was in Tucson, I took part in Borderlinks, a program that brought U.S. religious workers from around the United States to Tucson to study border issues. During this week-long program, participants crossed borders by staying at a soup kitchen, touring *maquiladora* plants,[9] visiting the Mexican squatter village of Los Tapiros, sharing a meal with Central American refugees, and sleeping on a Mexican activist's floor. These experiences were thought to give participants a new vantage point on social reality. As I noted in my journal:

> Furthermore, and this came out particularly in the group reflection times, there's a profoundness to everything. You don't just curiously walk through a squatters' camp, but rather you think about who you are, who they are, what is your relation-ship, what do you see in their eyes, what would Jesus do in this situation, how does it challenge your worldview, what new understanding does it give you, how would you see the world through the eyes of those in the squatters' camp, and so on. There's an experiential depth to it that becomes difficult to articulate. As one man said, "How will we relate this experience to others when we go back?" There's a feeling that they can never understand simply by hearing our words, because it goes beyond words. Furthermore, there's a feeling that we have been changed by this experience. In

other words, when we go back, we hear and see things in a different light. We hear what other people say, and we try to listen with an awareness of the existence of Los Tapiros. When people complain about the color of their wallpaper, we think, "Some people don't even have walls. "

Through this double vision, practices and assumptions that individuals had previously taken for granted were given new, usually negative, meanings. One Protestant minister who had had this experience observed, "All of our realities get shaken when you travel there." During a conversation among volunteers in the EBSC office, I found that my own reality was indeed shaken by my awareness of Central Americans' situations. When I joked to the other volunteers that the main difference between living together and being married was sharing each other's credit cards and insurance, I immediately realized how middle-class I sounded and that many undocumented Central Americans had neither credit cards nor insurance. Peter Lockhart, an East Bay volunteer, argued that such reevaluations occurred because the space between borders—a space from which multiple realities were visible—exposed the falsehood of life in the United States:

> You just cross the border [to Mexico], and you see this raw exposed reality. Nothing's painted. There's rusty wire, you have beaten-up cars that just look like raw material. A very crude kind of reality. ... There's a sort of telling it like it is, living with it, and not minding it. Whether it's flies, dogs, or just how people live.
> Then, in the United States, we like to pretty everything up. ... But in Mexico, you don't need to do that. It's functional. Especially for the poor. So that, the light bulb isn't hidden, it's exposed. It's a light bulb, not a fancy lamp hanging on the ceiling.
> ...
> There's something about poverty that by its very lack exposes the cosmetic, almost insincere pseudo-reality of wealth and power.

By exhorting individuals to cross boundaries that were not only physical but also cultural, socioeconomic, and religious, border crossings defined middle-class North American practices as inauthentic. The discourse that shaped and was produced through crossings proliferated as sanctuary workers used their experiences between borders as sources of insight and cultural critique. These insights and critiques then defined movement practices, encouraging those who engaged in these practices to more fully embrace the movement's vision of reality. Thus, as sanctuary workers created and reproduced the movement, the movement created sanctuary workers.

## Notes

1. I do not wish to imply that individuals have an innate need for order, that they "are unable to leave unclarified problems of analysis merely unclarified" (Geertz 1973:100). I agree that social analysis requires "look[ing] beyond the dichotomy of order versus chaos toward the less explored realm of 'nonorder'" (Rosaldo 1989:10; see also Taussig 1987). Certainly,

since it entailed dismantling assumptions, categories, values, and visions, sanctuary discourse created *dis*order as well as order. However, because movement actions built on prior incidents, sanctuary workers had to construct these incidents as events, even if this meant representing them as at least partially inexplicable.

2. Sanctuary workers themselves were ambivalent about the term "underground railroad." On the one hand, it harks back to the abolitionists, predecessors whose practices participants claimed as a precedent for their work. On the other hand, the term connotes civil disobedience, from which movement members differentiated their own efforts to enforce laws that they believed government policies violated.

3. For example, Arthur Theede, a San Francisco sanctuary worker, told me, "As an American, I have ... this 'know-it-all' attitude. Like, 'I really know what should be done here. I know how to run the church, run the family, run the world! '"

4. As sociolinguist William Labov noted, stories of brushes with death constitute "*narratives of personal experience*, in which the speaker becomes deeply involved in rehearsing or even reliving events of his past" (1972: 354, emphasis in original). Because they more fully recreate crossings than other crossing tales, stories in which protagonists face death may more accurately relate the thoughts and feelings that participants experienced at the time.

5. Orden was a paramilitary force accused of assassinations and human rights violations.

6. By temporarily leaving the middle class to cross social boundaries, sanctuary workers took part in the cultural quest for truth that anthropologist Roger Abrahams has termed "traveling on." Abrahams noted, "From the figure of the pilgrim-stranger to the romanticized hobo, our most admired protagonists are the ones who were able to move on ... and sometimes move up. Traveling on has been almost institutionalized through its connection with the missionary, the peddler, or the member of the Peace Corps" (1986:51). Indeed, traveling to distant places, living among a foreign people, and viewing one culture through the eyes of another are the essence of anthropological inquiry.

7. The belief, or what some might term the realization, that middle-class life obscures part of reality is not limited to the sanctuary movement. During the civil rights movement, some twenty years before he had joined the TEC's Task Force on Central America, Ernie Tarkington, a Tucson minister, unexpectedly crossed a border to find himself sharing the position of southern blacks:

> My views changed in Selma, [Alabama,] when I stood on the line opposite the church. We got a call from the Justice Department for someone who was at the rally. And so, like a good middle-class white northerner, the first thing I did was look for the police. I walked up to a policeman and I said, "We've got a call from the Justice Department, and we have to find this person." And he just looked at me and said, "You one a' them?" I said, "One of *them?* You don't understand! We've got the Justice Department on the phone, and we have to find—" "You get outta here! You get the fuck outta here!" And that was a changing point for my perspective. I hadn't believed that the police would act that way, especially on a federal level.

8. Not all sanctuary workers agreed that truth was to be found in Central America, and some criticized their colleagues' ambivalence about being American. Johann Braun, an East Bay sanctuary supporter, compared sanctuary workers' quick trips to Central America to General Secord of Iran-Contra fame, who, according to Johann, spent six hours in Central America before deciding he knew why he was supporting the Contras. Sonya Byrd, a Tucson

border worker, said of traveling to Central America, "I don't think that I need to go there to find out what it's *really* like. There was a time, five or six years ago, when I felt I did need to go there. People felt *compelled* to go; it was almost like a pilgrimage that they would make." Philip Kaspar, former Tucson sanctuary worker, was even more critical: "I've been to Central America a number of times, and I've seen how left-wingers go down there with an apologetic attitude. They say, 'I'm sorry that I'm from the U.S.' And you know, most of the Central Americans can differentiate between the people and the government. I'm pro-American. I'm not going to apologize for being a white male American!"

9. *Maquiladora* plants are American-owned assembly stations located in northern Mexico. These plants employ Mexican workers (the majority of whom are women) who are remunerated according to Mexican, rather than U.S., wage scales.

# 4

## Transformations

Genevieve Gallegos: *A lot of people don't even want to hear about what's happening down there [in Central America], because they don't want to be touched. They don't want to make themselves feel vulnerable to something. So, as long as they can ignore it—*

Susan Coutin: *There's some saying, "Once you know, you can't not know." I don't know where I heard that.*

Genevieve Gallegos: *Yeah. It's like, I can't [not know]! Sometimes I wish I could. Sometimes I think, "Oh, darn it! Why can't I just enjoy things? And live my life the way I used to? Why do I have to feel this responsibility for getting things done?!" But I can't ignore it.*
                    —Excerpt of interview with an EBSC staff member

Those who went on border crossings, housed undocumented Central Americans, volunteered in a sanctuary office, or served on their congregation's sanctuary committee not only constructed and reproduced the movement, they also found their worldview, faith, and sense of peoplehood changed in the process. As they crossed the border between their own and Central American reality—whether by hearing a Guatemalan's testimony, commemorating Salvadoran Archbishop Romero's death, or traveling to Mexico or Central America—sanctuary workers reinterpreted truth in ways that demanded action and personal sacrifice. Accepting and acting upon the movement's understanding of reality entailed shifts of consciousness, religious conversions (for Christians), or reinterpretations of history (for Jews). These transformations were not single events but rather ongoing processes embedded in the dialectic between meaning and action encapsulated in the border-crossing experience. For some, the personal changes wrought by sanctuary work were extreme, whereas for others, these were merely the latest expression of a lifelong commitment to peace and justice. Whether drastic or moderate, the personal changes experienced by sanctuary workers were an integral part of the social changes enacted by the movement.

The sharp line that is usually drawn between social change movements, such as organized labor, and personal change movements, such as religious cults (Jenkins 1983; Tarrow 1988; Garner and Zald 1985), has led researchers to underestimate the significance of the personal transformations that occur in the process of protest. In abjuring the once popular view that social movements are made up of maladjusted, alienated deviants, theorists have instead insisted that movement participants are rational actors who seek changes in the social order, not altered consciousness or spiritual enlightenment (Pichardo 1988; Oberschall 1973; Tilly 1978; McCarthy and Zald 1973; Zald and McCarthy 1979; Gamson 1975). Furthermore, researchers have largely assumed that the social changes achieved by successful movements take the form of observable political acts, such as repealing or enacting legislation, rather than cultural or religious developments that have more diffuse political implications (Jenkins 1983; cf. Melucci 1989). Those analysts who *have* examined personal change within social movements have deemed it either an inevitable but insignificant by-product of protest or a method of mobilizing commitment. To give an example of the former perspective, anthropologist Susan Harding concluded that personal change only affects society at large if it reaches those in power. Harding wrote: "All movements, by definition, transform their participants' conceptions of self and the social order, and are thus mechanisms of sociocultural change internally. When they succeed in altering the way state authorities perceive a matter, they become, through their reverberations of state, broader mechanisms of sociocultural change as they reshape the worldviews of a nation (1984:400)." Sociologist Craig Jenkins illustrated the latter, more instrumental view of personal change when he argued that to garner supporters, movements must "generate solidarity and moral commitments to the broad collectivities in whose name movements act" (1983:538). Neither of these approaches considers the changes experienced by protestors relevant to the social significance of a movement.

The personal changes realized by sanctuary workers were neither insignificant nor merely a means to an end. Rather, when taken cumulatively, sanctuary workers' ideological, religious, and cultural transformations constituted a significant part of the social change enacted by the movement. Personal transformations occurred when individuals interpreted reality through movement discourse rather than through other cultural frames. The processes that made movement discourse authoritative to participants were intertwined with those that created and reproduced movement culture. Both movement founders and subsequent participants entered into the reality of movement discourse through an initial experience, such as meeting a Central American refugee, hearing a refugee's testimony, attempting to bond a Guatemalan out of detention, and so forth. As they determined the significance of this initial experience, individuals created and accepted movement discourse. Defining events through movement discourse then led to further action, which reinforced their commitment while reproducing the movement.[1] Reinterpreting reality in light of Central American issues produced ideological, theological, and political changes that constituted significant developments in their own right. By adding to and altering existing cultural repertoires, these developments extended beyond the confines of the movement to the communities to which movement members belonged (see also Tarrow 1988). As the "worldviews of a nation" were not exclusively in authorities' hands, changing the views predominant in churches, communities, schools, and other social sectors and institutions changed society, regardless of whether government policy was affected. The personal changes wrought by sanctuary work thus incrementally altered society as a whole.

## Consciousness-Raising

The popular term for the process that takes place when the discourse of a particular movement becomes authoritative to individuals is "consciousness-raising." In the case of sanctuary, this process took many forms. When religious volunteers created the movement, they simultaneously created the discourse (or "consciousness") that compelled them to take action. Subsequent volunteers underwent consciousness-raising when they accepted the validity of this discourse, Such consciousness-raising reproduced the movement by leading additional individuals to engage in movement practices. At the same time, because each participant interpreted reality from a unique social position, consciousness-raising not only reproduced but also *redefined* the discourse that participants accepted. Finally, volunteers sought to bring about consciousness-raising in nonparticipants by promoting and recreating the experiences that had convinced them to join the movement. These forms of consciousness-raising followed a pattern. Meeting Central Americans introduced North Americans to a version of reality with which they had been unfamiliar. Because their new knowledge made it impossible for them to live as previously, these North Americans began performing the activities that constituted sanctuary work. Such actions in turn reinforced participants' commitment to movement discourse. It is important to note that the steps in this process did not follow inevitably, one from another. Not all individuals who agreed with the movement took action, while some volunteers—particularly those who lacked contact with refugees—found sanctuary *less* compelling after working with the movement. For participants who joined and remained involved, however, consciousness-raising was an ongoing process furthered by a deepening acquaintance with Central Americans.

Participants reported that what had made them inescapably conscious of human rights abuses in El Salvador and Guatemala was hearing Central Americans' accounts of persecution. Edward Radtke, a Tucson minister involved in the underground railroad, noted, "Once you spend time with the people who are coming here, once you have heard their stories, then there's no turning back." Ralph Lieber of First Church reached a similar conclusion:

> There's something unique about the way that it affects us culturally when we meet people face-to-face. We could hold endless meetings and discussions about El Salvador, but their effect would be nothing compared to the effect [that] getting to know one family has had on a congregation. I suppose Marxists would talk about the dif-

ference between ideology and material. In fact, leftists talk on and on about ideology and nothing happens, but when there's human contact, that's when change occurs.

Another East Bay sanctuary worker used an anecdote to convey the power of human contact:

> Once I went to a testimony where a woman passed around a picture of her son and then described how he'd been captured, tortured, and finally killed. You could hear the shock in the room! That's when people are won over in an instant. ... After walking away from that, when a person hears the news, he'll think "Now who am I going to believe? That trash that's printed in the newspaper, or this woman who came to my church last week and told me about her husband and two kids?"

For most participants, becoming conscious of the suffering in Central America also meant accepting that the United States was complicit in this suffering. During an interview, Anya Fischer—who had persuaded her synagogue to declare sanctuary—faulted U.S. authorities for failing to grant refugee status to Central American immigrants. She summarized the analysis that had led her to join the movement: "That refugees were fleeing, that they were fearing death if they went back to their own country, that the INS was deporting people like crazy, and they were not being granted asylum the way we all felt they should have, given the laws; and that this was an outrageous situation, parallel to what the Jews had faced historically, and that we had to speak up." Similarly, Samuel Durand, a Task Force member, commented, "The major issue for me has been the realization that the government wants to preserve its right to send the innocent to their deaths." Some sanctuary workers blamed the United States not only for failing to recognize Central Americans' refugee status but also for contributing to the suffering and human rights abuses that led Central Americans to flee. During an interview, Lindsey Martin, a Berkeley sanctuary worker, asked rhetorically, "Why is it that I should deserve to make $26,000 and live in a nice home and have all the food I can eat, and someone who earns $2,000 a year doesn't have the right to do this, and it's my tax-paying dollars that keeps the person in poverty through oppression and through that kind of regime?"

Conscious of human rights abuses in Central America and of their own society's complicity in such suffering, individuals found that they could not live with themselves if they did not become involved in the movement. Marty Finn, an EBSC Steering Committee representative, said of sanctuary, "There's such a need, that if you don't do it, then you can't be true to yourself." Sherrie Katz, a Tucson sanctuary worker, began to do border crossings so that she would have an answer when her children grew up and asked, "Mommy, what were you doing during the sanctuary movement? Why weren't you involved?" Jamie Porter, who had let border workers use his car during crossings, told me, "I didn't want to be like the Germans who said they didn't know about it [the Holocaust], which was bull."

Flora Grant, a Tucson border worker, asked, "How can you say no when someone comes knocking on your door?" Gina Holmes, another border worker, said, "When I knew about it [sanctuary], I just *had* to do it. I had no choice." Lindsey Martin, an EBSC Steering Committee representative who had traveled to Central America, noted, "My view now about sanctuary work is that it's like brushing my teeth or exercising. It's part of life, and it's part of my consciousness, and I wouldn't grow as a person if I didn't do it and commit to it on a regular basis."

Participants' growing willingness to take the physical, legal, emotional, and financial risks that sanctuary work entailed was reinforced by fellow sanctuary workers and by Central Americans themselves. Within the movement, those who took the greatest risks were admired by their colleagues. Sherrie Katz, who became a border worker shortly after the January 1985 indictments, explained, "The leaders of sanctuary and the people who had been the most active and who had taken more risks than I had, had been arrested. And that made me feel like, if anything, I needed to be *more* involved in the actual crossings to take up the work that they had been doing." Movement members were also impressed by the Central Americans who risked torture and death for the sake of their communities. A Tucson sanctuary minister recalled meeting such people during a trip to Central America:

> I guess the most extraordinary experience [on my trip] was to be with people who knew ... that they were not going to live much longer occupying the positions that they were, doing human rights work or working with the base communities. Their colleagues were killed right and left. They wouldn't last much longer. And we talked about it candidly. And I had never talked with people of faith before who were in that position. And I pressed them on it. The question that I asked all of them was, "Why are you doing this?" And to hear their responses out of faith: "Well, because Monseñor Romero would want us to." "Because God wants us to be here."

Peter Lockhart, a Bay Area Catholic and seminary student, found Archbishop Romero's sacrifice a model to emulate: "I believe it [the gospel] because others have believed it unto death. Oscar Romero is a perfect example of it for me. To be shot down in the middle of celebrating the Mass, the Eucharist, which for us is the ultimate thanksgiving, the ultimate symbol of our unity, what we're all about. Wow!"

To sway public opinion and to attract additional volunteers, sanctuary workers publicized the movement through tactics that replicated the experiences that had compelled them to join. The most important of these tactics were public testimonies in which Central Americans told church gatherings, college classes, high-school students, community groups, journalists, and others their stories of persecution and flight.[2] Because they brought North Americans into direct contact with the victims of persecution, testimonies were thought more persuasive than presentations by sanctuary workers. As one sanctuary worker said when explaining how he and others had arrived at the idea of sanctuary, "They could always dismiss us as bleeding hearts, or naïve, or liberals, or 'Oh, they're just church people,' or whatever. But they couldn't dismiss the refugees who told about their own experiences." Marty Finn, a Berkeley sanctuary volunteer, argued that direct contact between North and Central Americans would mobilize U.S. citizens to oppose aid for Salvadoran and Guatemalan regimes. Marty explained, "For Central Americans to meet with North Americans and just to talk and be friends and socialize is extremely important, because it shows people that when U.S.-backed governments of various sorts brutalize people, they aren't brutalizing animals, they aren't brutalizing robots, they aren't brutalizing Communist flunkies. They're brutalizing real people." Failing the availability of actual Central Americans, sanctuary workers sought to publicize Central Americans' *stories*. Randy Silbert, a Tucson border worker, concluded our interview by urging me, "Go out and spread the word about what's happening here. Tell people about the human consequences of the war. Publish the refugees' stories. Include pictures of their bullet scars and photos of the mutilated bodies."

Sanctuary workers also sought to promote consciousness-raising by publicly reiterating the arguments that justified movement actions, although such arguments were considered less compelling than refugees' testimonies. Participants felt responsible for countering what they perceived as widespread ignorance and misinformation regarding Central America. At a January 1988 sanctuary retreat in Tucson, participants characterized the news media's Central America coverage as a "terrible silence," wondered if there was a conspiracy against reporting criticisms of U.S. policy on Central America, and decided to investigate. Because they considered the press the body that defined reality for the general populace, sanctuary workers were highly media-conscious. A Berkeley minister explained, "Very early, we were concerned about people who were going to *speak*. And we had different levels of *speaking*. The people who were going to speak in churches and present slide shows and things like that, we said they should be people who are trained and know what to say and really understand [that] there are some things you say and some things you don't say." In addition to promoting sanctuary, public speaking was a method of opposing human rights violations. Whenever they learned of a detention, disappearance, or threat in El Salvador or Guatemala, participants spoke out. For example, when a Salvadoran refugee camp was threatened by military forces, Tucson sanctuary workers immediately called a press conference. In the Bay Area, office volunteers maintained an urgent action network that informed EBSC Steering Committee representatives of human rights violations and how to send telegrams of protest.

As sanctuary workers took the actions, including public speaking, that were mandated by their awareness of Central Americans' suffering, some underwent a transformation that was deeper than consciousness-raising. These participants reinterpreted religious as well as political reality in terms of movement discourse.

## Conversion

Christian sanctuary workers who reexamined their faith with an awareness of Central Americans' suffering went through not only consciousness-raising but also conversion. This did not happen to every participant. Many sanctuary workers had already experienced a conversion to social justice by being conscientious objectors during World War II, civil rights activists in the South, or draft dodgers during the Vietnam War. Others were acting out of a political or strictly humanitarian concern. Still others were involved in a peripheral way that required little commitment and brought little contact with Central Americans. In particular, Jewish sanctuary workers did not undergo conversions but rather identified with Central Americans out of their own history of marginalization—a subject that will be addressed in the next section. However, approximately one-fourth of the sanctuary workers I interviewed had experienced a conversion that, although resonant with other social movements, was specific to sanctuary and involved crossing a border to see reality from the perspective of the oppressed. I first heard of such conversions when Christian sanctuary workers publicly described the movement's significance for their own lives and faith. I originally conceived of conversion as something short and sudden; in actuality, it was an ongoing process that for some began decades before they met refugees from Central America. The conversions that were particular to the movement began when affluent, white, middle-class Americans crossed borders by trying to identify with the Central American poor, to act in solidarity with them, and in some sense, to *become* them. This desire to identify with the oppressed was caused by the belief that the persecuted were closer to God than were middle-class North Americans and hence were sources of knowledge about God, society, life, and spirituality. Identifying with the poor entailed questioning how one's social position had influenced one's faith. Conversions occurred when Christian sanctuary workers rejected what they characterized as their former, comfortable versions of faith to embrace liberation theology's risk-filled commitment to social justice.

The following narratives detail the conversions that two individuals experienced. I interviewed Matthew Scott twice in a busy Mexican restaurant in Berkeley during his lunch hour. Matthew, who was in his mid-thirties, was very active in EBSC. He was a professional, a father, and a Protestant. Gloria Murdock, in her late twenties, was a Tucson border worker and, like Matthew, a Protestant. We had breakfast together in a Tucson cafe and then met a month later for coffee one afternoon. My interviews with Matthew were tape-recorded while those with Gloria were not. These two narratives are excerpted from the interviews.

### Matthew Scott

I was a philosophy student at U.C. Berkeley, and I also was involved in Inter-Varsity Christian Fellowship. ... I.V. is an evangelical kind of group, and at one point, I was thinking about becoming a staff person. That sense of a personal relationship with God is still important to me and is something that motivates my work with sanctuary. I think that the people who have a personal relationship with God are more motivated because they have a sense that God is in charge, and that faith keeps them from getting burned out, or discouraged when things don't go the way that you want.

So, as a philosophy major, my own philosophy was something called Occasionalism, which means that you try out different philosophies, trying to believe them and living according to them for a short time, and then see how well it works. I tried this with a number of different philosophies. I was a Marxist for a month, and I tried being a Moslem for a month. But neither of those seemed right.

So, somehow, I don't remember how I did this, but I picked up a book by Gustavo Gutiérrez, and I decided to try liberation theology. And what struck me the most was that Gutiérrez wrote that to know God was to do justice. So I realized that I couldn't just try out this philosophy by believing it; I had to *act*. So that was how I first became involved in social justice, was from an abstract intellectual motivation. ...

I continued to read liberation theology, and found it more and more ... true. And the methods that get used in liberation theology seemed to me very sound and consistent. ...

It was May of '82 that I went to ... this one-day seminar on Guatemala. And there were these two Guatemalan women whose families had been massacred who were there at the seminar. ... The thing that struck me most was that even though almost everyone in their family had been killed, and basically, the whole village was wiped out, and they fled with nothing and they really had nothing, they were still hopeful. And they still had a lot of faith and a lot of hope [and] basically trust that one day they'd be able to return to Guatemala and continue living. ... The respect that I had for those two women did a lot to affect [me]. ... They talked a little bit about their culture, their Indian culture in Guatemala, and it started becoming more interesting. ...

I finally decided, ... "For two years I've been reading liberation theology and reading a lot about the culture, and what I really need to do is go down there and find out what's happening and see it first-hand." And so I went on this educational delegation down to Nicaragua. It was actually Mexico and Nicaragua, for three weeks, and I would say that that affected me pretty drastically in that up until that point, my working for justice was still a theoretical thing. I had discovered that working for justice *did* lead one toward knowing God, so I had pretty much decided and committed myself to doing justice for the rest of my life, but it was still doing justice for theoretical reasons. ...

Meeting the people [in Nicaragua] was pretty intense. There was a woman who asked me to take a picture of her baby, because after people are killed, they put up their picture in different places, and for them, having a picture taken was kind of a little piece of immortality, at least. ... What she said was, "He's never had his picture taken." He had just been born, and am I going to take his picture, because "in case he gets killed in the near future, I want to have a picture of him. Even if I don't have the picture, just the fact that he has his picture somewhere, I'll rest easy." ...

When I came back I went through ... a postvisit depression. ... I realized, "I wonder how many of the people I just visited two weeks ago or three weeks ago have been killed already? I wonder if that baby's been killed, or that woman's been killed? Or if some of the people whose testimonies we heard have been killed?" ... It made me realize the real urgency of the whole task, which was that there were people really dying, and I couldn't just sit around and not do anything. ...

There are a lot of people in the social justice movement who at one point or another rejected their faith, and then, seeing the churches take a lead[ing] role ... has made them reevaluate the church based on that. And so, I do see that in a lot of ways, it's a witness of your life rather than a witness of your words. ... Essentially, it's converting people or turning people back to the church who *have* a feel for justice. ...

I would say that in general, the American church has essentially really watered down the Sermon on the Mount [and] Matthew 25. Basically, it's made this very abstract and meaningless. ... Most churches have a little bit of a spark in them, but very few are really on fire, to use the analogy. ...

My conversion experience getting involved in social justice impacted me at least as much as my initial conversion experience of becoming a Christian. The major transformation has been from—I guess what it is is that when I became a Christian, it was all very much for myself, and everything that I was doing was egocentric. Even wanting to become more humble was an egocentric thing, because I thought it was becoming more godly to become more humble. ...

What I see is that social justice and loving your neighbor are intimately tied together, and that the heart of the gospel is [to] love God and love your neighbor. And if you're not doing social justice ... you're not really loving your neighbor. ... If you're not making, as the Catholic church says, the preferential option for the poor, then you're not loving your neighbor. And it also isn't just on a theoretical basis, loving your neighbor. I think the biggest conversion experience for me really is when I met the people down there, realized that they were dying, realized that, I guess, that God was calling me to love them and to do something for them, and that that loving other people has been a conversion experience. ...

One of the things—I've seen this happen to a lot of people that have gone down. That their experience in Central America *has been* a conversion experience. ... Getting people down to Central America is not only for protecting the people down there but also because of the conversion experience that people go through. ...

Another experience for me that was very [much a] part of my conversion—my second conversion—was in Mexico and [the experience] was [with] a family that lived on the street in a tent and was obviously extremely poor. ... We just happened to be passing by, and I was with a translator, and I just asked, "Can I take your picture?" And they said, "Oh yes, take our picture, come in." And they sat me down, and I ended up spending an entire evening there. They gave me some of their dinner, which I was reluctant to eat because I was worried about water and all that. They brought out these Oreo cookies that were obviously kind of old and stale, but it looked to me like they'd been saving them for a long time for a special occasion. And it just struck me, ... the people down there who were very poor, just in general, tend to be very giving, very open. "Come on and eat with us. We'll give you our best stuff." They ... redivided their dinner so that I could have some. And I guess it just shocked me that poor people tend to be much more generous than rich people. ...

Just seeing people who—I guess [you know] the old analogy of the faith going through the fire and being purified in the fire? A lot of them, I think, have a much more purified faith because it has been through the fire, and we just kind of stay a comfortable seventy-two degrees here.

### Gloria Murdock

Just to let you know what I was doing before all of this started, I moved here to do volunteer work with my denomination. During those years, I was doing a lot of work with the undocumented. I finished that in 1980 and went on to manage a political campaign. I was then asked to develop a border ministry with the undocumented, which is what I've worked on since. ...

Intellectually, I knew what was happening, but when I met Central American refugees face-to-face, it was transforming. When I heard their stories, when I saw them cry, it was gut-wrenching for me. I knew I had to do something. ...

In 1982, after the process of going to the detention center, being on the TEC Task Force, ... and after a lot of personal reflection on the Old Testament scripture, my own faith basis, the moral and ethical values I was raised with, and my understanding of the law, I came to the conclusion that more was required of my faith and my citizenship than what I was doing. I saw that I had to do more than the social service stuff that we were doing, even though that's important. So, I began doing the crossings. ...

I wouldn't say that it [the initial decision to do border crossings] was a conversion, because to me a conversion implies that there would be transformation. The conversion came later, when I took risks with the refugees. The decision I made after reflecting on my own life, on the law, on my values, on my everyday experience of doing social action here at the border, was more expanding the responsibility that I had [than it was a conversion].

My understanding of conversion comes from the notion of praxis as defined by Paulo Freire, and that is that first you have an active experience, such as in this case crossing refugees, and then you reflect on that experience, and then in turn you reflect on the time of reflection that you had. It's a series of events and a whole process that you go through. But for me, the conversion came from walking in the desert through the mountains with refugees, and the fears that I had. I was afraid of snakes, that we would be caught and raped by the *Mexicanos,* and so on. ...

The transformation came not so much from hearing their stories, but when I reached a point of talking with the refugees and hearing the risks that they had taken and that they would go on taking. I had never met people who were so dedicated to a cause! So for me, the conversion came out of my own experience of sharing their risks even a little bit. These experiences with refugees challenged my faith, and they made it more difficult for me to go to church. I was amazed at their ability to forgive someone who had tortured them. When I went to church, I would remember how the refugees had interpreted a particular Bible passage. They challenged me socially, politically, economically. ...

I began to feel that I was a stranger relating to those people who I'd grown up with! I say "who I grew up with," but actually, I didn't grow up in Tucson, but these were the people who shared my background, who had nurtured me, and who had challenged me to move beyond my status-quo-ness. And then, when I did, they weren't willing to go with me. And the worship services that nurtured their needs so well weren't meeting mine at all.

And then on the other hand, I wasn't with the refugees either, because I hadn't experienced torture, I hadn't had to flee my country. So I couldn't classify myself as in the same category that they were, much as I aspired to. I still had my middle-class values. ...

So the conversion came when my own fears and my idols were questioned and challenged by the refugees. And they didn't always know that they were doing it. Sometimes their very way of living caused me to question my own way of life. ... For example, their commitment to a cause. I was meeting catechists, community organizers, teachers, people who'd had brushes with the Treasury Police, or the National Guard, or with the military, and yet they didn't flee to the U.S. or Mexico right away. They stayed! They would just move to a different town where they could continue their work. That was beyond my experience! I don't know what it is to be tortured or to be pursued.

Their concept of community, which is something I can't integrate. They are willing to give their lives for their friends. They think of their community before themselves, before their own mothers and families. And I mean, I've been committed to a cause, but never to that extent!

Their concept of material goods. If I want something, whether it's something I really need or not, I just go and I buy it. And that's something that is beyond the ability of most Central Americans.

And things like, I don't think twice before reading a periodical that's critical of the government, or listening to a protest song, or indigenous music, which I happen to like. They could be picked up and killed for doing something like that! A friend of mine was washing the dishes one day, and everyone had gone to work, and she was playing a song by a Chilean political singer, and she had the music turned up way loud. And there was a refugee living with her who became very agitated, and she came in and asked, "Is it okay to play that music so loudly? Shouldn't we turn it down?" My friend answered, "Oh, it's fine, everyone's up and has gone to work, so we're not disturbing anyone." It took her a while, as it would have taken me, to understand that the woman was afraid because of hearing that.

So, even though I feel that we don't live in a democracy, I realize that it's relative. We take for granted many of the things that we are able to do here.

Well, Susan, I could go on and on. Those are just some of the things.

These two narratives reveal how border crossings brought about conversions. For both Matthew and Gloria, border crossings were life-changing experiences. Matthew was shocked by the suffering, poverty, and generosity of the poor, while Gloria was confronted with her own fears and with refugees' deep sense of commitment and community. Significantly, Matthew's and Gloria's conversions occurred in the highly meaningful space between borders. For Gloria, this space was the desert and the mountains, while for Matthew, it was Mexico and Nicaragua. By entering the reality of the oppressed, Matthew and Gloria moved from abstract to concrete knowledge of suffering. This knowledge led them to interpret reality in unique ways. Gloria felt separated from both her peers and the refugees she worked with, while Matthew discovered that his new commitment to social justice was missing in most American churches. Both Matthew and Gloria found that taking risks deepened their conversion to the movement. Matthew characterized risks as the fire that purified faith, while Gloria aspired to understand the torture and flight that refugees experienced. Matthew's and Gloria's conversions both resulted from and demanded deeper involvement in the movement.

The conversions experienced by Matthew and Gloria entailed questioning their own beliefs and turning to the oppressed for answers. According to Martin Reiner, an Arizona minister, "It's true as the Bible says, that the poor are a source of our salvation, and the reason is that they *know* that society isn't working, whereas the middle class believes that it is. So God *does* come to us through the poor. These aren't just empty words; this has been a historical reality." Similarly, Linda Allen, a minister who had been instrumental in the development of EBSC, described how a refugee had taught priests and nuns about faith:

> I had been invited to speak to a class of religious people, and so I thought to bring along a refugee. And I had the good sense to stop speaking after five minutes and to turn the floor over to him. ... And Susan, you can't imagine how well and how articulately he spoke! And his knowledge of the Bible! His story was *beautiful!* And there in that room were nuns and priests that had been stationed all over the world, and they sat at his feet and listened to his story.

Sister Anabel Marquet, a Tucson sanctuary worker, found that listening to refugees brought her into the sacred yet forbidden space where bread and wine were transformed into Christ's body and blood:

The usual idea is that we are the ones who are crossing a border to help them, but in this case, they're the ones who helped me cross a border. What I'm talking about is the separation of the Communion rail and the Eucharist. Only the priests can be behind the Communion rail. Women aren't allowed into the sanctuary, except when they get married. But what the refugees have done is enabled me to cross that rail. What is the Eucharist but the suffering and death of Jesus? As I've learned about the suffering and death of the refugees, it's expanding the whole meaning of "Eucharist" for me. They've expanded my borders and horizons.

As they listened to refugees, Christian sanctuary workers realized that their own theologies had been developed in a middle-class North American context. One Tucson pastor explained, "Where I find the conversion is people moving from viewing themselves and from reading the Bible from the point of view of North Americans, to reading the Bible from the point of view of Central Americans and of refugees." The results of such rereading were sometimes dramatic. Samuel Durand, a fifty-year-old minister of a fairly conservative church, told me:

> I have learned *incredible* things from the lives and the witness of the Central American people. Now I have an entirely different view of scripture, and I wonder how I could have read it before and have been so blind. And my new understanding came from the Central Americans, from *campesinos,* from people with no formal education, but who have rich insight that comes from their experiences.

Rev. Nathan Coffelt, a former minister of First Church, gave an example of this kind of rereading: "If you say, 'Who is Moses?' to a white, middle-class group, they almost always mention the Ten Commandments. If you mentioned it to a down-and-out group, they talk about Moses as the one that liberated them from the Pharaoh! And you know, it's the same story! In the same words!"

Through reinterpreting their faith from the point of view of the oppressed, Christian sanctuary workers underwent a conversion to liberation theology. Philip Kaspar, a Tucson sanctuary worker who believed that conversion was an ongoing process, explained, "The major conversion for me was the conversion to the poor. I went from a pietistic faith, focusing on my individual relationship to a transcendent God, to seeing God's immanence among the poor. Jesus was among the poor. Jesus said when you give food to the hungry, drink to the thirsty, clothes to the naked, you give those things to me." Nancy Michaels, a Berkeley social activist and a member of First Church's Sanctuary Committee, struggled against poverty and oppression until she became exhausted. Then, she found God. She told me, "Not only did I find a way to renew myself spiritually, so that I could basically get out of bed in the morning, but also found to my great delight that the Bible and Christian faith was full of the urge for justice! And full of solidarity for the poor!" Through working with Third World people, Marilyn Phillips of Tucson learned that faith "meant putting my life on the line for others. I came to understand the beatitudes, and I learned what Christ's life and teachings really meant. Christ spent most of his ministry working with the marginalized and the oppressed, and in the end, he was killed by the authorities for working to bring about the kingdom of God."

The religious transformations experienced by Matthew Scott, Gloria Murdock, and other Christian sanctuary workers constituted significant social developments. The individuals who went through conversions infused the liberal Christian community in the United States with a unique form of religious experience, a new interpretation of faith, and a dose of Latin American liberation theology. Like consciousness-raising, conversion committed individuals to acting on behalf of the oppressed. As they identified with and sought spiritual knowledge from Salvadoran and Guatemalan refugees, these individuals inverted and critiqued hierarchies between North Americans and Central Americans, the wealthy and the poor, citizens and the undocumented. One Berkeley monk whom I interviewed considered the very words "El Salvador" a synonym for Christ. This monk commented, "For me, by helping a refugee, it's my way of helping the church—the martyred church in Central America. ... It's where I see the Lord crucified—*El Salvador,* the Savior—being crucified." Similarly, Simon Portnoy, former pastor of a Tucson sanctuary congregation, compared the sacrifices demanded by social justice to those made by Christ, saying, "Jesus on the Cross means just that." Although likening the suffering of Central Americans to the martyrdom of Christ critiqued social hierarchies, such comparisons also produced idealized images of Salvadoran and Guatemalan refugees. A more direct, less idealizing means of identifying with refugees was provided by the parallels that Jewish sanctuary workers created between their own and Central Americans' histories of exile.

## An Exiled People

Rather than undergoing a religious conversion, Jews who became involved in the sanctuary movement made sense of Central Americans' suffering by comparing it to their own marginalization. Unlike Christians, who shared a religious tradition with Central Americans, Jewish sanctuary workers found few refugees knowledgeable about Judaism. Christians tended to identify with refugees by drawing on the view that God is among the poor—a tenet of liberation theology and the social gospel—and by comparing Central Americans' experiences to Christ's persecution and martyrdom. In contrast, in establishing common ground, Jews and Central Americans relied heavily on parallels in their peoples' persecutions. Most Jewish sanctuary workers whom I interviewed had relatives who perished during the Holocaust, who fled but were sent back, or who successfully immigrated despite daunting bureaucracies. To relate to Central American refugees, Jews viewed events in El Salvador and Guatemala through the lens of their own people's Diaspora, exile, and experiences of anti-Semitism and genocide. Unlike their Christian colleagues, Jewish sanctuary workers did not need to cross a border between security and suffering to enter Central American reality. Their own history placed them already on the other side.

It is necessary to qualify the Jewish-Christian contrast that I have just presented because the ability to relate to Central American refugees out of one's own history of persecution was not unique to Jews, nor was reinterpreting one's faith from the perspective of the oppressed limited to Christians. For example, Simon Portnoy, a Tucson Presbyterian, had had to flee Spain during the Spanish civil war. Simon told me, "I *know* what refugees are. I *know* what it is to be a refugee." Simon also felt that the refugee experience had been incorporated into his denomination at the time of its inception. He explained, "Refugees are part of our history. Even though Presbyterians are Scotch-Irish, during the Reformation, John Calvin went to Geneva, which had become a refugee city. Calvin was in the middle of it. So that history is in our bones; there's no getting away from it." Similarly, like Christians, some Jews reinterpreted their religious traditions in light of Central American reality. Sherrie Katz of Tucson believed that her sanctuary work fulfilled the Torah's command, "Justice, justice you shall pursue." Hilary Epstein of Congregation Aron Kodesh quoted Rabbi Hillel to explain the basis of her sanctuary work: "If I live not for me, who will live for me? If I live not for others, then what am I? If not now, then when?" Damien Rosenthal, also a Congregation Aron Kodesh member, said of sanctuary, "It's the Moses story. It's the enslaved and the slave, the free and the unfree, the Pharaohs and the saviors. ... It repeats itself. It's the symbols of our society in El Salvador." In Tucson, Freedom Seders open only to refugees and sanctuary workers had become a Passover tradition.

Though capable of each, Jews tended to identify with Central Americans by reinterpreting their history rather than their theology. One Bay Area rabbi explained that Jewish history informed all Jewish activism:

> We have been an exiled people and a persecuted people for two millennia, and our primary experience goes back to the enslavement in Egypt, which is a fundamental symbolic frame for a lot of Jewish values and activities and activism, whether on the Right or the Left. Whether it's Soviet Jewry, whether it's Israel, or whether it's Jews working on behalf of Palestinians, whether it's El Salvadorans and Guatemalans, it's a real touchstone.

Anya Fischer, who was instrumental in her synagogue's sanctuary declaration, found the parallels between Jewish and Central American history persuasive:

> We in recent history have known what it is to be rejected. If we were allowed out of the country, if we had the good luck to just be kicked out of the country, no other country would take in the Jews, and that's why so many more perished during World War II than should have. ... So [now] there are people who have to flee be-

cause of political oppression and have no place to go, and the parallels are common
to the Jewish experience. I thought, "My God! We've got to reach out and help people. *We've* suffered like that! We've suffered, so we certainly have to help other people."

The Holocaust, the most recent and severe instance of Jewish persecution, was
at the center of Jewish debates about joining the movement. Jews such as Adele
Tilberg of Tucson found the comparison between the Holocaust and persecution
in Central America apt. Adele related, "My son in particular became fast friends
with the little boy in the [Salvadoran] family that I was involved with, and every
time I used to see them together, I used to think of my own child, and I would
think 'What if the situation were reversed? What if it was Germany?' And I would
hope that someone would be there to help my kids." However, Jewish sanctuary
workers who made presentations to uninvolved synagogues discovered that some
Jews felt that such comparisons demeaned the Holocaust. Terri Segal of Congregation Aron Kodesh summarized the objections of such people: "Six million Jews
were killed during the Holocaust. It was the prejudice and hatred of a people,
whereas in Central America, it's more indiscriminate. You can still live in Central
America, but if you were a Jew in Germany, you couldn't live at all." Yosef Meyer
of Congregation Aron Kodesh told me that when such arguments were raised
during his own presentations about sanctuary, he usually responded by distinguishing the *lessons* of the Holocaust from the experience of the Holocaust. He
explained that because Jews honored the Righteous Gentiles for putting themselves in jeopardy to save Jews, it would be hypocritical for Jews to remain silent
when another people was being persecuted. A Tucson rabbi told me that when
Jews objected that the Holocaust was not an appropriate analogy, he would argue:
"You can't bring back the six million Jews. And you don't honor the dead by creating memorials and by setting up plaques. You honor the dead by creating a situation where the living don't have to repeat the horror that the dead experienced."
      Unlike certain Christians (such as Gloria Murdock) who struggled to know
what it was to be a refugee, many of the Jews I interviewed *were* refugees, refugees'
children, or refugees' grandchildren.[3] At a Congregation Aron Kodesh sanctuary
brunch organized to honor donors and a refugee family, one Jewish man related
that his family had entered the United States illegally by bribing officials in Washington, D.C. At the same gathering, while watching a sanctuary videotape during
which a talk show host commented that he had never seen a refugee, the woman
sitting next to me said indignantly that there are many refugees in the United
States and that she herself had fled Germany at the age of seven. Similarly, a Tucson rabbi reported:

> My father was an undocumented alien. And I figure that it's the same thing whether
> you escape from the Kaiser in 1913, or whether you escape from Central America in
> the 1980s. And I had an aunt and uncle that escaped to France, and they couldn't

find anyone to take them in, and so they were sent back to Germany, and they were killed in a concentration camp, so I know. I know what happens to people when you don't let them in.

Even financially secure Jews who had never been persecuted felt the impact of fellow Jews' maltreatment. Damien Rosenthal of Congregation Aron Kodesh noted, "I, as a North American, I mean, that never happened to me. I never got holocausted. I live well! ... But [regarding] my Jewishness, finally, [through sanctuary] I have an avenue to go back to my roots."

In contrast to the more vicarious Christian efforts to identify with the poor through Christ's suffering and martyrdom, Jews related to Central Americans out of their own experiences. This contrast was brought home to me during an interview with Lisa Rothstein, a Jewish sanctuary worker in San Francisco. When I asked Lisa to describe the connections between Judaism and sanctuary, she noted, "It's a little different from Christianity, because I see Christians [as having] more of a sense of—it's quite different, I think. It's more of a—like they see Christ, I guess, *in* the refugee. Or something like that." Lisa explained that she understood exiled Central Americans because she understood exiled Jews: "They [Central American refugees] remind me of my own people. I mean, I can say that because the Jewish people were in exile for a couple of thousand years. It's that same kind of feeling that these people have about their country. They maintain the rituals, the culture. ... I can understand how they feel because I know my own people." Such comparisons between persecuted Jews and persecuted Salvadorans and Guatemalans were common among Jewish sanctuary workers. A Tucson rabbi told me that when Jews balked over sanctuary's legal implications, he usually asked them to put themselves in the shoes of Central Americans:

> I tell them, "Now, I want you to look me straight in the eye, and answer me a question. Suppose there was a Christian family in Germany and they were discussing whether or not to take in a Jew. And they were trying to decide whether or not to break the law, because it was illegal at the time. And suppose you were there to advise them about what to do. Tell me, would you tell them not to do it because it was illegal?" And whenever I've asked someone that, I've always won on that point. I've never had a Jew look me in the eye and tell me that they shouldn't do it.

Similarly, during an interview, when I asked Yosef Meyer of Congregation Aron Kodesh what North Americans could learn from Central Americans, he answered by considering what North Americans could learn from the Holocaust survivors he had known. He concluded, "That's going to differ from refugee to refugee in the same way that it differs from Holocaust survivor to Holocaust survivor."

Because of their past marginalization, there is a sense in which Jewish sanctuary workers did not cross a border to identify with the oppressed but rather found themselves already on the other side. Martha Madeira, a Jewish sanctuary volunteer, linked her commitment to sanctuary to "just being a member of a group that's been persecuted, oppressed, and singled out throughout history. ... Even though I've never studied it and I never learned much about it specifically, I've just always been conscious of that." David Hoffman, Lisa Rothstein's husband, told me, "We as Jews know what it's like to be underdogs, and ... out of our special knowledge and insight comes a responsibility to stand up and to see the predicament of a people who are without a voice." According to Hilary Epstein of Congregation Aron Kodesh, "Jews, I think, always have an insecurity that they could be put out of the mainstream due to anti-Semitism." In addition to using their knowledge of Central American societies to expose the shortcomings of middle-class U.S. life, some Jewish sanctuary workers looked to their own past for models to emulate. The rabbi of one Bay Area sanctuary synagogue wrote, "Many of us carry with us the image of a time in the past when Jews had a home, a community where life was integral and whole, where the spirit mattered, and one's daily actions related to something ultimate. Now that time is gone, and we find ourselves longing for something precious that has been lost." The shtetls destroyed by the Holocaust, like strafed Salvadoran and Guatemalan villages, provided images of community for a people in exile.

## Conclusion

The consciousness-raising, conversions, and reinterpretations of Jewish history that sanctuary workers experienced and promulgated were important religious, cultural, and political developments. Interaction with Central American refugees convinced middle-class North Americans that human rights violations had occurred in El Salvador and Guatemala and that the U.S. government had supported or at least ignored these abuses. Their personal acquaintance with the victims of such persecution compelled these North Americans to speak and act against abuses, even at great personal risk. Some of the Christian North Americans who learned of Central Americans' suffering reinterpreted their faith from the perspective of the poor and thus experienced a conversion to liberation theology. The Jewish North Americans who encountered Central Americans' plight connected Jewish history to the history of Central American refugees. Each of the individuals who, to a lesser or greater extent, experienced these transformations was part of a personal network that extended beyond the confines of the sanctuary movement. Even if other members of these networks (and society as a whole) did not fully adopt sanctuary workers' views, the forms of personal change created by members of the movement added to existing cultural repertoires. Social change does not have to be all-encompassing to be significant.

The ways that the sanctuary movement was created, perpetuated, and made compelling to participants illustrate how cultural innovation, reproduction, and imposition are interrelated. First, the sanctuary movement was constructed through a complex interplay of agency, structure, and history. Though the choices available to participants were to some extent historically and culturally predetermined, by acting, sanctuary workers made history and improvised on preexisting social forms. Innovation was ongoing, as participants continually sought to shape and respond to changing historical and social conditions. Second, once created, the sanctuary movement was reproduced through a dialectic between meaning and action. Border crossings gave participants a set of shared experiences out of which to construct the movement's vision of reality, and this vision, in turn, influenced participants' interpretations of the crossing experience. Because border crossings occurred at different moments and under different conditions, reproducing the movement entailed innovation as well as simple recreation. Third, movement culture was made authoritative to participants through consciousness-raising, conversions, and reinterpretations of history. As sanctuary workers became involved in the movement, their experiences with Central American refugees changed their ideological, cultural, and religious views, which in turn led to further action and deeper transformation. Such personal changes reproduced the movement by leading nonparticipants to become sanctuary workers. Cultural imposition[4] was also connected to innovation, as the changes experienced by participants constituted significant social developments. Innovation, reproduction, and imposition were ongoing and intertwined within the movement, as within society.

To understand the political implications of the culture of protest that sanctuary workers created, reproduced, and embraced, it is necessary to examine how movement practices challenged and reinforced particular systems of power. When movement members crossed and sheltered undocumented Central Americans, they both defied and invoked the authority of laws that called such actions crimes. Sanctuary practices engaged U.S. immigration law not only through direct conflict with authorities but also by altering the social relationships that defined undocumented Salvadorans and Guatemalans as illegal aliens.

## Notes

1. Gerlach and Hine's (1970) description of how people become committed to a movement is similar to mine, except that I see this as a dialectical process that produces not only participants but also the movement itself.

2. There may be parallels between the ways that Central Americans' testimonies led sanctuary workers to revise their understandings of reality and the ways that the civil rights movement challenged white hegemony by publicizing the views of southern blacks. See Harding 1984.

3. Being a refugee did not necessarily mean supporting sanctuary. One Jewish sanctuary worker told me that when the issue of sanctuary arose in her synagogue, the main opposition came from Jewish refugees from Cuba. She explained, "They felt that this country had done so much for them that they didn't want to be involved in anything like this. But of course, coming from a Communist country, this government had given them legal status right from the start."

4. By "cultural imposition," I do not mean to imply that individuals were forced to join the sanctuary movement or to accept its tenets. Rather, I refer to the ways that preexisting cultural concepts and practices are rendered authoritative to individuals. Cultural imposition does not only occur when individuals join protest movements or other unique social groupings. Whenever social beings accept, reproduce, and live according to cultural concepts and practices, imposition takes place.

# PART TWO

# SANCTUARY

# 5

# Alienation

*As we were leaving [a political asylum hearing], one of the men [who had been granted asylum] walked up to me and said in Spanish, "So, Susan, this piece of paper is my political asylum!" I said yes, and how happy I was for him that they'd won. He then said, "¡No más mojado!" No longer a wetback. No longer illegal.*
—Excerpt from Susan Coutin's fieldnotes

When religious volunteers attempted to define undocumented Central Americans as legal refugees rather than illegal aliens, they engaged a set of meanings, practices, and institutions—in short, a discourse—that pervaded U.S. social life.[1] On the surface, it would seem that the inequity that the movement addressed was relatively straightforward: Legitimate refugees were being denied asylum by government officials who placed Cold War ideology and foreign policy objectives above human life and their own legal obligations. Righting this wrong would mean persuading (or forcing) the U.S. government to recognize Central Americans' refugee status—a difficult task, to be sure, but one that involved the overt competition for public support and moral legitimacy that characterizes politics in the United States. However, the problem that sanctuary workers faced was actually more complex than this description implies. The Central Americans whom the movement sought to aid were entangled in a system that constituted them as illegal beings, made their abilities to work, travel, study, and receive medical care dependent on juridical status, and compelled them to define themselves within legal categories at every turn. Sanctuary workers found their efforts to aid these immigrants predefined within this system. Delivering a box of food to a Salvadoran family could be construed as furthering the presence of an illegal alien; paying a Guatemalan to do yardwork could be defined as unlawful hiring; and driving a Central American into the country could be considered alien smuggling. Members of the sanctuary movement thus confronted not only government authorities but also their own notions of law, justice, and legal identity. Moreover, this confrontation largely took place outside legislatures and courtrooms, within the everyday actions that determined individuals' immigration statuses.

Michel Foucault's (1980a, 1980b, 1979) concept of power is particularly useful for analyzing the insidious nature of "alienation"—the process of defining individuals as illegal aliens and the process with which sanctuary workers had to contend. Foucault rejected the view, popular among liberal political theorists and neo-Marxists alike, that politics is a contest between two or more groups with competing interests. He argued instead that power inheres in social systems *as wholes,* within the discourses—such as jurisprudence, medical science, education, and the like—that govern social life. In contrast to the notion that power is *repressive,* that it inhibits thoughts, censors speech, and constrains action, Foucault argued that power is *productive,* that it creates thoughts, elicits speech, and compels action. In particular, power constitutes individuals as beings (delinquents, madmen, deviants) within particular systems of meaning. Unlike theories of domination that view meaning or ideology as something produced by a ruling class and imposed on subordinates (Williams 1977; Althusser 1971; Lukes 1974), Foucault contended that meaning is constructed through interactions of the most intimate nature—between parents and children, physicians and patients, therapists and clients, teachers and students, and so on. The political implications of producing meaning derive not only from the deliberate intentions of actors but also from the system of knowledge in which meaning is produced.[2] Thus, Foucault proposed:

> Let us not, therefore, ask why certain people want to dominate, what they seek, what is their overall strategy. Let us ask, instead, how things work at the level of on-going subjugation, at the level of those continuous and uninterrupted processes which subject our bodies, govern our gestures, dictate our behaviours etc. ... We should try to discover how it is that subjects are gradually, progressively, really and materially constituted through a multiplicity of organisms, forces, energies, materials, desires, thoughts, etc. (Foucault 1980b: 97).

When applied to the system that defined Central American immigrants as illegal aliens, Foucault's theory of power reveals that U.S. immigration law consists of more than legal codes, government policies, and bureaucratic apparatuses. Immigration law is also a set of practices and categories that are woven into daily life. It is true that immigration law produces a two-way conflict between undocumented immigrants and the border patrol agents responsible for capturing and deporting them. In addition, however, immigration law affects and is carried out by employers who ask job applicants for proof of work authorization, children who need social security numbers to enroll in kindergarten, and admissions officers who charge undocumented college students out-of-state tuition. It is also true that there are clear examples of repression within the immigration system. For instance, the undocumented are denied jobs, detained, and deported. Yet immigration law is overwhelmingly *productive* in that a myriad of practices, usually carried out by people who have no connection to the government, produce knowledge that constitutes individuals as citizens, illegal aliens, legal residents, asylees, and so forth. Though the most definitive of these categorizations are made by government officials, private individuals are also agents of their own and others' subjection. Given the pervasiveness of this system, any act that constructs individuals' legal identities has political implications—a truth that religious volunteers discovered when they attempted to aid undocumented Central Americans.

## Central American Immigrants

The events that would eventually situate Central Americans within the category of "illegal alien" were set in motion by political violence that led the Salvadoran and Guatemalan governments (and their adversaries) to seek out, torture, and kill presumed political opponents. During an interview in Tucson in 1987, Ramon Palacios, a Salvadoran student who had come to the United States with the assistance of sanctuary workers, described his own experience. Ramon showed me the newspaper article where his name appeared on a death list along with others who had organized a student protest. He also showed me newspaper photos of the bodies of the American nuns and of a fellow student who'd been shot in the face by the armed forces. Pointing out how bloody the bodies were, Ramon urged me to look closely. He then related:

> In 1985, the students organized the first demonstration that they had had in ten years. The reason was that the budget for schools had been cut, and they had increased the tuition fee charged to students. All students from the university were regarded suspiciously, although not at the private universities, because those cost more. So we organized it secretly, so that the leaders wouldn't be known. But several of the organizers were picked up, and someone must have given out our names, because otherwise how would we all have appeared on the list? They let the people they picked up go, but they don't do that just to be nice. They do that so they can kill you later. This is the history of how the refugees have fled, because of the death squad killings.

Because of such violence, being defined as "political," whether right-wing or left-wing, was life-threatening in El Salvador or Guatemala. With the air of one whose knowledge derived from experience, Ramon Palacios explained:

> All of the guerrilla work is carried out clandestinely. There were many who wanted to enter the guerrilla forces but who couldn't because they were closed. You couldn't join the guerrillas unless you knew someone or were known by them. The guerrillas were chosen by the other guerrillas. ... They were very secretive for security reasons and to avoid infiltrations. Both the FBI and the CIA wanted to enter into the guerrilla forces, so they developed something called compartmentalization, in which the guerrillas are divided into little groups and only know the people within their own group, so that if someone is arrested and tortured, that person can't give out the names of the leaders or other information. No group knows the leaders of other

groups, and they use false names. They do this to protect their families, and many of them use nicknames. ...

When I was living in El Salvador it was terrible. My wife didn't know that I was involved in politics, although she suspected, because sometimes I knew about things that were going to happen before they happened. But I didn't have any arms around the house, so she never thought I was a guerrilla. Why should I have arms? I was one of the ideologues. ... I ran a lot of risks while I was there. I used to carry political propaganda around in my notebooks, and if anyone had found it there, I would have been dead.

Because authorities (and, to a lesser degree, their opponents) viewed noncommitment as support for their adversaries, Salvadorans and Guatemalans often found it difficult to define themselves as politically neutral. Clemente Rivera, a young Salvadoran living in private sanctuary in a Bay Area church building, described himself as a simple student who, while in El Salvador, had attempted just this. Clemente recalled:

It was very hard for me there. There, I was going to school. I had plans for what I wanted to do with my life. I was going to study and then get a job. I knew what I was doing. And then, in around 1980, the civil war started. And the repression grew. And it was so hard for me, because I was trying to walk the fine line between the two sides in the war. I was trying to remain neutral and just to continue my studies. But I couldn't do it. The time came when I would see bodies lying in the streets. All of the students were afraid of being picked up. At first, when I was in the university, I took classes three hours every evening. But then there were various military emergencies and states of siege. And the director of the school decided to end classes after an hour and a half, and all of the students would rush out of the schools, trying to get on the buses and rush home before the curfew.

Once targeted by the government (or, less often, the guerrillas), Central Americans sometimes fled, desperately and suddenly, leaving money, jobs, possessions, even children, behind. Marisol Hernandez, a Guatemalan whom I interviewed in Tucson, took this course of action after her husband had been detained and tortured. Marisol recounted:

We crossed from Guatemala into Mexico with nothing. We had absolutely nothing, except my father had given us some money. And you know how that is. We got to Mexico City and we were so excited to be there, in such a big city, that we checked into a hotel and stayed for a few days. It was my husband and I and my little son. I left my other four children in Guatemala with my mother. Then, when the money ran out, we had nothing. We walked to a park, and I was crying, Susan. I didn't know what to do. My husband couldn't find work. And so my little son said, "Mother, I can ask for money!" I said, "And how will we do that? With me with you, people will look at you and say, 'Why is this child begging when his mother is so strong? Couldn't she work?'" And so my son went by himself begging in the park. I've never done such a thing before, and I felt terrible. I was crying.

The scrutiny that Central Americans fled and that they would once again encounter in the United States continued on the journey northward. Marisol
Hernandez related that, after having sent her son begging:

Then, someone told me about a place where I could go and they would give me
work. I went there, and the first thing they said to me was, "Where are you from?" I
couldn't say I was from Guatemala, because then they would say, "From Guatemala?
You Communist!" So I said, "I'm from Chiapas," because of the accent. "Oh, very
well then, we'll help you. But, you have to come back and show us your papers." I
left there, and they closed the door behind us, and they were no help to us at all. My
husband couldn't find work either, because of not having papers. We slept in the
park that night, the three of us, because we had no money.

The next day we thought, "There must be some Guatemalan here who will help
us." So we went to the university, and we were looking everywhere for a Guatemalan.
Finally, we met a man who was from the EGP [Ejercito guerrillero de pobres, Guerrilla Army of the Poor], and he asked us what had happened to us. And we said,
"this, and this, and this," and we showed him my husband's scars, which were still
fresh. We told him that two peasants had been killed in our house, and my husband
had been taken away. And so he said he would help us. And he loaned us 5,000 pesos. We were able to rent a hotel room.

After entering the United States, Central Americans, like other exiles, faced the
loneliness of leaving friends, family, and connections. Clemente Rivera related
that, despite sharing the dwelling of a large group of seminary students, he felt he
lived alone. When I asked what he missed most about living in El Salvador, Clemente became sad:

What do I miss the most? I miss my parents. That's what I miss the most. And my
sister. I miss the way that my parents spoke to me and taught me, and they guided
me down the right path. Whenever I felt depressed, I would go to them and talk to
them, and they would give me words of comfort and love. That's the main thing.
They gave me love, and they taught me how to love. It is a very beautiful thing to
love.

And my sister. I would go to my sister when I couldn't talk to my parents. Because
there are some things that you don't talk to your parents about. And she would help
me, and she would say to me, "Clemente, it will be all right tomorrow. Tomorrow it
will be better. Just remember to think before you act." And she also gave me a lot of
love. Love. That's the main thing that I miss here. ...

When I was in El Salvador, I was studying at the university. I used to go to class in
the morning, and then come home late at night. And my parents would be there,
waiting for me to come home. They would greet me and ask me how my day had
gone, and my mother would go and get me something to drink. And they would be
there in the morning to say goodbye to me as I left to go to my studies. Sometimes I
think about going back, but if I return, there's no future. There's no future in El Salvador.

The main thing that I haven't found here is love. There is no one here who really loves me. Here, I have nobody. I feel isolated. I never lived by myself like this; I always lived with my family. And sometimes I feel really bad, and I think that I have nothing here.

Also like other exiles, Central American immigrants feared losing their culture, particularly when their children began speaking English and adopting North American customs. Such losses were exacerbated by the difficulties they faced attempting to live and work without papers in an economy where costs were pegged to middle-class incomes. Marisol Hernandez found these problems so overwhelming that, despite Guatemala's widespread human rights abuses, she felt she had had more freedom there than in the United States. Marisol told me:

Here in the U.S., it's very difficult. It's work, work, and more work. Everything here is very expensive; the electricity, the phone bill, everything.

And also, I don't want to lose my culture. I miss the people, I miss the places I used to go, I miss my family, and more than anything else, I miss the freedom that I had there. It's true that things were oppressive. But there, I could go out, I could visit a friend, I knew where to go and what to do. ...

It's so difficult here just to make ends meet. There, one can live with the family. If I didn't have the money to pay the rent, I would move in with a friend or with a relative. If I didn't have enough food to eat, I would call a friend and have some of hers. But here, if I don't pay the rent every month, they'll kick me out. I know what it is to suffer.

Here, we shouldn't want everything. I can't take my children to the clothing stores, or to other stores, because they want everything. I have to tell them, "We will have what we can get. " I tell my children, "Remember how we lived in Guatemala and how we suffered? Why should we have things here that we couldn't have had there?" But my children want to wear the latest fashions, they want to have the latest hairstyles combed this way or that way. And they speak English, which is good, but I want them to also speak Spanish. I want to learn English also, because I need to know English while I am here. We should not be ashamed of who we are.

Finally, like other refugees from war-torn and repressive societies, one thing that Central American immigrants did not leave behind them was fear. Ramon Palacios felt that even in the United States it was dangerous to be politically active:

The refugees in the U.S. don't want to walk with the [former Salvadoran] National Guardsmen. The guardsmen want to silence those here who are opening their mouths. The death squads are operating here. They sent a death threat that was, *"El florecito morirá en el desierto"* ["The little flower will die in the desert"].[3] We asked ourselves what that meant, and we realized that by the desert, they meant Tucson. They're saying that they're coming here. ...

Refugees here in the U.S. have a complex that they're being *perseguidos* ["followed" or "persecuted"], and this is something that they will carry with them always, even in the U.S.

Unlike immigrants who either were legally admitted to the United States or entered clandestinely from countries whose citizens were routinely granted asylum (e.g., Cuba), Central Americans remained undocumented. Although the 1980 Refugee Act made it possible to apply for political asylum after arriving in the United States (Kennedy 1981; Zolberg 1990), the U.S. government contended that Salvadorans and Guatemalans were economic (and therefore deportable) immigrants. Because the United States supported the Guatemalan and Salvadoran governments, the Reagan administration was loath to declare that their citizens had suffered human rights violations.[4] As a result, the vast majority of Salvadoran and Guatemalan asylum petitions were denied (U.S.C.R. 1986; Dominguez 1990; Zolberg 1990; Fuchs 1985). Well aware of the obstacles to obtaining political asylum, the majority of the Salvadorans and Guatemalans who entered the country clandestinely did not submit asylum claims unless they had already been apprehended by the INS.[5] Even then, ignorance of U.S. immigration law and lack of legal representation prevented many from requesting asylum. Therefore, with the exception of the few asylum recipients and the immigrants whose applications were pending, the majority of the Salvadorans and Guatemalans who immigrated in the 1980s lived in the United States without documents. Clemente Rivera described what such a life was like:

> It feels very negative, it feels as though one is discriminated against. It makes it very difficult to find work. And also, for example, when a person wants to go forward with their studies. I can feel deeply motivated internally in my desire to study and then go to the school and say that I want to study. And they ask me if I have documents, and I say no, and they say, "I'm sorry, I can't talk to you. You don't meet the requirements." But I look at another person in line next to me who also wants to study but who does have documents, and I think, "I am just as worthy as that person." I feel like I'm discriminated against. It is a very difficult situation.
>
> When a person has documents, that person feels the equal of any other person.

Because numerous social practices required identity documents, undocumented Central Americans found that, even if they succeeded in avoiding U.S. Immigration authorities, everyday life in the United States inexorably defined them as illegal aliens.

## Illegal Aliens

The category "illegal alien" has become such a part of common parlance that it is useful to pause a moment to explore the origins and significance of the term. Although people have crossed national boundaries since these were first created, the category "illegal alien" and the immigration discourse of which it is a part are products of modern culture and history. Historian Michael Marrus noted that "premodern times ... needed no special category to suspend ... [masses of civilians] outside the framework of the civilized community" (1985:4).[6] In the United

States, such a category was created when the colonies became a republic. The newly created citizens swore allegiance to a document,[7] the U.S. Constitution, and as a result, what had been a concrete relationship between subject and monarch became an abstract linkage between individuals and the law. Their relationship to the law granted citizens a *legal* existence in addition to their *physical* existence, a juridical form of being that continues to be affirmed through birth certificates, death certificates, and the like.[8] The creation of citizenship simultaneously produced its antithesis: alienage. All those who were not party to the social contract embodied in U.S. law were defined as aliens. Unlike citizens, aliens lacked a juridical existence.[9]

Though "aliens" were created along with "citizens," there was no such thing as an *illegal* alien until the U.S. government assumed the authority to regulate travel across its borders. The days of open immigration, when "aliens simply arrived on our shores, found lodging and jobs, and were assimilated by degrees into the society" (Harwood 1986:2), ended in 1882 with the Chinese Exclusion Act. Over the years, the United States established quotas to regulate immigration from different nations and criteria to exclude such people as homosexuals, Communists, and felons. By 1986, the federal prosecutor who tried eleven sanctuary workers on alien-smuggling charges could proclaim, "Every nation has the absolute power to control its borders, to determine who comes in their country, when they come in, where they come in, how long they are going to be here, what they are going to do, how they are going to support themselves and when they are going to leave" (U.S. v. Aguilar 1986:14191). Once travel across U.S. borders became a matter of state control, the entity known as an "illegal alien" was born. *Actions*—such as crossing a border or overstaying one's visa—were made *states of being.*[10] Aliens who were in the United States without the government's permission now became illegal aliens—jurally nonexistent persons whose physical presence inherently violated the law.

As governments around the world assumed similar authority, illegal aliens and other nonjuridical persons found themselves in the tragically absurd situation of having differing sites of legal and physical existence. The upheavals of World War I created stateless people unable to prove "who they *were* in a juridical sense" (Marrus 1985:94, emphasis in original). Because they lacked a legal existence, stateless people were refused a physical one as well: "Constantly questioned about who they were, what their status was, and what was their destination, these people could not cross international frontiers, could not remain where they were, and were often not supposed to be at liberty at all" (Marrus 1985:179). The uniquely modern problem of people who exist in a physical sense but lack a legal existence has produced camps that separate such ambiguous beings from the rest of the population. Around the world, refugees dwell indefinitely in centers such as the Site 2 Camp in Thailand, where 162,000 Cambodians have lived for as much as nine years, unable to work and raising children who have been refugees since birth (Williams 1988). The position of illegal aliens is equally ambiguous; therefore, when the U.S. government apprehends such entities, it restores juridical order by either deporting them to their places of jural being or setting them apart in detention centers until their legal statuses are defined.[11] Even when not physically separated from other individuals, illegal aliens are set apart by their lack of documentation. Metaphors for the undocumented reflect this invisible, but material, barrier.[12] A congressional policy study warned that illegal aliens were becoming a "fugitive underground class" (Harwood 1986: 20), and even an author sympathetic to the rights of the undocumented wrote that "immigration agents operate in a nether world, seeking 'shadow' people who slip in and out of sight" (Hull 1985:14). As it is clear that illegal aliens live a flesh and blood existence like other people, such talk of "shadowy underworlds" does not refer to *physical* reality but rather to a *legal* reality in which illegal aliens are in, but not of, society.

Because they are legally nonexistent, illegal aliens are conflated with another group of juridically paradoxical beings: criminals. Criminals are citizens who have violated the social contract, while illegal aliens' threat to the rule of law derives from not being party to the social contract in the first place. For example, political scientist Elizabeth Hull wrote, "Public alarm [over illegal immigration] is nevertheless not inappropriate because the institutional health of a nation is imperiled whenever sizeable communities live outside the law; indeed, a large contingent of undocumented migrants challenges the very notion that the United States is a country under law" (1985:80). Similarly, Lawrence Fuchs, executive director of the 1978 Select Commission on Immigration and Refugee Policy, cautioned, "The United States should not permit the buildup of an underclass society living outside the protection of the law" (1985:21). Because they are intrinsically "outside the law," illegal aliens are viewed as a threat to law and order (Malkki 1992). In San Diego County, local law enforcement officials, despite lack of statistics on the matter, believed that illegal aliens were committing more than their share of crimes (Bailey and Reza 1988). During the 1992 Los Angeles riots, reporters and police officials accused illegal aliens of carrying out much of the looting.

Because the United States requires all within its bounds to be known to government officials, the category "illegal alien" connotes not only criminality but anarchy. In contrast to the arborescent metaphors used to refer to the "rooted" (Malkki 1992), illegal aliens are compared to uncontrollable, even chaotic bodies of water. Those who write about illegal aliens use such phrases as "steady stream" (Esper 1987:B13), "shut off the flood" (Shields and Morris 1987:1A), "wet" versus "dry labor" (Harwood 1986:4), and "the trickle of illegal crossers became a torrent" (Harwood 1986: 50). The border patrol's expression for legalizing immigrants is to dry them out (Bach 1990:128). These metaphors express fears that uncontrolled immigration will undermine social stability by overloading schools, hospitals, and other services with vast, even unquantifiable[13] numbers of needy people. For example, R. Jensen of Anaheim, California, wrote to the *Los Angeles Times*, "Are we really obligated to solve the poverty of the 5 billion people in the world by trying to stuff them all into this country?" (1988:sec. 2, 8). Similarly, Arizonan John E. Earl wrote to the *Arizona Daily Star*, "Having noted the rising tide of environmental degradation, crime, poverty, unemployment, traffic jams, drugs, housing shortages, child abuse and other social ills, I feel we should slow our population growth. Besides birth control, we need immigration control. We can't accept all the world's poor and remain a stable democracy" (1986:14A).

Thus, crossing an international boundary without governmental authorization, an act that was once neither legal nor illegal, [14] has become not only a crime but a threat to democratic stability and national order. When Salvadorans and Guatemalans performed this act, their legal existences vanished, their physical existences were criminalized, they were kept apart from the U.S. populace, and they were viewed as sources of lawlessness and anarchy. In short, they became illegal aliens. Examining how this transformation occurred delineates the system of power that sanctuary workers confronted when they sought to define Salvadorans and Guatemalans as refugees.

## Alienation

The question of how a particular discourse becomes authoritative to individuals is one that I have already addressed. In Chapter 4, I argued that religious volunteers accepted the validity of sanctuary discourse—and thus became sanctuary workers—through a dialectic between meaning and action. The same dialectic is at work within immigration discourse, although being defined as an illegal alien, unlike becoming a sanctuary worker, is not a voluntary act. Immigration law pervades a variety of social relations; alienation takes place when these social relations produce knowledge that places individuals within the category "illegal alien." Such categorizations then shape the activities in which the individuals so designated engage. Materially, undocumented immigrants *are* illegal aliens, and they interact with others as such even if they are attempting to construct alternative identities. For example, the fact that many Salvadorans and Guatemalans claimed to be refugees did not prevent them from being detained if apprehended, nor did it exempt their employers from legal sanctions for hiring undocumented individuals. Defining individuals within immigration discourse, whether as citizens, illegal aliens, seasonal agricultural workers, or another status, reproduces immigration discourse over time.

As I mentioned at the outset of this chapter, alienation creates a conflict between two competing groups: border patrol agents and undocumented immigrants. Even this struggle, however, involves more than the immediate parties, as the border patrol scrutinizes the entire population in order to extricate the juridically nonexistent from the mass of the documented. Along the U.S.-Mexico border, armed agents guard against those who would enter the country without government permission. Agents' vigils are aided by an optical arsenal that includes "technological gadgetry (such as seismic and electronic sensors) placed strategically in areas where the heaviest crossings occur along with helicopters, all-terrain cycles, horses, spotter aircraft, and vans" (Harwood 1986:49). In the interior, plainclothes INS officers police bus and train stations, highways, farms, ranches, workplaces, and anywhere that the undocumented are likely to congregate (Harwood 1986) . In Orange County, California, police questioned day laborers who gathered on street corners. Those who lacked proof of residency were turned over to the INS (Schwartz 1988). In New York City, the INS ordered 100 agents to surround subway stops and question those who looked ethnic (Hull 1985:93). During job raids, INS agents scrutinized employee records for details such as place of birth, foreign handwriting, schools attended, and suspicious social security numbers (Harwood 1986:96–102). In Los Angeles, one INS raid netted fifty-one ice-cream vendors from Mexico who were captured in the warehouse where they had been sleeping (Arax 1988).

Alienation is brought about not only through conflicts between the border patrol and the undocumented, however, but also through a variety of everyday social relations. In recent years, surveillance has increasingly been displaced from Immigration authorities to private citizens. Because they can be held legally liable for the immigration status of those whom they hire, drive, and assist, individuals involved in these activities must now scrutinize those around them. The 1986 Immigration Reform and Control Act requires employers to document the work authorization of every new employee. Immigration statutes make it illegal to knowingly house, transport, or further the presence of an illegal alien.[15] Vehicles used to bring illegal aliens across the border may be confiscated by Immigration officials, even if the driver is unaware that the passenger is undocumented and if criminal charges are never filed (McDonnell 1988). Procedures that detect and deny services to illegal aliens are increasingly performed by individuals who are not part of the INS. In Arizona, the Systematic Alien Verification for Entitlement program screens welfare applicants by tapping into INS computers (Fischer 1986). College admissions officers sometimes require proof of citizenship from applicants. Hospitals and physicians sometimes check patients' immigration statuses. In Los Angeles, a dying child was initially denied a liver transplant because he lacked legal residency (James 1988). Even religious charities sometimes ask clients for identity documents. According to Tucson sanctuary workers, as of 1988, the Tucson branch of the Salvation Army required proof of legal status from aid recipients.

Through these social relations, in conjunction with the surveillance conducted by the border patrol and other Immigration agents, the Salvadorans and Guatemalans who immigrated during the 1980s were materially constituted as illegal aliens. Denied social services, detained,[16] and deported, these Central Americans were continually set apart from the rest of U.S. society. Clemente Rivera, a Salvadoran living in the East Bay, commented, "When a person asks [me] for a green card, and when I say I don't have one, then the person says, 'I'm sorry. I can't talk to you.' It makes a person illegal. I feel very rejected when that happens. And it happens all the time. In banks, in schools. Wherever I go, I always wonder whether or not they're going to ask me for a green card." The surveillance that pervades social life shaped Central Americans' daily activities, leading them, like it or not, to live as illegal aliens. Because they lacked work authorization, many were unemployed. A Guatemalan day laborer whom I met in Tucson was so desperate to work that he actually chose to forgo surgery on his hand so that he would be available if a job opportunity arose. Lacking documents also made Central Americans vulnerable to those with knowledge of their legal status, as the INS used tips from friends, relatives, and neighbors to identify deportable immigrants (Harwood 1986). Ramon Palacios described the difficulty of being without documentation in a society that demanded it:

> Those who don't have documents live a very untranquil life. At bus stops and parties the Immigration could stop someone and ask for documents. Even at the movie theaters and other places. So you're never calm. You don't buy a lot, because you know that if you're deported you'll just lose it. There's no point in putting money in the bank, because you'll have to leave it there if you're picked up and deported. Those who don't have documents can't get social benefits, can't work, can't get back their money paid as income tax, and can't apply for health benefits.

Like the stateless people created by World War I, Central Americans who were defined as illegal aliens confronted a system that essentially forbid them to be anywhere. Salvadorans and Guatemalans, having found physical existence in their home countries nearly impossible, were then denied a juridical existence in the United States. As one Berkeley sanctuary worker commented:

> They're damned if they're damned if they're damned. They go down there [to Central America] and they get shot, they come here and they're not welcome, they go to Mexico and they're not welcome, they get threatened in Guatemala. No answers, dead families. Totally under siege. They're better here, but as long as they're undercover. Is that a life? Is that a life for people? For good people?

Mario Aguirre, a Salvadoran I met in Tucson, had just arrived and was desperate because of his lack of options. Without legal status he could not work, and without work he could not survive. He feared that if he applied for political asylum and obtained a work permit, the information in his application could reach his government and endanger his family. Scars from torture and bullet wounds attested to the difficulties he would face returning to El Salvador. Mario's desperation was shared by other immigrants, such as the eighteen Mexican men who suffocated to death hidden in a boxcar (*San Francisco Chronicle* 1987), a seventeen-year-old Mexican boy who died during an immigration raid in the San Joaquin Valley (Kendall 1988), and two Cubans who spent eight days floating to the United States on inner tubes (*San Jose Mercury News* 1986). The immigration system permeated the lives and deaths of these people.

To challenge the system that constituted Salvadoran and Guatemalan immigrants as illegal aliens, sanctuary workers invoked the authority of another subset of immigration discourse: the political asylum process.

## Political Asylum

The discrepancy between illegal aliens' legal and physical existences is not always resolved by suspending them from the population, detaining them, or deporting them to the country of their legal existence. Sometimes the juridically nonexistent undergo procedures that grant them a legal existence in the United States. These procedures take many forms, including applying for amnesty under the 1986 Immigration Reform and Control Act, applying for suspension of deportation due to having been in the United States illegally for more than seven years, or—the form most germane to Central Americans—applying for political asylum. Unlike applying for *refugee* status, in which persecuted individuals request refuge while abroad and, if successful, enter the United States as legal refugees, political *asylum* was established as a recourse for those who reached the United States and faced persecution if deported to their home countries.[17] Sanctuary workers became familiar with the asylum process in the early years of the movement when they began aiding Salvadoran and Guatemalan detainees. Filling out Central Americans' asylum applications convinced volunteers that these immigrants met the legal definition of refugee, and the overwhelming denial of these petitions led participants to resort to crossing and sheltering undocumented immigrants. Many of the movement's legal arguments derived from its critique of the asylum process.

Like alienation, political asylum constructs legal identities by producing knowledge, situating individuals within immigration categories, and shaping the material existence of those so constituted. Like requests for identity documents, the political asylum process compels applicants to produce knowledge that makes them subjects within immigration discourse. To apply for asylum, immigrants must complete forms that ask them to note any experiences demonstrating that they cannot return to their countries "because of persecution or a well-founded fear of persecution on account of race, religion, nationality, membership in a particular social group, or political opinion" (Sklar et al. 1985:1012). Next, through repeated questioning, the applicant's attorney[18] elicits a more detailed account of torture, fear, threats, warnings, detention, massacres, and flight—an account that, if related in El Salvador or Guatemala, could make the speaker a target of death squads. The attorney then carefully reorders this jumble of details, creates chronologies, and reconstructs the connections between the characters in order to retrospectively reconstitute the applicant's experiences as instances of persecution as it is legally defined. Finally, the hearing itself elicits further knowledge through questioning and cross-examination.

The knowledge elicited through the asylum process is, like an individual's juridical existence, substantiated by documentation. To corroborate the applicant's case, legal workers accumulate relevant medical reports, personal letters, statements from the Red Cross, newspaper clippings, human rights reports, and affidavits from family members. For example, Tucson legal workers used an applicant's daughter's birth certificate and an Amnesty International report describing the public execution of the applicant's husband to certify that the applicant and her daughter would be in danger if deported to Guatemala. Ramon Palacios told me how difficult it was to obtain such documentation:

> The problem is that when people come to the U.S. from Central America, most of them don't have any proof of what happened to them. You have to have proof to get political asylum. I carried the newspaper with the death threats with me, but I had it well hidden the whole time. Because in Mexico they're the same as they are here. If they had found it when I was in Mexico they would have called me a guerrilla and sent me right back to El Salvador.

Together, the application, testimony, and supporting documentation form a record that transforms asylum applicants' lives into discourse.

To define individuals either as illegal aliens or political refugees, the asylum process measures knowledge about applicants' lives against the legal definition of refugee. This measurement takes place during hearings before an Immigration judge.[19] Like most court proceedings, these hearings are an adversarial process. The applicant's attorney and an INS attorney construct competing interpretations of the applicant's narrative of persecution. The applicant's attorney, of course, argues that the applicant's experiences meet the definition of refugee, while the INS attorney argues that they do not.[20] The case of a man who had fled El Salvador after being identified as a guerrilla sympathizer and as the relative of guerrilla soldiers shows how hearings retrospectively evaluate applicants' experiences according to legal categories. In court, the applicant told the following story. While still in El Salvador, he had entered the army only to find himself serving under a sergeant who had been involved in a relative's assassination. The sergeant persecuted the applicant, trying to make him desert the armed forces so that the sergeant could kill him. The applicant was afraid and deserted at his first opportunity. He stayed away from his home, but he was nevertheless recognized. He fled to the United States several days later.

The INS attorney tried to counter the applicant's account with a different interpretation of events. First, the attorney argued that the Salvadoran government was looking for the applicant because he was a deserter—a legitimate concern—rather than because he was a guerrilla sympathizer. Second, he argued that the applicant was at no more risk than the general population. Third, the attorney tried to demonstrate that if the government had actually intended to persecute this man, it had had plenty of opportunity to do so. The INS attorney asked why, if the applicant was known to be a sympathizer for years, he had only encountered problems after joining the army. The applicant responded that the persecution came from the sergeant in question. The attorney then asked why, if the army actually wanted to persecute him, they did not kill him while he was in the service. The applicant answered that they could not kill him while he was in the headquarters and were therefore trying to provoke a desertion. Finally, the INS attorney wanted to know whether the authorities had searched for the applicant after he deserted. The applicant answered that he had no way of knowing, because he had avoided his own home while in El Salvador and his family was afraid to include such details in their letters to him here in the United States. The judge granted asylum.

The arguments used in the above example demonstrate the difficulty of proving the likelihood of a future event. On the one hand, if an individual either escapes before being persecuted or is detained, tortured, and released, then there is no proof that the individual continues to face danger. On the other hand, if an individual is captured, tortured, and either executed or detained indefinitely, then the danger of persecution is clear, but obviously, in such a case the person would not be in the United States applying for political asylum. During one asylum hearing, an INS attorney asked an applicant who had been threatened with death at the hands of guerrilla forces, "But they in fact didn't kill you?" She answered no and pointed out that if they had, then she would not be in the courtroom testifying. After the hearing, she laughed at the absurdity of this question. Another applicant who was denied political asylum was more bitter. He commented, "They want you to come here crying and begging, with bullets in your chest. But here, there's more freedom, so some of our fear leaves us. If they want to have another court hearing [to appeal the decision], then that's fine. Only let's have it in El Salvador next time, and then I'll prove what I say."

Another asylum hearing that I attended illustrated the artificiality of measuring a person's life against a legal definition.[21] During this hearing, the INS attorney tried to prove that an instance of persecution, although unfortunate, did not fall into the categories of persecution listed in the 1980 Refugee Act. He asked the applicant, "Were you and your family persecuted due to your family's race?" Not understanding, the applicant replied, "No, I don't know what you mean, 'race'?" After this question was repeated several times with no progress, the judge intervened, pointing out that the applicant did not understand the meaning of "race." The INS attorney then explained that he was trying to establish that this instance of persecution did not meet the legal definition of "refugee." He continued, asking, "Was it because of your nationality? Because of your religion?" Finally, the applicant simply explained that her family was being persecuted because of a personal vendetta on the part of a man who wanted to steal their land.[22] The judge ruled that because the man with the vendetta had used his connections with the military to persecute the applicant, the applicant's experiences constituted political persecution and she therefore merited asylum.

Finally, judges' decisions in asylum hearings, like the evaluations made by individuals who request identity documents before providing services, produce material reality by constituting individuals either as political asylees or illegal immigrants. Judges' decisions determine whether applicants legally exist, where they can physically exist, whether they can work, and whether they remain in custody.

Regardless of the outcome, this decision, and the process that produces it, is imbued with power. Through the asylum process, immigrants who have previously been unknown to the legal system are brought within its confines and made subjects within its categories. Repeated questioning transforms applicants' fear and suffering into claims for particular legal and political identities—claims that, if made in El Salvador or Guatemala, could endanger the claimants. Rather than the applicants themselves, it is legal experts, including applicants' attorneys, INS attorneys, and ultimately judges, who interpret the significance of these claims. To do so, the authorities measure applicants' constructions of life events against legal definitions, thus reducing highly complex and usually tragic events to instances of a general rule. Applicants are not empowered to determine their own immigration statuses; rather, they only become asylees through government officials' rulings. Though such rulings can be appealed, they situate individuals within immigration categories.

Though parallels between alienation and the asylum process abound, alienation constitutes social reality through a dialectic, whereas asylum does not. Individuals are constituted as illegal aliens through social relations that have been influenced, shaped, even created by immigration law. These relations produce knowledge that categorizes individuals within immigration terminology. Such categorizations have material force, leading the individuals in question to interact with others according to their immigration statuses. This interaction simultaneously reconstitutes individuals within immigration terminology and reproduces immigration law. In contrast, individuals become political asylees when, usually after having been detained, they submit asylum applications. Immigration law shapes the application process, leading individuals to produce narratives that are measured against immigration categories. This measurement results in rulings that then determine the individuals' immigration statuses. Individuals subsequently interact with others according to their status; however, such interaction does not reshape and reproduce the asylum process. Instead, whether they have been constituted as illegal aliens or political asylees, immigrants once again participate in the informal but nonetheless binding categorization that takes place in daily life.

## Conclusion

Whether ruthlessly imprisoning undocumented children or benevolently granting asylum to the politically persecuted, the U.S. immigration system is imbued with power. Immigration discourse entangles *all* individuals within its categories and practices. Immigrants who lack documentation are separated from the documented through detention, deportation, and the denial of services. Citizens involved in certain social interactions, such as hiring employees or admitting college students, police the population. Asylum applicants are required to redefine their lives in legal terms. All those with legal status, native born citizens and legalized immigrants alike, have to document their existence, both to government officials and to the private individuals who request identity documents. Individuals facing life-threatening circumstances find it difficult to flee to the United States or to survive if they succeed in immigrating.

This discussion of U.S. immigration discourse demonstrates that when people protest, they do not only confront external phenomena, like unjust laws, that can be addressed through the formal political process. In addition, the power that such movements challenge is embedded in the practices and categories through which people—including protestors themselves—live their lives. By changing these practices and redefining these categories, individuals can challenge power relations. This is what occurred within the sanctuary movement as participants devised actions that both invoked and defied the authority vested in U.S. immigration discourse.

## Notes

1. I am drawing on three meanings of the term "engage": join, converse, and do battle with. Sanctuary workers "joined" movement practices to immigration discourse by connecting these to immigration categories and procedures. The movement "conversed with" immigration discourse by addressing legal issues that this discourse presented. Finally, participants "did battle with" immigration discourse by opposing the system that constituted Central Americans as illegal aliens. See Chapter 6 for a description and analysis of this "engagement."

2. Let me address a possible criticism of invoking this understanding of action. Some readers may wonder if I am saying that when people protest they do not know what they are really doing and that only researchers can see what is actually happening. I would say that while the complete implications of an act of resistance may be essentially unknowable, when people protest, they know what they are doing; the idiom in which they express this understanding, however, is not necessarily the rational, strategic language that current thinking considers a hallmark of political dissidence.

3. Ramon was referring to a death threat received by Central American activists in Los Angeles, where a Central American woman was raped and tortured.

4. Zolberg pointed out that "the recognition of a group as refugees by the constituted international community was tantamount to a formal charge that one of its members was engaging in illegitimate acts toward its citizens" (1990:105). Similarly, in a 1984 government report, Jerry M. Tinker, minority counsel to the U.S. Senate Judiciary Committee's Subcommittee on Immigration and Refugee Policy, wrote, "[N]othing more clearly documents the inability of a government to provide basic human services and protection to its people than a flow of refugees" (Subcommittee on Immigration and Refugee Policy, Committee on the Judiciary, United States Senate 1984:31).

5. After the passage of the 1986 Immigration Reform and Control Act, which criminalized the hiring of illegal aliens, many undocumented immigrants found it impossible to live in the United States without work permits. Salvadorans and Guatemalans reassessed the risks of applying for asylum, and many concluded that the necessity of obtaining a work permit

(which would be granted while their application was pending) outweighed the chance that they would be deported if their applications were denied.

6. Prior to the nineteenth century, "large masses of people simply could not move from place to place supported by meager social services. Winters, generally, would finish them off" (Marrus 1985:5). With the exception of the affluent, who could usually arrange a welcome abroad if the need presented itself, the few individuals who moved across borders simply joined the ranks of the poor (Marrus 1985).

7. Even those who are citizens by birth and never formally swear allegiance to the Constitution are assumed to have agreed to accept the authority of this document (Foucault 1979).

8. The artificiality of separating individuals' physical and legal existences is captured nicely in a passage from Maxine Hong Kingston's *China Men*. This excerpt describes the experience of a Chinese immigrant who sought to enter the United States at an Immigration Station on Angel Island:

> The interrogators liked asking questions with numbers for answers. Numbers seemed true to them. "How many times did your grandfather return to the United States?" "Twice." "Twice?" "Yes, twice. He was here once and returned twice. He was here three times altogether. He spent half his life in America and half in China." They looked into his eyes for lies. Even the Chinese American [interpreter] looked into his eyes, and they repeated his answers, as if doubting them. He squelched an urge to change the answers, elaborate on them. "Do you have any money? " "Yes." "How much?" He wondered if they would charge him higher fees the more money he reported. He decided to tell the truth; lying added traps. Whether or not he spoke the truth didn't matter anyway; demons were capricious. It was up to luck now.
>
> They matched his answers to the ones his relatives and fellow villagers gave. He watched the hands with yellow hair on their backs turn the copies of his grandfather's and father's papers. ...
>
> "Your grandfather's papers are illegal," the Chinese American translated. "And your father is also an illegal alien. " One by one the demons outlawed his relatives and ancestors, including a Gold Rush grandfather, who had paid a bag of gold dust to an American Citizenship Judge for papers. "There are no such things as Citizenship Judges," said the Immigration Demon and put an X across the paper that had been in the family for seventy-five years (Kingston 1980:58–59).

9. U.S. courts have long debated whether aliens are legal persons. See Hull 1985:86–88.

10. My understanding of the ways that actions became states of being draws on Talal Asad's (1983b: 304–305) distinction between a sinful *act* and a sinful *condition*. The former is an event whereas the latter is a temporary or permanent state of existence.

11. Detainees who are unable to post bonds remained incarcerated for months or years. A federal court recently ruled that Cuban detainees who were not legal residents had no rights and could be kept in an Atlanta prison "until they die" (*Tucson Citizen* 1987b).

12. The similarity between identity documents and the bars of detention centers was captured in an advertisement for a Tucson newspaper's feature story on the 1986–1987 amnesty program. The ad depicted a Hispanic-looking man behind a wire-mesh fence, with the caption, "They overcame their fears, came out of the shadows and walked into legalization offices" (*Tucson Citizen* 1987a). In fact, the majority of amnesty applicants were not behind metal bars but only behind the barrier of illegality.

13. A newspaper article about the amnesty program begins, "A state agency trying to count the uncountable has concluded that there are 1.7 million illegal immigrants in California who qualify" (McLeod 1987: 8).

14. My argument here is based on Michael Marrus's extensive research about the history of European refugees. Marrus wrote:

> Throughout the nineteenth century there were no serious administrative impediments to the movement of persons between states. The English author Norman Angell remembered his own youth in the 1890s, when he decided abruptly to leave the European continent for America: "I had no passport, no exit permit, no visa, no number on a quota, and none of those things was asked for on my arrival in the United States." Angell simply went. Passports existed at the time, and a handful of states, including the tsarist and Ottoman empires, required them for internal travel. ... But these documents had largely fallen into disuse internationally. ... Up to the First World War "civilized" countries considered that no more formal arrangements were necessary to designate people moving from place to place (Marrus 1985:92).

15. According to legal scholar Ignatius Bau, a lawful resident who warned an undocumented coworker of Immigration officials' arrival by "pointing in the direction of the INS agents and uttering a single phrase" was convicted of facilitating the presence of an illegal alien (1985: 98–99).

16. Ramon Palacios' experience shows that even relatively brief detention is a hardship:

> If you're foreign and are in the U.S., you have to have all your documents with you, or you could be taken away. Once, after I had been granted political asylum, I went near the Mexican border. I didn't cross the border, but just for going near the border, they picked me up. I had my driver's license, an I.D., and my social security card, but I had forgotten to carry the piece of paper that said I had political asylum. My friend had crossed the border into Mexico and he was deported. Luckily for me, I stayed on the U.S. side. Even so, I was detained for three months until I had a court hearing and my lawyer got me out. The judge said to me, "Why should you have to be harassed like that? I'm going to give you residency so that you won't have to go through this again. ... " Meanwhile, while I was in there, I lost all my possessions and the apartment I was renting because I wasn't working for three months. I also lost my car, which they claimed had been illegally parked. Moreover, I couldn't send money to my family, who I had been supporting, because I couldn't work.

17. See Kennedy 1981 and Zolberg 1990 for histories of political asylum.

18. Here I assume that the applicant has legal representation. In many cases, applicants did not.

19. When decisions are appealed, they go before a higher-ranking judge at the Bureau of Immigration Affairs and then, if further appealed, leave the immigration court system altogether to be heard in a federal circuit court of appeals (U.S.C.R. 1986).

20. The reason that the INS attorneys invariably argued against applicants is that these hearings were the second stage in the application process. Applicants who filed affirmatively first presented their applications to INS authorities in a nonadversarial format. After brief interviews with Immigration officials, Salvadorans and Guatemalans were almost invariably denied asylum. The hearing, was, in a sense, the first step in the appeal process. If the INS

interviewer had granted asylum, then no hearing would have been necessary (Sklar et al. 1985). Immigrants who applied after being detained were already under deportation proceedings. They had no interview with INS officials and instead presented their claims directly to an Immigration judge. The burden of proof was on the immigrant rather than the INS (U.S.C.R. 1986).

21. Applicants' attorneys' efforts to place their clients in the category "refugee" were as artificial as INS attorneys' efforts to place them in the category "illegal alien."

22. While volunteering at TECLA, I helped document the asylum application of a Salvadoran woman whose husband had been killed, whose friends had been murdered, and who had herself been threatened. TECLA staff believed that this woman had a weak asylum case because she could not prove that these events were due to her race, creed, political opinion, social group, or nationality.

# 6

## The Refugee

*When I talk to a Central American who has crossed the border illegally, with nothing but the clothes on his back, who has lost his family and his country, I am talking to someone who is like the dry bones that God breathed life into. It is from situations like this that God creates life. Because when I see how these people, who have lost so much, still have faith and hope, then I know that I am closer to God.*
—Ralph Lieber, First Church's pastor, speaking during a Sunday morning sermon

In order to define undocumented Central Americans as "refugees" rather than "illegal aliens," the sanctuary movement both challenged and invoked the authority of U.S. immigration discourse. Drawing on the legal expertise acquired during bail-bonding efforts, public speaking, and the 1985–1986 Tucson sanctuary trial, sanctuary workers intervened in the dialectic that constituted undocumented Central Americans as illegal aliens. By allowing their own interpretations of the law to shape their interaction with Salvadoran and Guatemalan immigrants, movement members reconstructed social relations in ways that defined these immigrants as legal refugees. Convinced that Salvadorans and Guatemalans merited asylum and that the U.S. government's denial of refugee status to these immigrants violated the law, movement members assumed responsibility for carrying out U.S. refugee law. Volunteers began interviewing Central Americans who wished to enter the United States, bringing those judged to be refugees across the border, sheltering undocumented Salvadorans and Guatemalans in churches, synagogues, and private homes, and creating opportunities for immigrants to speak publicly about their experiences. By manipulating the notions and practices that situated individuals within immigration categories, sanctuary workers used immigration discourse to legitimize their work and, in the process, to create novel notions of citizenship, legal identity, and law.

Examining how sanctuary workers reinterpreted U.S. immigration law to define Central Americans as refugees requires employing a broader concept of protest than is usually applied to organized movements. Recent studies of U.S. protest movements have assumed that protestors focus on clear-cut grievances, such as unjust policies or discriminatory laws, that can be redressed through political change (Jenkins 1983).[1] As a result, analysts have also assumed that protest is geared toward measurable outcomes, that strategizing focuses almost exclusively on these goals, and that protest itself is a means to such ends (Marwell and Oliver 1984; Tarrow 1988). If, however, in the course of addressing specific grievances, protestors engage the structures of power that make up society (structures like capitalism, racism, or, in the case at hand, immigration discourse), then acts of protest have political implications that may differ from their authors' intentions. Altering and redefining power-laden practices and notions not only addresses narrow goals but also, in diffuse ways, defies, deconstructs, and reconstitutes oppressive systems. Of course, altering discourses of power is not inherently oppositional, because societies can become more, as well as less, oppressive. For example, as the enforcement of immigration law has been displaced from government officials to private individuals, surveillance has become more deeply embedded in the general population. Nor is reproducing discourses of power inherently or entirely oppressive, as these systems can empower as well as subjugate, as the next chapter will show. Moreover, because power and resistance are intertwined within cultural discourses, it is impossible to take advantage of a discourse's potential for resistance without creating practices and categories that are simultaneously power-laden (Foucault 1980a; Abu-Lughod 1990; Willis 1981).

When members of the sanctuary movement invoked and redefined U. S. immigration discourse, they simultaneously resisted and reinforced the power that inhered in alienation and the political asylum process. On the one hand, crossing, sheltering, and publicizing the stories of undocumented Central Americans overcame divisions between the documented and the undocumented, empowered private citizens to interpret and enforce law, and challenged U.S. immigration policy regarding Central American immigrants. On the other hand, these practices compelled Salvadorans and Guatemalans to reveal their experiences to movement members, reinforced distinctions between legal and illegal immigrants, and defined Central Americans within immigration categories. By drawing attention to the political ambiguity of sanctuary practices, I do not mean to imply that there is a "purer" form of resistance in which movement members could have engaged. Every form of political action engenders its own contradictions, and had the movement foresworn legal arguments, it would have abandoned a powerful source of legitimacy and allowed authorities to define the movement's legal significance. Rather, by examining how sanctuary practices deconstructed and recreated power relations, I seek to uncover the ways that sanctuary workers engaged not only the U.S. government's interpretation of refugee law but also the immigration categories and practices that shape social reality.

## Civil Initiative

By crossing, sheltering, and publicizing the stories of undocumented Central Americans, sanctuary workers pursued a legal strategy that the Tucson branch of the movement called "civil initiative"—a means of creating law by carrying it out.[2] Through civil initiative—so named to distinguish this tactic from civil disobedience—movement members reshaped immigration discourse on an ongoing basis. First, participants reinterpreted U.S. immigration law. Sanctuary workers contended that if individuals merited asylum, they *were* refugees whether or not a court had declared them to be so; that private citizens could recognize individuals' refugee status as accurately as could government officials; and that citizens were obligated to enforce laws when governments failed to do so. Second, sanctuary workers acted on their reinterpretations of immigration law by manipulating the formal and informal practices that defined individuals as illegal aliens and as refugees. Sanctuary workers structured their own relations with Central Americans such that these in some ways imitated and in some ways critiqued the definitional scrutiny characteristic of both alienation and the asylum process. Finally, as participants sought to establish the validity of their legal notions, sanctuary workers constituted Central American immigrants as legal refugees. On a continual basis, movement practices produced a different legal reality than that which is normally created by interaction between the documented and the undocumented.

Though both Tucson and East Bay sanctuary communities practiced civil initiative,[3] the version that developed in the East Bay was less complex than its Tucson counterpart. In the East Bay, from the moment the movement began, sanctuary workers took pains to establish a legal basis for aiding undocumented Central Americans. The original EBSC covenant statement cited the United States's obligations to international law, proclaiming, "The United Nations has declared these people [Central Americans] legitimate refugees of war. ... The 1951 United Nations Convention and the 1967 Protocol Agreements on refugees—both signed by the U.S.—established the rights of refugees *not* to be sent back to their countries of origin" (emphasis in original). Because undocumented Central Americans were refugees, sanctuary workers reasoned, sheltering, assisting, and transporting them in the face of government opposition *obeyed*, rather than violated, the law. In December 1983, less than one year after the movement began, the EBSC Steering Committee minutes noted: "Discussion: How to speak when the press is listening. The consensus is that we try to stress that ... this group does not think of itself as a group of lawbreakers. ... This discussion was brought up because it seems that every time we 'get in the news,' so to speak, we are pictured as people willing to break the law." Over the years, EBSC deliberately avoided anything smacking of civil disobedience, such as being arrested during rallies or accepting phony I.D.'s from undocumented refugees.

In Tucson, border workers devised a form of civil initiative that enacted participants' understandings of the relationships between citizens, law, and the state by explicitly incorporating court rulings and elements of law into movement actions. Unlike their East Bay colleagues, Tucson sanctuary workers initially perceived aiding undocumented Central Americans as civil disobedience. At the time of the original sanctuary declarations, the pastor of All Saints Church informed the U.S.

attorney general that his congregation would "publicly violate the Immigration and Nationality Act, Section 274(A)" (Corbett 1986:36). As news of the sanctuary declarations spread, however, attorneys began advising participants in Tucson and elsewhere that their actions could be considered legal under the very laws they accused the government of breaking. For example, in July 1983, Ira Gollobin, the immigration law consultant for Church World Service, informed sanctuary workers that the United Nations protocol on refugees, which was made part of U.S. law in 1968, prohibited returning individuals with a well-founded fear of persecution to their country of origin, even if they had entered another country illegally. Gollobin concluded, "In granting sanctuary to the Salvadoreans [*sic*] seeking asylum here, the Churches act in conformity with the letter, as well as the spirit, of constitutional rights and statutory law" (Corbett 1986: 64).

As they became convinced that their actions were legal, Tucson sanctuary workers devised the notions of citizenship, law, and state that became the basis of their version of civil initiative. According to Tucson practitioners, citizens had legal notions that were more fundamental than the formal legal codes.[4] One border worker explained that despite the fact that it was often unwritten, communities knew this common law "at a practical level, at the level that most of us know our rules, the way that we manage to speak language without knowing how we would write a grammar about it." Tucson participants contended that the rules that make up common law are so basic that they are universal. As evidence, they cited parallels in U.S. refugee law, international refugee law, and religious law regarding the treatment of strangers, outcasts, and the politically persecuted. In the case of Central American refugees, border workers argued, the problem was not the law itself but rather authorities' *interpretation* of the law. The challenge that sanctuary workers felt that they faced, and that civil initiative was designed to meet, was to make the U.S. government interpret refugee law in a manner consistent with community legal norms.

To validate their understanding of U.S. refugee law, Tucson border workers assumed responsibility for enforcing the law. In essence, they created a partial substitute for the immigration system. Movement members began evaluating Central Americans' asylum claims and bringing those judged to be refugees across the border. One border worker told me with pride, "We are carrying out the 1980 Refugee Act, whereas the INS is not." Border workers believed that acting on their interpretation of law could create legal precedents in one of two ways. Either the government would fail to prosecute border workers, thus tacitly legitimizing their arguments, or authorities would indict sanctuary workers, thus giving them the opportunity to state their position before jurors who, as fellow members of the community, would presumably share border workers' interpretation of immigration statutes.[5] Carl Fonde, a Trsg member, stated the goal of this strategy: "Sanctuary must establish foundations that ... serve others beyond Central Americans. The organizations themselves will pass. But if the principles themselves are woven into society, if the principle that citizens must act to see that refugee rights are respected [is woven into society], then sanctuary will have been established soci-etally."

The "Merkt" letters that Trsg members sent to immigration authorities illus-trate how participants sought to establish precedents through citizens' practices. In 1985, when a federal court overturned sanctuary worker Stacy Merkt's alien-smuggling conviction on the ground that she was bringing undocumented aliens to U.S. officials to help them apply for legal status, Trsg incorporated this ruling into its border-crossing procedures. Beginning in August 1985, Trsg began notify-ing Immigration officials of each crossing by means of a "Merkt" letter stating, "The Tucson refugee support group is helping the following refugees reach legal counsel in order to determine the best way for them to obtain legal status in the United States."[6] The times and sites of crossings were not given in the letters, and the Central Americans in question were identified only by nationality, sex, and year of birth. Trsg members did sign their letters, however, and the first such crossing was filmed by newspeople. Because they encountered no reprisals for their actions, Trsg members reasoned that the government had recognized sanc-tuary as a legal practice. In a January 16, 1988, letter to the INS, Trsg members ex-plained their position:

> As civil initiative for the protection of refugees' rights to safe haven, sanctuary is
> now firmly established in the Arizona-Sonoran borderlands. It will eventually yield
> a body of common law that assures refugees' rights to safe haven, even if the INS
> continues to try to nullify the treaties and statutes that have been enacted to protect
> these rights. Everyone's interest would be served, though, if the federal government
> would itself establish procedures for the admission of first asylum refugees, proce-
> dures that make civil initiative unnecessary. In the interim, sanctuary-providing
> communities on the border must make-do with the checks and balances that civil
> initiative introduces.

Through the Merkt letters and other practices, sanctuary workers intervened in the dialectic that reproduced immigration discourse. Taking advantage of the ways that immigration discourse made private citizens responsible for the legal status of those around them, movement members altered their own relations with Salvadorans and Guatemalans so that these relations continually constituted Cen-tral Americans as refugees. Each of these alterations was politically contradictory in that it both challenged and reinforced the power relations inherent in immi-gration discourse. A case in point was the screening process that movement mem-bers used to decide which Central Americans merited the movement's aid.

### Screening Procedures

One of the ways that sanctuary workers carried out civil initiative was to screen Central Americans to determine who met the criteria for particular types of movement assistance.[7] In the East Bay, screening procedures evaluated whether

Central Americans interested in sanctuary were appropriate for such a living situation, whereas in Tucson, these procedures decided who would be assisted in border crossings. (It is important to note that in both Tucson and the East Bay, other forms of assistance—such as food and clothing donations—were provided to "unscreened" refugees, who outnumbered the "screened" refugees housed and crossed by sanctuary workers.) Believing that it was legal to cross, shelter, and transport legitimate refugees regardless of their official immigration status, sanctuary workers devised procedures to ensure that those they assisted merited asylum. These procedures mirrored asylum hearings by eliciting knowledge about immigrants' lives and using legal definitions of "refugee" to evaluate this knowledge. Screening procedures also improvised on the asylum process by authorizing private citizens to assess asylum claims. Because sanctuary workers' reinterpretations of asylum recreated some of the power-laden elements of this process, screening procedures were politically contradictory.

In the East Bay, screening procedures evaluated Central Americans' asylum claims, emotional stability, and willingness to speak publicly. The December 1983 Steering Committee minutes explained: "'prepared for sanctuary' means 'refugees who have no legal status and thus are in need of the protection of a congregation, who are mentally stable in spite of the persecution and dislocation they had suffered, and who are willing to speak to North American congregations about the reasons for their flight here'" (EBSC 1983). Screening was performed by a committee consisting of EBSC Steering Committee members and Central Americans. The Central Americans on the committee were responsible for evaluating the truth of their compatriots' accounts of persecution. The committee screened refugees for emotional health because of difficulties that arose when local congregations first began sheltering undocumented Central Americans. A member of one of these congregations described her church's experience:

> Early on, we had a refugee in sanctuary, and it was in the days before they had really perfected the screening and evaluation of individuals. We had the misfortune of getting this young man who had a very severe drinking problem. We struggled along with him for a long time. He was in treatment in a halfway house, but his idea of fun when payday came was to go to bars. And so he got himself murdered in a bar, probably over some worthless gal.

Willingness to speak publicly was a screening criterion because participants believed that publicizing refugees' stories could transform the congregations and community groups that listened.[8] Sam Gersch, minister of a Berkeley sanctuary congregation, explained, "What's been the genius of the sanctuary movement is that you can't start necessarily with trying to teach people what's happening in Central America. But you *can* start by introducing them to refugees." When I was in the East Bay, the screening committee had become fairly inactive because few Central Americans were interested in being placed in congregations at that time.[9]

As a result of the screening process, most East Bay sanctuary workers only saw a politically active, emotionally stable, centrist or left-of-center slice of the Central American immigrant population. Because willingness to speak publicly was a screening criterion, the screening process necessarily selected for individuals who were politically active. A second result of the screening criteria was that the Central Americans who worked with the local movement usually did not have severe emotional or social problems. A volunteer who worked with Salvadoran and Guatemalan detainees noted:

> A lot of other [nonsanctuary] refugees are *mas travieso,* more mischievous, not as clean-cut. So they have alcoholic problems, drug problems, emotional problems. They're not pretty, see? They're not these nice, neat, pretty little saints. "Oh, we've got a martyr from El Salvador. We'd better take good care of him." No. Not every refugee can fit into a sanctuary—a *public* sanctuary situation.

Finally, although I do not know that those fleeing persecution by the political Left were deliberately screened out, I never met any such person during my time in the East Bay. Certainly, East Bay sanctuary workers tended to assume that Central Americans were fleeing persecution from the Right rather than the Left. For example, a questionnaire that asked potential asylum hearing witnesses to state their areas of expertise had no question regarding knowledge of persecution by the guerrilla forces.

In Tucson, the procedures for deciding which Central Americans to bring across the border did not evaluate emotional health or willingness to speak publicly but only asylum claims. Because of the 1985–1986 Tucson sanctuary trial and the legal risks of border crossings, Tucson screening procedures more closely mirrored the asylum process than did East Bay screening procedures. When Trsg— the group responsible for crossings at the time of my research—learned through Mexican or Central American colleagues of Central Americans who desired sanctuary workers' assistance, a Trsg counselor was sent to the border to find out why the Central Americans had left their countries, whether they had experienced persecution, and what they feared would befall them if they returned home; in short, counselors compiled the knowledge that constituted a political asylum claim. In addition, like immigration attorneys, Trsg counselors sought corroborating documentation. For example, while volunteering in the Task Force office one morning, I was asked to translate a letter from a Salvadoran man in order to determine whether he had a valid asylum claim. As this was a task I had performed for immigration attorneys, I assumed that this man was preparing for a court hearing. I later learned, however, that the man was still in El Salvador and that at its next meeting Trsg would decide by consensus whether he met the definition of refugee contained in the United Nations Refugee Protocol and the Geneva Conventions on War and War Victims.[10] When, based on the counselor's report and any corroborating documentation, Trsg members concluded that individuals such as this man were refugees, they brought them across the border. Those not deemed refugees were left alone or given another form of assistance.

Because their screening procedures adhered closely to the asylum process, Tucson sanctuary workers (like those in the East Bay) enforced the legal distinction between deportable economic immigrants and nondeportable political refugees. According to U.S. refugee law, individuals could only be granted asylum for being persecuted on account of their "race, religion, nationality, membership in a particular social group, or political opinion" (Sklar et al. 1985:1012). Economic deprivation, no matter how severe, was not a legal ground for asylum. The fact that the INS denied 98 percent of the asylum applications filed by Salvadorans and Guatemalans proved to sanctuary workers that the INS was failing to distinguish between political refugees and economic immigrants. Sanctuary workers reasoned that if the movement were to cross *all* Central Americans, it would be guilty of a similar charge. Therefore, to participants, refusing assistance to some immigrants became a way of proving that sanctuary work enforced, rather than violated, the law. I attended a meeting in Tucson at which a member of a sanctuary group that had splintered off from Trsg defended his group to Task Force members by noting that it had refused half of the people requesting the group's assistance. A Trsg member whom I interviewed noted, "To keep up the credibility, you need to say no sometimes. There was a case just last week when we were called to the border to take someone across, and it turned out that he just wanted a job, so we gave him some money and wished him luck." Another sanctuary worker whom I interviewed observed proudly, "We are better at separating political refugees from economic refugees than the INS is!"

Despite their commitment to these criteria, some Tucson sanctuary workers expressed misgivings about the economic versus political distinction. One border worker summarized the problem: "By adhering to Trsg standards, we're playing a role in trying to change refugee law. ... [But] what do you do when an economic refugee comes to you and says that their children are dying? They're just as dead whether they're economic or political. " Some felt that economic oppression required different solutions than political oppression. For example, Carl Fonde asked rhetorically, "What about refugees who are facing life-threatening conditions of deprivation? How do you respond? Do you get them dishwashing jobs in the U.S., or do you go to where they are to try to help them?" Other sanctuary workers believed that both groups deserved to immigrate but were only willing to take risks for the political refugees. Still others considered the distinction a question of priorities, reasoning that political refugees faced worse risks than economic immigrants. Marilyn Phillips, a former border worker, cited Matthew 25, in which Jesus tells his disciples that when they aided the needy, they aided him, to convey the dilemma posed by the economic versus political distinction:

> Once, when I was in Hermosillo, we went down to talk to what we thought were seven people who were interested in crossing the border, but once we got there, we

actually met twenty-five—including ten people with babies who were just emaciated from hunger. And we really had to struggle with what our decision was going to be as to whether or not to cross them. Were they politically persecuted? And we had to conclude that they weren't. The way that we reached that decision was to go back to the Refugee Act of 1980, which is what sanctuary is based on. I realized that those people could probably cross themselves at some point, and that if you're going to be doing border work, you *have* to have criteria. And for me, it was a dilemma between the 1980 Refugee Act and Matthew 25. Matthew 25 called me to help all those who are in need. So what we did in the end was that we assisted them with food and with advice about how to come to the U.S., but we didn't cross them. Crossing them wouldn't help the goal of sanctuary.

Tucson border workers (unlike East Bay activists) also legitimized their claim to be upholding the law by *not* differentiating between refugees from the Left and the Right. Sanctuary workers contended that official asylum procedures were biased against applicants from non-Communist nations and therefore in violation of the law. As evidence, they cited higher acceptance rates for asylum applicants from Poland and Nicaragua than from El Salvador and Guatemala. Sanctuary workers sought to avoid such bias—and make their procedures superior to those of the INS—by ignoring refugees' political views.[11] For example, Ernie Tarkington, a Tucson sanctuary minister, seemed to relish the words as he told me of his assistance to a Nicaraguan refugee: "He had fought for the Sandinistas, and then had quit that, and had fought for the Contras, and then he quit and fled to the U.S. Now, I don't believe that he's in any real physical danger if he were to go back to his country. ... But I helped him. And the reason that I helped him was because he was in a situation that was hopeless." Similarly, Marilyn Phillips, the former border worker quoted above, described the dilemma presented by a group of women and children connected to the political Right:

> There were some allusions by some members of Trsg that by helping them, you're helping Hitler. And so I did a lot of soul-searching on that one. And what I realized, especially as I came to know them, is that they are human beings who were afraid, and who were heading for Canada. And it was a very real fear for them. We spent a lot of heavy nights discussing that one, and we had a lot of debates about who you help. And my position in the end was that some of them were children and babies, and that the humane thing to do in those circumstances is to help. Because what I realized is that for me, sanctuary isn't political. It isn't Left or Right, it isn't black or white, but instead there's a lot of gray.

By incorporating such legal notions and practices into their screening procedures, East Bay and Tucson sanctuary workers both resisted and reinforced the power relations inherent in immigration discourse. On the one hand, defining undocumented individuals as legal refugees implied that persecution inherently entitled an individual to asylum. This redefinition made the designation "refugee" intrinsic to persecuted individuals rather than a status that could only be conferred by the state. Moreover, by enabling ordinary citizens to evaluate individuals' asylum claims, screening procedures made immigration a matter of community control as well as of state control.[12] When a Phoenix minister told me simply, "I knew they were refugees because I had heard so many of their stories," he was establishing a truth that bypassed the official immigration process. Finally, by constituting Salvadorans and Guatemalans as refugees rather than illegal aliens, screening procedures challenged the U.S. government's view of human rights abuses in El Salvador and Guatemala. On the other hand, because they were constructed out of discourses whose oppositional potentials were also power-laden, screening procedures also created relations of power. Screening procedures, like political asylum hearings, compelled Central Americans to produce the discourse that situated them within immigration categories. By assuming the authority to define individuals' immigration status, sanctuary workers created an asymmetry between themselves and those whom they defined. Last, when they asserted that political refugees had legal rights that were not shared by economic immigrants, sanctuary workers were essentially saying that political refugees' life experiences granted them a jural existence wherever they physically existed, but that economic immigrants' jural and physical existences did not coincide within U.S. borders. This contention reinforced the notion of legal personhood that made some immigrants deportable.

The power relations inherent in screening procedures also pervaded the practice from which the movement derived its name: giving sanctuary to undocumented Central Americans.

## Sanctuary

Like screening procedures, housing undocumented Central Americans both invoked and defied the legal discourse that suspended the undocumented from society. Although U.S. immigration law made individuals criminally liable for the legal status of those whom they sheltered, East Bay and Tucson sanctuary workers declared that it was legal to give sanctuary to undocumented Central Americans. When they acted on this contention, sanctuary workers not only challenged the U.S. government's view that El Salvador and Guatemala were democracies with improving human rights records, they also proclaimed that, regardless of whether the U.S. government had authorized their presences, Central American refugees existed jurally *and* physically within U.S. borders. By treating undocumented Salvadorans and Guatemalans as legal refugees rather than illegal aliens, sanctuary workers sought to establish the validity of their understanding of law and thus prevent Central Americans from being deported to face persecution and death. Despite the fact that sheltering Central Americans overcame some of the divisions between the documented and the undocumented, however, the definitional scrutiny that pervaded screening procedures also entered into these living arrangements. By protecting undocumented Central Americans from the deporting gaze of the INS, participants subjected them to the gaze of sanctuary congregations.

The prototypical sanctuary arrangement consisted of a congregation openly sheltering a refugee family in a church building, synagogue, or member's home. To educate North Americans about repression in Central America, refugees were expected to recount their experiences to congregation members, journalists, and other public audiences. However, actual sanctuary arrangements often differed from this prototype. A number of sanctuary congregations in both the East Bay and Tucson never housed a Central American but instead donated money for bail bond, sent volunteers to provide social services through sanctuary or Task Force offices, wrote letters to Congress urging changes in U.S. foreign policy, funded delegates to Central America, organized community-wide events relating to Central American issues, and performed countless other tasks. In the East Bay, First Church had joined a half dozen other sanctuary congregations in contributing toward the rental of a refugee house where seven Central Americans lived. All Saints Church in Tucson regularly showed visitors its "bedroom"—the sanctuary where the congregation worshiped on Sunday mornings and where newly arrived Central Americans slept until more permanent quarters could be arranged. In Tucson, many sanctuary workers quietly housed Central Americans who arrived on the underground railroad for days, weeks, months, or years, neither publicizing their actions nor requiring presentations from the immigrants they aided.

Despite its varied forms, sanctuary work derived its meaning from the model that it imitated. For example, consider the experience of Gustavo Alvarez, a fifty-five-year-old Salvadoran immigrant whose relationships with two Tucson congregations approximated, but never matched, the sanctuary prototype. I first met Gustavo at a luncheon where he spoke to an international women's group that was meeting with Tucson sanctuary leaders. Through an interpreter, Gustavo told the group that as a Christian, he had struggled against injustice by trying to help the needy in the small Salvadoran town where he formerly lived. Gustavo described fleeing to San Salvador after two of his companions were murdered and after he had been named as the next victim. In San Salvador, he said, he had joined a union and had again been persecuted. At this point in his presentation, Gustavo was overcome by emotion. He told his listeners, "I regret that I won't be able to say any more about my country or the situation there, because it is too difficult for me. I still have family there, and also, many of my family members have been killed. There are many who are dead. And so, I would like to thank you for listening to me, and I would like to ask that you pray that there be peace in El Salvador." Gustavo walked off, weeping.

During interviews with Tucson sanctuary workers, I learned that Gustavo's family had entered the United States on the underground railroad and then had been given private sanctuary in a local church. A member of the church told me that this "was probably to the family's disadvantage. It was supposed to have been temporary, but we didn't exactly launch them out." Gustavo said of this period:

Being recently arrived, they gave us a home and food and clothing. For the first six months, we got lots of help. The help that they give is humanitarian. At the same time, we got a lawyer ... to apply for political asylum for us, and the lawyer didn't charge a fee or anything. During the first six months, we did very well, and we got lots of help from the churches. They got us work as painters, and they got a childcare job for my wife. The moral and spiritual support that they gave us was great. In return, we collaborate in the various churches, telling about the terrible experiences that we've had in El Salvador.

After the first six months, Gustavo and his family moved into their own apartment. To Gustavo's frustration, however, they continued to rely on social services programs: "If it wasn't for the social services program of the church, we couldn't get help. It is hard on us, for example, when we need to consult a doctor, because we can't call them and speak to them directly. We don't speak English. But sometimes we need to see a doctor and there's no one in the social services office."

Through public speaking, Gustavo and his family formed a relationship with a local church that had not officially declared itself a sanctuary. One of the clergy at this church told me how this relationship evolved:

I suggested to Jennie Haight [a local pastor] that we have a course on liberation theology. "Great!" she said, "but let's make it *real*." So we began a Bible study with the refugees. ... We brought in Gustavo's family. They had come into the United States ... with the help of sanctuary, and their story was so horrendous that they got immediate temporary asylum. About thirty to thirty-five people came to the Bible study. Using the book of Luke, the family told their story. And I'll tell you, there was not a dry eye in the house. They'd experienced rape, murder, disappearances. Both the inquisitive and the supportive were moved by what they heard.

However, Gustavo's wife, Marta Rodriguez, told me that she felt used by those to whom she spoke. While still in El Salvador, Marta had decided that when she came to the United States she would publicize her experiences. So, after arriving, she was eager to speak to congregations, reporters, and others. One day, she noticed that a church collected quite a few checks as a result of her testimony. She told me that someone in the church had said to her, "You are a blessing to the church." "Why?" she had asked. "Because lots of money came into the church as a result of the testimony that you gave," the woman had replied. Marta decided to give no more testimonies.

When congregations gave sanctuary to immigrants such as Gustavo, they provided much-needed material assistance. Echoing Gustavo's appreciation of the aid he had received, Erica Castillo, a San Francisco refugee organizer, told me:

We see that truly, without them [members of the U.S. religious community], we would not exist here. They have helped [to] free people from prison, helped people who were going to be deported. ... And that is like giving life to a person who might encounter some form of repression in his own country, [such as] disappearance, or being thrown in prison, or being assassinated.

Similarly, Marisol Hernandez, a Guatemalan immigrant, commented:

I admire the volunteers who expose their own lives to pass us [across the border]. It's a question of doing something voluntarily for us, because they are not paid or reimbursed or given any kind of compensation for what they're doing. ... They have helped me so much! First they crossed me and my husband, and then later, they brought my children. They gave me medicine and they gave us a place to live. They have been wonderful.

As these living arrangements aided Central Americans and challenged U.S. policies, they also imbued immigrants with a quasi-sacred power to represent truth. As anthropologist Michael Taussig noted of the persecuted's brushes with death, "We may think of the space of death as a threshold that allows for illumination as well as extinction. Sometimes a person goes through it and returns to us, to tell the tale" (1987:4). In hearing Central Americans' tales of persecution, sanctuary workers inverted the negative powers that immigration discourse conferred on illegal aliens. Rather than viewing undocumented immigrants as lawless beings and sources of anarchy, sanctuary workers considered undocumented Central Americans sources of wisdom. For example, a sanctuary announcement distributed by a West Coast church referred to the Central Americans it hoped to shelter as "ambassadors of the suffering people of Central America" who, in sharing their stories, would teach congregants about their faith, their struggle, and their culture. This inversion of the implications of legal categories drew upon the religious notion that the persecuted are closer to God than are others. Thus, in the case of Gustavo Alvarez, the liberation theology class proposed by two Tucson ministers became *real* when Gustavo's family told its story of persecution.

As bearers of truth, refugees were believed capable of transforming the congregations that assisted them. In addition to consciousness-raising, conversions, and reinterpretations of history, Central Americans produced *juridical* transformations in those around them. Sheltering people whom the U.S. government defined as illegal caught sanctuary workers in a web of illegality. Carl Fonde, a Tucson border worker, defined sanctuary as "protective community with the violated," and noted, "To the extent that the violated are viewed as 'illegals', the community itself becomes 'illegal'—in quotes." Becoming "illegal" had religious implications for sanctuary workers. As congregants risked arrest, they joined the ranks of the persecuted—thus, in their own eyes, making the sacrifices required by their faith. By, in the words of one immigrant, "giving life" to Central American refugees, citizens whose government supplied El Salvador with bombs and bullets *found* life. As one Tucson border worker exclaimed, "I believe that the refugees can save our American souls!" Similarly, a San Francisco activist stated, "I think it's the classic situation, where they [refugees] get money from us, and we get life from them."[13] Because of their transformative power, refugees were subjected to invasive, if well-meaning, scrutiny by the congregations that sheltered them. Gustavo spelled out the nature of the exchange between refugees and sanctuary workers when he noted, "In return [for their assistance], we collaborate in the various churches, telling about the terrible experiences that we've had in El Salvador."

Some of the Central Americans I interviewed participated in the poetic discourse that imbued refugees with the power to educate and even transform North Americans. During an interview, José Martín, an organizer in the San Francisco refugee community, used rich biblical imagery to explain how such transformations occurred:

> The sanctuary movement provides a vision of the exoduses of our peoples. When I left my country, I found many pharaoh-like *pueblos,* with their kings who tried to enslave. But the sanctuary movement is the conscience and the voice of the North American people against these pharaohs. And the sanctuary movement is also an exodus for those people who act within it. It brings them persecution and sacrifice, and it causes them to renounce the luxuries that they have. Sanctuary is moving in the exodus, even though physically people aren't moving. Rather, sanctuary is transforming North Americans as they come to identify with *our* exodus. ...
>
> We are the guests and the North Americans are the hosts, but they share in the pilgrimage that we are on.

Not all Central Americans shared Jose's views. Like Marta Rodriguez, some felt that Central Americans were being "used" by the movement. One Salvadoran I interviewed accused the sanctuary movement of using the refugee situation as a flag to attract attention. He said that the movement made a show of the refugees and that participants' attitude toward Central Americans was, "Poor little refugee! We'll help you!" Central Americans also resented the objectification that resulted from being the subjects of sanctuary workers' gazes. For example, while I was talking with a minister and a Salvadoran, the minister asked the Salvadoran, "Remember when you were being a refugee?" He answered, "Oh, yeah, I used to go around and they would look at me, the exotic refugee, and say, 'Wow! You have two legs just like white people and you walk just like white people!'" Similarly, Clemente Rivera, a Salvadoran living in private sanctuary, noted that he preferred relationships that were "person to person instead of person to refugee." Finally, some Central Americans noted that sanctuary relationships created hierarchies between those who defined and those who were defined. Clemente Rivera found being designated a refugee constricting. He said, "I would prefer to live freely and to free myself from the word, 'refugee.' ... I mean, I left my country due to the violence and due to the fear and danger of disappearing, *not* in order to become a refugee. To me, the word 'refugee' implies inferiority and superiority." A Salvadoran active in the Bay Area refugee community spoke eloquently about the paternalism that sometimes occurred when congregations or individuals sheltered Central Americans:

> A refugee can feel like a bird in a cage. And while the cage may be beautiful, it's still a cage. A person can feel very overprotected. And being overprotected isn't the same as being a refugee and yet being free. ...
>
> Like, they say that you shouldn't work, because it could be dangerous. Or they tell you to forget your country and to learn English. They try to tell you how to raise your children, explaining how they raised their children. They tell you to cook a certain way, and to eat a certain way, and to view your own community a certain way. For example, maybe they think that it's important for you to go to church every Sunday at eleven o'clock. And maybe you would rather go to a community event on Sunday.

These immigrants' remarks demonstrate that imbuing refugees with life-giving power was not the same thing as empowerment. To understand why not, let us look more closely at telling the tale of the space of death. Such tellings, which were central to sanctuary work, were known as giving testimonies.

## Testimonies

Within the context of the sanctuary movement, "testimony" referred to Central Americans' accounts of the events that led them to seek refuge in the United States. Testimonies reiterated the same stories of persecution elicited during political asylum hearings and screening procedures—stories that, according to Gustavo Alvarez, were painful to tell. Testimonies were given during church services, interviews, meetings, gatherings, public presentations, and workshops. Typically, a sanctuary worker would introduce the refugee and give some background about Central America, sanctuary, and U.S. policy. Then the refugee, speaking through an interpreter, would present a narrative that moved from his or her personal experience to statements about stopping the violence in El Salvador or Guatemala. The testimony was often followed by a question-and-answer period and was usually accompanied by fund-raising appeals or announcements about how to get involved. In the Bay Area, sanctuary workers requested refugee speakers through CRECE, a local refugee group, whereas in Tucson, sanctuary workers arranged testimonies more informally, by contacting Central Americans who were willing to speak publicly. In both Tucson and the Bay Area, the interpreter's role during testimonies was crucial, as English-speaking members of the audience listened to the translation rather than the original Spanish. Testimonies were clearly performances.[14] When I volunteered as a translator, Central Americans frequently rehearsed their testimonies with me in advance in order to clarify the events and to explain difficult vocabulary. In one case, a Salvadoran man brought a typewritten version of his talk for me to review.

The following unedited transcript of a tape-recorded testimony was made in May 1987. At that time, EBSC was preparing a booth for a local festival, and volunteers suggested that, along with brochures about sanctuary, Central American crafts, and suggestions about how to get involved, the booth feature a tape recording of a Central American's testimony. Volunteers sought out an English-speaking Central American for the recording so that festival-goers would be able to listen to the refugee's words directly, without translation. Through CRECE, an EBSC volunteer arranged to tape-record an eighteen-year-old Salvadoran woman at the CRECE office. According to the volunteer, the woman had told her story publicly only once before. The volunteer told me that when she first tape-recorded this testimony, the woman spoke in general terms about politics and about life in the United States. The volunteer stopped recording and asked the woman to tell her personal story. As she told her story, the woman began to weep. When the woman finished, the volunteer made what she said was a very difficult request. Because the tape recorder had been turned off during the second rendition, she asked the woman to tell her story a third time. Here is the transcript that resulted, and that EBSC office volunteers placed in the booth along with the cassette recording:[15]

I came here about ... I have been here for three years now. I came with my mother. I'd like to explain a little bit about why I came here. One time ... one afternoon in 1979 we were home, my sister ... my younger sister and I and my mother. My father had just come from work. He was working at a factory when ... My mother was almost ready to serve dinner. My sister and I were with her when someone came to the door. My father opened the door—he was in the living room—and suddenly we heard noise in the living room and we heard like someone drop and when we came in the living room it was my father and there were three people there wearing plain clothes and they had machetes and a forty-five, each of them. I saw one of them hitting my father with his machete. My father was ... had wounds all over and they were saying that they were doing that because he was a guerilla fighter and because they had seen him in several strikes, labor strikes, and therefore they knew that he was a guerilla fighter.

My mother tried to talk some sense into them. She cried and begged them; she went on her knees begging them to leave my father alone and they just would insult him and kept hitting him. He was just ... I just thought he was dead. I was in the corner with my sister just looking at him. And my mother, when she tried to help him, they just ... one of them just grabbed her. And then the other one started to hit her with the machete also. My mother tried ... asked us to leave. She just cried, "run!" I just don't know how or why, I just ran. ...

My sister, we ran as fast as we could and I just went to the police. There was a station. I don't even know why I went there. At the time it was the only thing that made sense to me, to come to them. We got there and explained to them what was happening. They didn't really seem to care. The following day they got into a pick-up and asked us to show them where we lived. When we took them there they had ... the men who had come earlier to kill my father had already left. People said that they had just left a few minutes ago and that maybe if they followed them they could catch them still, but they said that that was not important at the time, that they shouldn't go after them—that they might be gone by now.

So they took my parents to a hospital but they wouldn't even help them because they said they were not ... that they didn't have a chart in there, that they didn't have their names on their list so they couldn't help them. They finally took them to another hospital in San Salvador where they could help them. My father died there. My mother was unconscious for, I just ... I don't know how long, a long time.

After a month she was able to be seen. My sister and I were too young to go into the hospital to see her so she asked the doctor if she could leave the hospital because she couldn't stay there. A friend of hers was taking care of us and she just wanted to be with us.

So when she left the hospital we moved to another place and went to see a lawyer and told him—my mother said that she could recognize the guys who killed my father and they advised us not to say anything because they said that our lives would just be in danger and not just because of her life, but for us—my sister and I.

We were five children. Actually we were eight, but three of us died at a very young age because my parents were in a real bad situation, and there was ... they were sick, and they didn't have any medical attention so they died. My other two sisters, they were very grown up. One was living with my father's sister and she was a student. My other sister had already gotten married. It was just my younger sister and I.

When we were living at this place, we thought that maybe what had happened to us was just ... that some people maybe pointed at us and said that my father was part of a union maybe or a guerilla or that they. ... . At that place where we lived a lot of people started to disappear and my mother was really afraid for us because most of them were young children. I should say that because some of them were even 11 years old. They would just disappear them and kill them. A lot of young girls my age—at that time I was 11 years old, near 12—disappeared. They were raped and then killed.

When my mother saw this and noticed that a lot of my friends had already been disappeared and killed, we were really terrified. We managed to save some money so that we could leave the country. We only had enough to make it to Mexico, but when we got there we talked to a coyote and explained to him why we had to leave. He was moved too, from our testimony. He said he would help us come to the United States. He helped us cross the frontier. We paid him here later. We didn't have any money at that time.

When we came here we thought that things would be different since in my country there's a great violation of the human rights and when I was there I was just not the same because of what I've seen because I kept remembering these people—these men [who] came into my house and killed my father, every night over and over. I just thought it would be different. I just thought I would learn to live a normal life here because I wouldn't be under the fear of being persecuted, of being killed for nothing. I just thought that it would be different.

Because down there my sister and I were under psychological treatment for nearly two years and a half. And I just had to learn to cry again. I just had to learn so many things. I had to learn to talk to people again because I was so afraid, because I was so afraid that when I talked I would say something wrong that would put my mother's life in danger. I was so scared of saying anything wrong that would put my sister's life in danger. I just didn't know how to speak. I just didn't know how to express myself before people. And I thought that when I came here it will be different.

But here, this country does not recognize our status as refugees. They say that we just come here as economic refugees and it is not true because we come here running from the war. If people here would recognize that and help us, I know that we could stop the war. But in order to stop the war in our country we have to stop the economic aid that this country is sending to El Salvador. Because they are not just sending the money, the bombs and the guns, the Marines. But they are also sending the victims—we the Salvadoran refugees. And we have come here running from the war and we are deport[ed]—we go down there to a death sentence.

Because in our government there is no justice. They just don't understand. I don't know but I guess those people become unhuman. I don't think they'll feel anymore what pain means. I don't think that they stop to think about the families they are going to leave helpless because they have killed the head of the family—the father, they kill the only source of income in the houses. And they just don't think and they don't even respect the children's lives.

It is just sad and I just wish that the people who is listening to me now will stop to think about it and will think that we are also human and we also deserve to live in peace. We also deserve to have a normal life like you do; like anybody deserves to. Sometimes I just feel helpless because I feel that the people here don't care. I just feel that the people don't even realize what being in El Salvador is because they haven't gone through and because they might never go through it. They think that what is happening in El Salvador is just normal and they just don't stop to think that there is just humans in El Salvador, that we are only humans asking for peace, that we want to stop the aid that this government is sending because that is just prolonging the war.

We want to [??] because we want to stop the war but our government, Mr. Duarte don't want [??] because he's just never going to understand the poor people. They just give them repression when they ask for a better salary for their families, to support their families, when they ask for hospitals, when they go on strikes because they don't have anything to feed their children. They just give them bullets—they come and kill our families. And we just feel helpless.

And I just hope that the people who is listening to me today will help me build a peace that we want so much, and that we need so much in our country. Thank you.

When the eighteen-year-old Salvadoran woman produced this narrative, she participated in a Latin American tradition in which common people relate their personal experiences in order to educate others about oppression. For example, in the preface to the book *Let Me Speak! Testimony of Domitila, a Woman of the Bolivian Mines,* Domitila Barrios de Chungara explained the meaning of testimony:

I don't want anyone at any moment to interpret the story I'm about to tell as something that is only personal. Because I think that my life is related to my people. What happened to me could have happened to hundreds of people in my country. ... I want to testify about all the experience we've acquired during so many years of struggle in Bolivia, and contribute a little grain of sand, with the hope that our experience may serve in some way for the new generation (Barrios de Chungara and Viezzer 1978:15).

Similarly, during sanctuary testimonies, speakers' particular stories assumed the authority to represent those who could not speak. For example, one Salvadoran for whom I frequently translated always began her testimony by saying, "I am one of the thousands of Central American refugees."[16] Another Salvadoran activist said of refugees, "We have become like an open book, and [a] radio which switched from silence to sound, the throats of thousands, and like the biblical reference [to] the voice in the desert." In this metaphor, the refugees could be read, they were known, they were the subjects of their own speaking. As "the throats of thousands" they spoke not only for themselves but for their people. Like John the Baptist ("the voice in the desert"), they heralded the coming of change.

Despite the fact that immigration discourse did not define listening to the undocumented as a criminal act, the sanctuary workers who heard testimonies like the one quoted above often experienced these words as forbidden knowledge. Refugee testimonies publicized the voices of "illegal aliens" who lived "in the shadows," émigrés from a land where fear, torture, and death had silenced many. Listeners were aware that, by advertising their presence, undocumented speakers risked being captured and deported. To people from countries where political knowledge endangered its possessor, words could be dangerous. Ramon Palacios, who used to risk death by carrying political literature around in notebooks, told me, "Now that my family is here, I don't want to do as much speaking to get publicity. There's fear among refugees even being in the U.S., although not like there." Sanctuary workers also believed the U.S. government would have preferred to silence the victims of wars that it had helped finance. For example, Marty Finn, an East Bay volunteer, argued that interaction between Central and North Americans would make it difficult for the U.S. populace to support military aid to Central American governments. Similarly, Central Americans whom I interviewed believed that by denouncing the oppression and human rights violations in El Salvador and Guatemala, they would influence U.S. policy and effect social change in their own countries.

Their revelatory quality gave refugee testimonies the power to transform North American listeners. Testimonies recited the same narratives of persecution and flight that asylum applicants produced under oath during asylum hearings; however, unlike asylum hearings, sanctuary testimonies aimed the transformative power of the victims' words at listener as well as speaker. Just as asylum applicants' stories defined them as either illegal aliens or political asylees, each repetition of a Central American's testimony reconstituted the speaker as a refugee rather than as an illegal alien. Though both courtroom and sanctuary testimonies were designed to persuade, sanctuary testimonies caused a deeper transformation. These testimonies represented truth by confronting listeners with the physical presence of those who were forbidden, the voices of those who were silenced, and the suffering of those who now pricked the consciences of the comfortable. Testimonies were integral to the conversions described in Chapter 4, and many sanctuary volunteers traced their involvement to hearing a refugee testimony. The depth of the changes wrought by refugees' words was expressed by Sam Gersch, an East Bay minister, who told me, "The blood that is shed on the soil of Central America is sprouting forth and bringing new life to the church of North America."[17]

The transformative nature of refugee testimonies derived not only from law but also from religious notions of "witnessing," a form of evangelism in which Christians seek to communicate their faith to others through their life and words (Greenhouse 1986). In fact, refugee testimonies were sometimes called "witnessing," as in the following observation by a Bay Area sanctuary worker: "In the sanctuary movement, it's a very fine line you walk between having people *witness* and give testimony and tell about their lives, and putting them on parade." Sanctuary workers' use of testimonies probably resulted from the same evangelical tradition that led pre–Civil War abolitionists to travel with former slaves who spoke publicly about their suffering (Tyler 1944:506). For religious activists, Central Americans' lives and words were a source of life-giving truth, as shown by a Bay Area "Covenant for Compassion" gathering at which a minister told the audience "We came to see the face of Jesus in the Central Americans. ... God is speaking to us through the Central Americans."

Just as refugee testimonies mirrored the Christian practice of witnessing, they also resembled a practice from recent Jewish history: the testimonies of Holocaust victims. Like Holocaust testimonies, Central Americans' stories were a means of alerting the world to human rights violations. For example, Lisa Rothstein, a Jewish sanctuary worker, told me, "They're like the people in the Holocaust. ... They're in a desperate situation, trying to get the word out about what's happening in their home. They can't concentrate on living their lives, and so we have to help them." A member of Congregation Aron Kodesh believed that refugee testimonies established a personal connection to suffering, a connection that had not been possible during the Holocaust. He explained, "When the Jews left Eastern Europe, there was no way for them to come to the United States and talk about the horror of the concentration camps. People did not want to hear about it, and there was a real resistance to even believing that it had happened. ... But in this case, they've been arriving from Central America and they've been telling their stories."

Despite the fact that testimonies transformed listeners and challenged the status quo, there was still a power relationship—analogous to that between a listening judge and a testifying asylum applicant—between the sanctuary workers who knew and the refugees who were known. Although Central Americans were often eager to give testimonies, it was North American audiences, rather than Central American speakers, who had the authority to elicit accounts of persecution and judge their significance. Though individual North Americans often told Central

American friends and colleagues about their life experiences, no movement practice required North Americans to relate personal experiences to Central Americans or authorized Central Americans to judge North Americans' identities. As a result, knowledge went primarily from refugees to sanctuary workers rather than vice versa. The eighteen-year-old Salvadoran woman's tragic story of her father's assassination was heard by volunteers, disseminated at a public fair, and now is reproduced in this monograph. Similarly, during an interview, a Tucson sanctuary minister criticized a church's misconceptions about the refugee family it was sponsoring. He then exclaimed, "Some churches don't get to know their refugees at all!" During fieldwork, I never heard anyone worry about whether a refugee family got to know "its" congregation.

Thus, imbuing refugees with the power to speak truth was also a power-laden process of knowing an oppressed and foreign other. Though insurrectional, the sanctuary movement's quest for transformative knowledge of refugees' lives in some ways derived its power from foreign governments' searches for dissidents, the INS's search for illegal aliens, and the political asylum process's search for discourse and documentation. The two-edged process of imbuing power while extracting knowledge that was begun during screening procedures, continued through giving sanctuary, and celebrated during public testimonies demonstrated that the sanctuary movement could not avoid recreating some of the power relations intrinsic to the legal discourse from which its legitimacy derived.

## Conclusion

When they set out to challenge the U.S. government's contention that the vast majority of Salvadoran and Guatemalan immigrants were illegal aliens, sanctuary workers did not intend either to resist or reinforce the power inherent in immigration discourse. As sanctuary workers struggled to devise ways of changing U.S. refugee policy, however, they found themselves manipulating categories and practices whose meanings were, to some extent, already defined. When they used the legal definition of refugee to screen Central Americans requesting the movement's assistance, sanctuary workers reinforced distinctions between legal and illegal immigration. Crossing, sheltering, and publicizing the stories of Central Americans overcame divisions between the documented and the undocumented, but refusing to cross those Central Americans deemed economic immigrants constituted such individuals as illegal beings and set them apart from the rest of society. Eliciting and publicizing Central Americans' accounts of suffering challenged the U.S. government's view of human rights violations in El Salvador and Guatemala but also created asymmetries between the sanctuary workers who knew and the refugees who were known. Constructing an alternative immigration system challenged the exclusivity of the U.S. government's control over international travel yet placed sanctuary workers in a position of power vis à vis Central Americans. In short, participants could invoke the legitimacy of legal notions, improvise on preexisting practices, and create new meanings, but they could not avoid reproducing some of the power relations in which these notions, practices, and meanings were embedded.

The contradictory nature of protest does not tip the scales against protestors, as their adversaries' actions are *also* politically contradictory. In fact, as the U.S. government discovered when it indicted movement members, efforts to repress can promote resistance in unanticipated ways.

## Notes

1. Melucci criticized such studies for having "a 'myopia of the visible,' which leads the analysis to focus all its attention on the measurable aspects of collective action (e.g., confrontation with the political system, and movements' effects on the policies of organizations)" (1989:44).

2. Merry noted that actors develop legal expertise through particular experiences with the legal system. She termed this expertise "legal consciousness," defined as "the ways people understand and use law" (1990:5). Civil initiative was one form of legal consciousness.

3. A minority of sanctuary workers in both Tucson and the East Bay adopted other understandings of the legality of sanctuary work. A few accepted the appellation "civil disobedience" and claimed that aiding the undocumented obeyed a higher law than U.S. legal codes. Others agreed that sanctuary work was legal but, in sharp contrast to civil initiative's careful precedent-setting activities, considered legality irrelevant. Still others rejected the distinction between citizens and aliens entirely and insisted that no human being could be illegal. For a more detailed description of these perspectives, see Coutin 1990.

4. Tucsonans' distinction between the formal legal codes and communities' understandings of the law was a variation of the contrast between natural and official law that is part of U.S. culture. According to anthropologist Carol Greenhouse, Americans conceptualize official law as "rules imposed externally by elite institutions" (Greenhouse 1989:269). In contrast, they conceive of natural law as the community's collective understanding of the norms that govern relationships.

5. Participants did not consider the 1985–1986 Tucson sanctuary trial a true test of this theory because court rulings prevented defendants from presenting many of the arguments they used to justify sanctuary work. See Chapter 7 for more details.

6. Contrary to a popular misconception within the sanctuary movement, Tucson border workers did not force Central Americans to apply for asylum. While in Tucson, I met Central Americans who had entered the country with the assistance of the movement but who, after meeting with attorneys, had elected not to submit asylum applications.

7. I am describing the screening procedures that were in effect at the time of my research.

8. In describing the battle over defining reality that took place between civil rights workers and authorities, Harding noted that "whose interpretation requires proof is an indicator of who has and who lacks hegemony" (1984:391). One reason that the sanctuary movement publicized refugee testimonies was to prove that Salvadorans and Guatemalans faced persecution if deported. An indication that the movement's (and other refugee advocates') arguments were persuasive is that the government eventually began citing reports that Central American deportees were not harmed after arrival.

9. During interviews, I heard several explanations for this lack of interest: (1) The number of Central Americans placed in public sanctuary during the early years of the movement was greatly exaggerated by the movement, the press, and the public, so the contrast between the numbers in the past and at the time of my research was not as great as it seemed. (2) During the early years of the sanctuary movement, there were fewer Central Americans in the United States than there were later on, and therefore, refugees had few alternatives to public sanctuary. As the number of Central American immigrants grew, it became easier for immigrants to settle with friends or relatives in Latino areas of major U.S. cities. (3) Public sanctuary was stressful for Central Americans because it isolated them from other Latinos, was sometimes paternalistic, and required people to speak publicly about painful events. (4) In the early years of the sanctuary movement, the Central Americans who came to the United States had been targeted by the government because they had been involved in specific political activities, such as organizing a union or opposing the government. Such immigrants saw sanctuary as an opportunity to continue their struggles by speaking out to the North American people about the repression and atrocities in Central America. After years of war, however, many of the more recent immigrants were not politically active in Central America. Instead, they were fleeing general conditions of violence and were not interested in speaking publicly in the United States.

10. According to Trsg handouts, the UN Refugee Protocol—which was incorporated into U.S. law through the 1980 Refugee Act—"defines a refugee as anyone who is outside the country of his or her nationality and who cannot return because of 'well-found fear of being persecuted for reasons of race, religion, nationality, membership in a particular social group, or political opinion.'" Handouts described the Geneva Conventions as

> applicable to areas of armed conflict. The Conventions protect civilians from the dangers of war. Direct military attacks on the civilian population as well as "acts or threats of violence whose primary purpose ... is to spread terror among the civilian population" are forbidden. Murder, torture, mutiliation [*sic*], corporeal punishment, collective punishments, taking of hostages, acts of terrorism, degrading treatment (such as rape, enforced prostitution, indecent assault), and threats to commit any of these abuses are forbidden. Refugees, for the purposes of the Geneva Conventions, are persons who do not enjoy the protection of any government. Under the conventions, refugees cannot be forcibly returned to their homeland until after the cessation of hostilities and armed conflict.

11. Some of the Central Americans I interviewed in Tucson felt that the local movement's concern with legality blinded it to the potential danger of bringing former members of the Salvadoran Armed Forces into the United States. For Guatemalan Marisol Hernandez this potential became an actuality. When Marisol accompanied her compatriot Felipe Arguelles to meet a newly arrived Guatemalan woman and her children,

> My children saw her children [and] started to run away. I said, "Why are you doing that?" because I didn't recognize the children. And then I saw the woman, and I recognized her, and I said to Felipe, "Come on, let's get out of here. I know these people." I knew them very, very well. The woman lived near my mother-in-law, and her husband was with the National Guard and he had been one of the people involved in my husband's capture and torture. For three months my husband was held in a house and tortured, and when he came out, he was covered with scars.

So I said to Felipe, "I don't want them to know me, or to know where I live or to know where I work. Because they know about the problems that I had there in Guatemala. If sanctuary wants to bring them into the U.S., then I'm not opposed, but I don't want them to know anything about me."

12. That such citizen empowerment threatened authorities was shown by the federal prosecutor's argument to the jury that would judge eleven indicted sanctuary workers: "The people of the United States ... intended for there to be only one Immigration Service in the United States and that is the Immigration Service that operates under the control by statute of the United States Government" (U.S. v. Aguilar 1986: 14198).

13. From the point of view of Gustavo Alvarez's wife, Marta Rodriguez, churches used refugee testimonies to raise money. From the point of view of sanctuary workers, however, money raised by testimonies and other events funded social service programs that ultimately benefited Central Americans.

14. I do not wish to imply that because they were performances, testimonies were somehow "fake" or "untrue."

15. This transcript is reprinted from the original transcript prepared by EBSC office workers. The punctuation, spelling, capitalization, and so forth are the ones used in the original document. I have not omitted any part of the transcript. Therefore, in this quotation, ellipses do not indicate that text has been deleted, but rather that the speaker did not complete her sentence. Bracketed question marks denote unintelligible portions of the tape.

16. In contrast, Clemente Rivera, a Salvadoran immigrant who was critical of the subordination that he felt resulted from being defined as a refugee, told me, "I don't like to call myself a refugee. I don't like the word 'refugee.' When I give a talk, I don't start out by saying, 'I am a refugee from El Salvador.' I simply say, 'I am from El Salvador.'"

17. Sam's comment borrowed this metaphor from Oscar Romero, who said that his blood would be a seed of new life for his people.

# 7

# Prosecution

*"Ladies and gentlemen, we can best describe this case as an alien-smuggling case."*
—Prosecutor's opening statement to the jury
during the 1985–1986 sanctuary trial

To construct acts of repression, authorities, like protestors, draw on cultural discourses. While sanctuary workers were reinterpreting immigration discourse to constitute Central Americans as refugees, the federal government was using the same discourse to constitute sanctuary workers as conspirators and alien-smugglers. Through an undercover investigation of the movement, immigration authorities intensified their scrutiny of those members of the general population who were involved in sanctuary work. This surveillance, like that which defined undocumented immigrants as illegal aliens, produced knowledge about sanctuary workers' lives. In January 1985, the government used this knowledge to situate sanctuary workers in such legal categories as "alien-smugglers," "conspirators," and "felons." Reasoning that, because undocumented Central Americans were illegal aliens, those who crossed, transported, and sheltered them were, by extension, criminals, the government indicted fourteen movement members. The indictments initiated a trial that, like political asylum hearings, produced legal truth by eliciting discourse, constructing competing legal interpretations of this discourse, and definitively constituting defendants either as criminals or as individuals who could not be proven guilty of crimes. Prosecution shaped material reality such that, after the trial, the former defendants acted, willingly or no, according to the identities that they had been given. Moreover, their awareness of continuing surveillance led nonindicted movement members to reshape their practices in anticipation of possible future indictments.

Because, as the previous chapter demonstrated, power and resistance are interwoven, acts of repression create corresponding potentials for resistance. The sanctuary defendants took full advantage of these potentials. Although the government defined defendants within legal categories and compelled movement members to monitor their behavior, defendants and their supporters used the trial to embarrass the government and promote defendants' legal notions. Before indictments were even issued, while the government was using surveillance to define movement activities as crimes, sanctuary workers were already affirming their understanding of legal reality. During the trial itself, when the government used the knowledge produced by surveillance to define defendants as criminals, sanctuary workers publicized their view that the movement enforced rather than violated the law. Following the trial, participants took advantage of ongoing surveillance of the movement to leave a record that they felt would define reality in their own terms rather than those of the government. The sanctuary trial thus demonstrated that, like incorporating immigration discourse into oppositional practices, using the law to repress dissidence is politically contradictory.

My analysis of the sanctuary trial is based on official trial transcripts, accounts in the Tucson press, bulletins published by the Arizona Sanctuary Defense Fund, my fieldwork in Tucson and East Bay sanctuary communities, and interviews with defendants, defense attorneys, and sanctuary workers whose lives were touched by the trial. I did not interview the prosecutor, his staff, the undercover informants, or the judge because I was concerned that, in the event of future indictments, I and my research materials could be subpoenaed, and I did not want to bring myself to the attention of government authorities. Nor was I able to attend the trial itself, as it had ended before I began research on the movement. The trial's impact on communities where I did fieldwork was so profound, however, that this event has become quite vivid to me. When I first approached Bay Area sanctuary activists during the spring of 1985, the trial was just concluding. Though no local movement members had been indicted, participants believed that their own fates hinged on that of the Tucson defendants. An acquittal would vindicate East Bay sanctuary workers, but convictions would increase the threat of arrests. A little over a year later, I arrived in Tucson, where the trial seemed an ongoing process. Sanctuary workers traded stories about the principal actors, about attending church the Sunday following the indictments, about fighting traffic to get to the courtroom for the verdicts, and so on. Being prosecuted shaped Tucson sanctuary practices, contributing to the notion of civil initiative described in Chapter 6. To the extent that movement members continue to attempt to defend themselves against the charges they could face in any future indictment, the trial is still taking place. Perhaps this is not surprising, given the fact that the competition over the movement's legal significance began long before movement members were indicted.

## Operation Sojourner

On March 24, 1982, the date of the first sanctuary declarations, religious volunteers held a ceremony and press conference at All Saints Church in Tucson as a border patrol agent surreptitiously observed the proceedings. The construction of competing legal interpretations of sanctuary work had begun. By declaring that they would shelter undocumented Central Americans, members of All Saints and its fellow sanctuary congregations in the East Bay and elsewhere had proclaimed that Salvadoran and Guatemalan immigrants were refugees who deserved asylum. This proclamation critiqued the U.S. government's application of refugee law, implied that individuals could be refugees without having been so designated by government officials, and suggested that private citizens were capable of enforcing the law. In inviting the press to the declaration ceremony, organizers not only sought publicity but also attempted to distinguish the participants from law-breakers, who usually hide from authorities. At the same time, when authorities sent an undercover observer to All Saints, they implied that the Salvadorans and Guatemalans in question were not refugees but rather illegal aliens, that sheltering these aliens was a criminal act, and that far from enforcing the law, sanctuary workers were forming a criminal conspiracy. Participants' desire for publicity notwithstanding, government surveillance implied that sanctuary was illegal.

Just as sanctuary practices continually reconstituted Central Americans as refugees, so too did surveillance continually constitute sanctuary workers as criminals. Covert observation by government agents did not simply *record* reality; rather, by implying that sanctuary was a crime and that sanctuary workers were criminals, it *constructed* reality (Marx 1988). From 1982 to 1984, immigration agents merely collected movement literature and attended public sanctuary events. In 1984, however, this relatively noninvasive surveillance escalated into an undercover investigation called "Operation Sojourner," presumably an ironic twist on sanctuary workers' invocation of Leviticus 19:33, a biblical commandment to aid sojourners from other lands. In March of that year, Jesus Cruz, a government informant, approached Padre Quiñones, a future defendant, at his church in Nogales, Mexico, bringing a truckload of oranges, grapefruit, and tangerines for the needy. (The irony of an informant named "Jesus" infiltrating a religious movement was not lost on volunteers. One participant later commented, "What a name! It should have been Judas!") Professing to be sympathizers, Cruz and several colleagues began attending sanctuary meetings, worshiping with participants, and volunteering with the movement. Government informants wore hidden microphones, noted participants' license plate numbers, had their pictures taken with movement members, and gave regular reports to their superiors. By constructing a body of knowledge about the movement, government officials took the first step toward reconstituting sanctuary workers' words and actions as "evidence" to be introduced in a criminal trial.[1]

Largely unaware of the extent of the government's investigation, sanctuary workers believed that they had constructed a discourse that would make it difficult for the government to infiltrate the movement. Some argued that the movement's religious composition protected it from infiltration. One former defendant told me, "We did have discussions about it, ... but I felt that people [in the movement] were getting paranoid. I saw that there was something strange about those two characters [Jesus Cruz and a colleague], but they came into church and worshiped with us, and I thought, 'The government would never send agents into the churches.'" Others hoped that if the government *did* use undercover agents, then once these individuals heard refugees' testimonies and learned about Central America, they would be converted to the movement's cause. Still others felt that an undercover investigation posed no additional risk because the movement already publicized its activities. The few with strong suspicions of Jesus Cruz either avoided him or concluded that the risk of falsely accusing a legitimate participant outweighed that of allowing an infiltrator to proceed without hindrance.

On January 5, 1985, three years after the original sanctuary declarations, the government indicted fourteen sanctuary workers on charges of conspiracy and alien smuggling. (The government later dropped charges against two of the indicted, while a third individual plea-bargained to a lesser charge.) The dramatic moments when government agents arrived at sanctuary workers' homes to deliver indictments, search dwellings, and detain Central Americans were often recounted within the movement. Upon learning that Jesus Cruz had been an infiltrator, one Phoenix minister rushed to warn undocumented Central Americans who had participated in a Bible study attended by Cruz. More than half had already been taken into custody. Taking advantage of the delay afforded by an error in the way his address was written on the indictment, a Tucson volunteer destroyed several documents, then calmly awaited the authorities' arrival. In Mexico, a priest who had been forewarned by his U.S. colleagues turned the tables on the government by hiding a microphone in his desk and secretly recording his encounter with the U.S. agents who came to indict him. In addition to those charged with crimes, more than 100 unindicted citizen and alien coconspirators were named in the indictment. With the indictments, the stage was set for the formal ritual that would produce and authenticate defendants' legal identities.

## The Pretrial Hearings

The conflict over the legal implications of sanctuary work moved into the courtroom with pretrial hearings; during this stage, the prosecution and defense would debate and decide how defendants' actions could be interpreted during the trial itself. Because they believed themselves to be enforcing U.S. refugee law, the defendants were prepared to argue that the acts of which they were accused were not, in fact, crimes. Anticipating this possibility, the federal prosecutor filed a motion to prohibit defenses that questioned the legality of crossing, transporting, and sheltering undocumented individuals. This motion sought to bar evidence about U.S. Central American policy, danger to civilians in El Salvador and Guatemala, the defendants' motives, the defendants' religious beliefs, international law, and the political asylum process (Turner 1985a). Banning such evidence would essentially predefine sanctuary work as alien smuggling and narrow the legal issue to whether the defendants had committed the acts listed in the indictment. Defense attorneys responded by moving to dismiss all charges on the grounds that the defendants' actions were legal under international laws ratified by the United States, that sanctuary was a religious act protected by the First Amendment, that infiltrating Bible studies and worship services violated the separation of church and state, and that the evidence obtained through Operation Sojourner stemmed from an illegal search of a defendant's car in 1984 (A.S.D.F. 1985a).With these motions, the formal legal proceedings began.

The issues debated during pretrial hearings centered on competing notions of law, religion, and church-state relations. Not surprisingly, the defense attorneys advanced the concept of law that was the basis for civil initiative. They argued that citizens are obligated to enforce laws when their government's failure to do so jeopardizes lives. Moreover, they cited conditions in Central America and flaws in the immigration process as proof that the only way for defendants to have obeyed U.S. laws granting safe haven to the persecuted had been to help undocumented Central Americans avoid the U.S. Immigration Service (U.S. v. Aguilar 1986:778–853). Defense attorney Stephen Cooper asserted that for the defendants to have brought Central Americans to Immigration officials would have been like rescuing someone from a burning house and then taking the victim back inside while the fire yet raged (U.S. v. Aguilar 1986:848). Defense attorneys contended that their clients ought to be allowed to tell the jury how their understandings of federal and international law had compelled them to aid Central Americans (A.S.D.F. 1985a).

In contrast to the defendants' view that under certain circumstances, private citizens can enforce law, the prosecutor contended that only the government has the authority to make, interpret, and carry out law. Declaring that defense attorneys should not even be allowed to refer to Central Americans as "refugees," the prosecutor asserted that determining immigrants' legal status "is a proceeding that the statute clearly provides is first to be made ... by the Attorney General and his designates. It is not to be made by the defendants" (U.S. v. Aguilar 1986:765–766). According to prosecutor Don Reno, allowing individual citizens to make such decisions would create anarchy. Reno told the judge:

> The basic issue here ... is are we going to have two Immigration Services? Are we going to have one that has been duly constituted, controlled and funded by the federal government or are we going to have a secondary and perhaps a third and a fourth immigration service funded and controlled and created by the defendants here and their colleagues across the country? (U.S. v. Aguilar 1986:383).

Reno argued that legal justice depended on the impartiality of the law. He stated, "If this Government is going to represent all the people of this nation, it cannot favor those which commit criminal acts and contend that they are immune from prosecution, because they are motivated by a higher authority or a higher power" (U.S. v. Aguilar 1986:1049).

During pretrial hearings the attorneys also debated what could legally qualify as religious practice. The defense argued that sanctuary was a religious act protected by the First Amendment, while the prosecution contended that defendants were using religion as a guise for criminal activities. To prove that sanctuary was grounded in the Judeo-Christian tradition, defendants called experts from each of their denominations. One expert testified that on judgment day, "Those who welcome strangers, will be given reward, and those who do not, will fail" (U.S. v. Aguilar 1986:214). The prosecutor cross-examined, asking witnesses whether the asylum procedures delineated in the Immigration Act violated their faith. The judge, seemingly in search of a clear-cut religious doctrine, asked witnesses if sanctuary was not a matter of personal conscience rather than a corporate stance of the church. Though witnesses insisted that individuals' consciences were informed by the church body (U.S. v. Aguilar 1986:212–240), prosecutor Reno pointed out, "There are millions and millions of people attending church that certainly do not want to be party to any of these activities which the defendants have engaged in" (U.S. v. Aguilar 1986: 1063). In the end, the question remained, if (as was the case for liberal Christians) individual believers had some authority to define the content of their faith, then how could courts affirm that a particular act was religiously mandatory? The defendants' understanding of religion confronted the doctrinal requirements of an evidentiary system and was found wanting.

Competing notions of law and religion also informed the defense's and the prosecution's characterizations of the undercover investigation. At issue was whether Operation Sojourner was an unprecedented government intrusion into the privacy and fellowship of congregations or if sanctuary was an unprecedented manipulation of churches for illegal ends. Defense attorneys took the former stance, comparing Operation Sojourner to the infiltration of churches in Nazi Germany, Czechoslovakia, and the Soviet Union (U.S. v. Aguilar 1986: 558). (The pastor of one infiltrated sanctuary congregation lamented that church members had been "as gentle as doves but maybe not as wise as serpents" [U.S. v. Aguilar 1986:472]). The federal prosecutor adopted the latter position, stating that what was extraordinary about this case was that for the first time, churches had been used to hatch criminal conspiracies (U.S. v. Aguilar 1986: 1050). The judge himself indulged in a debate with defense attorney Ellen Yaroshefsky over this issue. Suggesting that the government resorted to infiltrating churches because of these churches' criminal activities, he asked Yaroshefsky to cite a prior occasion on which congregations had publicly planned to break the law. After she listed the abolitionists and Martin Luther King, the judge suggested that if Martin Luther King had been in charge, sanctuary would have been different. Yaroshefsky responded, "I doubt it," and continued, "I would suggest to this Court when history looks back on this case that many of the defendants … may be honored in the way that Martin Luther King has been honored by our country." The judge countered, "They may be honored, but I don't think it will be of that character" (U.S. v. Aguilar 1986:1023–1024).

The judge announced his decisions shortly before the trial itself was to begin. On all significant motions, the judge ruled in favor of the prosecution and against the defendants, thus prompting a flurry of charges that he was biased. The prosecutor's interpretations of law, religion, and the undercover operation had been vindicated, and crossing, transporting, and sheltering undocumented Central American immigrants had been defined as criminal acts. Despite the prosecutor's victory, however, the trial itself created opportunities for the defendants to reassert their notions of legality and to thus resist being defined as criminals.

## The Courtroom Ritual

The 1985–1986 Tucson sanctuary trial produced legal truth by situating defendants within legal categories. By saying that the trial *produced* truth, I draw attention to the fact that individuals are not inherently criminals any more than they are inherently illegal aliens or refugees. What defines them as such are the legal practices that locate them within juridical discourse.[2] This view of prosecution runs counter to the commonsense notion that what defines individuals as criminals is the act of committing a crime. From the commonsense point of view, a trial is not a method of *creating* truth but rather an empirical, though not infallible, means of *uncovering* a preexisting truth, of ascertaining who did what to whom on what date and how. Yet, making such determinations produces constructions of events and their authors. Take a murder trial, for example. Suppose that individual A shoots individual B, who then dies. Despite the materiality of this incident—A pulled a trigger, a bullet entered B's body, B died—the *legal construction* of this reality, the construction on which subsequent social action will be based, has yet to be created. For this to occur, law enforcement officials must produce a body of knowledge (similar to that created through Operation Sojourner) about participants. Various legal authorities, including prosecutors, defense attorneys, judges, and court officials, must then interpret this knowledge (was the incident self-defense, a mercy killing, involuntary manslaughter, second-degree murder?). Next, following complex rules about who can speak and when, what speakers can say, and so on, the principals must present this knowledge to a judge, jurors, and public spectators in such a way as to render competing interpretations of the event compelling. Finally, the judge and/or jurors validate one of the interpretations presented, thus defining the event's legal significance. Only after this process is complete would individual A be constituted as a murderer.

When the U.S. government indicted members of the sanctuary movement, it sought to use this process to constitute sanctuary workers as alien-smugglers and conspirators. All trials situate individuals within legal categories (including the category "not guilty") and therefore have constitutive force (Geertz 1983; Bourdieu 1987), but this trial went further than most because it defined the legal significance of activities that had not yet been definitively constructed in legal terms. Prior to the 1985–1986 Tucson sanctuary trial, the majority of alien-smuggling cases concerned individuals (known as coyotes) who were accused of charging immigrants fees to bring them across the border. Bringing immigrants into the country free of charge for humanitarian purposes fell into a gray area; such activities, though technically illegal, had been largely tolerated by authorities. Prior to the 1980s, the INS rarely prosecuted employers who brought undocumented workers into the country, private individuals who brought relatives across the border, or religious groups that provided social services to undocumented immigrants (Harwood 1984, 1986). By developing a movement that performed similar sorts of activities in a highly publicized way and claiming that to do so was legal, sanctuary workers presented a legal challenge to the government. As prosecutor Reno noted while defending the government's decision to infiltrate the movement, "This Government cannot tolerate essentially what is anarchy by individuals taking the law into their own hands ... and flaunt and taunt these criminal acts to the Government and the Government in this case virtually ignore this conduct for a period of almost two years" (U.S. v. Aguilar 1986: 1052–1053). When the government responded to the movement's challenge with indictments, it sought to definitively constitute movement actions as crimes and thus deter future participants.[3] Like sanctuary workers who used immigration discourse to construct movement practices, however, the government found that it could not control the meaning of the discourse it invoked. Not only did the sanctuary trial create opportunities for sanctuary workers to formulate and publicize their interpretations of the law, it also enabled movement members to define authorities, their actions, and the trial itself within movement discourse.[4]

Attorneys' opening statements and closing arguments summarized the interpretations of sanctuary work that each side hoped to validate through the legal process. Not surprisingly, prosecutor Reno consistently deployed language connoting criminality, rendering the defendants and their colleagues "conspirators," "unindicted co-conspirators," and "illegal aliens." The prosecutor characterized the movement as a three-tiered alien-smuggling conspiracy, the third tier being "the Nogales Connection"—presumably a reference to *The French Connection,* a film about drug-smugglers (U.S. v. Aguilar 1986:2612–2615). To refute defendants' claims that sanctuary work served humanitarian rather than criminal purposes, Reno told jurors not to base their verdicts on politics, religion, morality, or the ultimate good (U.S. v. Aguilar 1986:12683). He noted, "We don't have to prove in this case that they [the defendants] are bad people. All the United States Government has to do is to prove beyond a reasonable doubt that they are violating the law" (U.S. v. Aguilar 1986:14201–14202). The prosecutor also rejected the notion that private individuals are capable of interpreting and enforcing the law. Reno reminded jurors that in the United States, the law is made by Congress on behalf of all the people, not by the defendants "[at _____] church on a Monday night when they ... make a decision about who is going to come into the United States, when they are going to come in, and where they are going to go" (U.S. v. Aguilar 1986:14197). Because the law is a codification of the collective will, prosecutor Reno reasoned, it has an inviolability that demands that any transgression be punished.

In contrast, defense attorneys, deprived of the arguments that had been declared inadmissible during pretrial hearings, contended simply that their clients' actions were good and therefore legal.[5] Defense attorneys characterized the defendants as church workers who were being prosecuted for ministering to the poor and the persecuted. Defense attorney James Brosnahan stressed the noncriminal nature of the defendants' actions, telling the jury, "This conspiracy is one of Jesus Cruz running around frantically trying to give the appearance of criminality to certain activities of these defendants" (A.S.D.F. 1986b:3). Brosnahan argued that the allegedly conspiratorial interest that motivated defendants was nothing more than the biblical verse, "For I was hungry and you gave me meat, I was thirsty and you gave me drink, I was a stranger and you took me in, naked and you clothed me, I was sick and you visited me, I was in prison and you came unto me" (U.S. v. Aguilar 1986:13360). Similarly, defense attorney Yaroshefsky told jurors that her client had been "caught in the act of helping someone" (U.S. v. Aguilar 1986:13387). By distinguishing between the letter of the law and moral good, defense attorneys implied that formal legal codes (in this case, the statutes prohibiting crossing, harboring, and transporting illegal aliens rather than the refugee law defended through civil initiative) do not always reflect community norms. Echoing sociologist Emile Durkheim's (1933) contention that crime is that which offends the collective conscience, Yaroshefsky asked jurors:

> When you go around helping people, ... giving people places to stay, giving them a roof over their head, giving them food, giving them shelter, do you think ... they walk around thinking, Hmm, is it legal? Is it legal to give someone a sandwich? Is it legal to give someone a roof over their head? You assume it is legal. You assume doing good is legal (U.S. v. Aguilar 1986:13451).

The bulk of the trial was devoted to producing and displaying the knowledge constructed through Operation Sojourner in ways that supported and undermined these competing representations. During the four months between opening statements and closing arguments, the prosecution called two government agents and seventeen Central Americans to the witness stand in order to substantiate the criminality of the defendants' actions. The prosecutor questioned witnesses regarding who brought whom across the border, how border crossings were executed, who housed Central Americans once they had entered the United States, and who transported Central Americans to other parts of the country. When possible, the prosecutor also sought testimony that weakened the defenses that had been ruled inadmissible during pretrial hearings. For example, one Salvadoran witness who had been assisted by defendants testified that he had entered the United States to find a job, thus contradicting defendants' claims that they only aided political refugees (Durazo 1986). Witnesses' words became legal facts that recreated and displayed defendants' actions within a framework established by the prosecutor. The prosecutor's power to elicit and shape the significance of testimony, however, like that of defense attorneys, was limited by the adversarial nature of this process. For example, the judge sustained defense attorneys' objections to government agent Jesus Cruz testifying in Spanish about conversations that took place in English (A.S.D.F. 1985b). In addition, Central American witnesses who were hostile to the government sometimes tried to undermine the prosecutor's characterizations of events. For example, when asked to identify a defendant accused of illegally harboring him, a Salvadoran man responded, "She [the defendant] was the only person who offered me a roof over my head when I was most in need. ... I remember her with much love" (Varn 1986).

Defense attorneys called no witnesses, contending that cross-examination—their own interrogation of witnesses subpoenaed by the prosecution—had discredited undercover agents and affirmed the humanitarian, noncriminal nature of the defendants' actions. During cross-examination, defense attorneys challenged government agent Jesus Cruz's credibility with questions about his own previous alien-smuggling activities and about the deceptions he had practiced to infiltrate the movement (A.S.D.F. 1985c, 1985d). Defense attorneys sought testimony that disputed the prosecutor's characterizations of events. For example, they asked Cruz if prayers and religious ceremonies occurred at meetings that the prosecutor had portrayed as conspiratorial (Browning 1986a). Whenever possible, attorneys elicited testimony that cast doubt on whether their clients had actually been present at a particular meeting, driven a given Central American into the United States, or harbored individuals as alleged in the indictment. Finally, defense attorneys tried to circumvent the judge's restrictions on admissible defenses by eliciting testimony regarding persecution in Central America, the defendants' religious beliefs, flaws in the asylum process, and so on. Cross-examination became, to quote one former defendant, "an interesting game to see how much we could get in in spite of his [the judge's] restrictions." The judge limited the very words permissible during testimony, ruling that such graphic terms as "killed," "tortured," "death," "cut off ears," and "electroshock" had to be replaced by euphemisms (Browning 1986c). Testimony was not primarily *restrictive*, however, but rather *productive*, as the threat of being held in contempt of court hung over those who considered remaining silent. Four government witnesses who refused to testify were sentenced to house arrest for the duration of the trial.

The trial reconstructed the knowledge produced through Operation Sojourner through material exhibits as well as through testimony. Among other things, attorneys introduced a refugee rights statement that defendants had distributed to imprisoned Central Americans, payment vouchers that undercover agent Jesus Cruz had received from immigration officials, and transcripts of the government's secret tape recordings. Because the significance of these items was defined by attorneys and by the trial context, material exhibits were as much a construction of reality as the words spoken during testimony. For example, during his final closing argument, the prosecutor told jurors of a remark caught by one of the government's hidden microphones. Prosecutor Reno quoted Rev. John Fife, one of the defendants, as saying that a film director was coming to Tucson to make a movie "About all of this—." Reno (who, as a fundamentalist Christian, apparently found this term too offensive to verbalize) completed Rev. Fife's sentence by writing out the word "bullshit" for the jury and said, "That was the statement of the Reverend Fife in the privacy of his home" (U.S. v. Aguilar 1986: 14187). Through prosecution, this remark, uttered casually in private conversation, became legal knowledge employed to impugn the character of a minister who would use obscenities.

The trial officially situated the defendants in legal categories through its final act: the verdicts. In order to determine which of the competing constructions of sanctuary work they would validate, jurors scrutinized the legal facts created though testimony and material exhibits, weighed the prosecution's and the defense's competing interpretations of these facts, and measured all of the above against legal definitions. After a suspenseful two-week deliberation, jurors convicted eight of the eleven defendants, thus transforming these individuals retroactively and incontrovertibly (barring appeals)[6] into criminals. These verdicts authenticated the prosecution's interpretation of sanctuary work and invalidated the defense's. The convictions did not make the trial a complete victory for the government, however, because publicity surrounding the defendants' representation of their actions threatened to undermine the authority of the verdicts. For, as legal examination had created truth within the courtroom, publicity had made this ritual a public spectacle and a locus of resistance.

## Public Spectacle

When the government chose to prosecute movement members, it inadvertently enabled them to promote their own understanding of the events in question. Just as sanctuary workers who invoked immigration discourse unintentionally recreated power-laden practices, the sanctuary trial in some ways reproduced subversive categories and practices. The government's effort to constitute sanctuary workers as criminals was subject to interpretations that the government could not control. In and of itself, the defendants' competing representations of legal reality did not greatly threaten the government: If the government were to win convictions, then the defendants' construction of events presumably would be invalidated. But the sanctuary trial not only *created* such representations; it also *publicized* them nationally and internationally. Of course, the publicity that surrounds politically controversial trials can be in the prosecution's interests as well as the defense's. Publicity can help launch the political career of a promising prosecutor and can deter activities similar to those performed by defendants. Yet, the circumstances of the 1985–1986 sanctuary trial (with religious workers—including priests and a nun—being arrested for aiding refugees) favored the defense rather than the prosecution. Public interest in the case enabled defendants to promote not only the arguments made in court but also the defenses that had been

prohibited by pretrial hearings and the movement's representations of the trial itself. The result was a spectacle, bordering on the carnivalesque, that portrayed the
defendants as heroes, Immigration authorities as villains, and the trial and the infiltration as religious persecution.

Oddly enough, the government contributed to the conditions that lent themselves to spectacle by summoning the defendants to court on the first day of a previously scheduled national sanctuary symposium to be held in Tucson. One of the
symposium organizers wrote of this coincidence, "We knew we were involved in
an event that was truly a kairos ('opportune occasion') in the deepest sense of that
Greek word" (Schmidt 1985:3). The defendants received an immediate affirmation of their interpretation of the law when registration for the symposium
jumped from several hundred to 1,500 after word of the indictments spread. Because of the indictments, the symposium was covered by national news media.
Sanctuary workers from around the United States came to Tucson, met with the
defendants and their supporters, and returned enthused to their local groups. In
yet another extraordinary coincidence, on the symposium's second day, a Texas
jury acquitted sanctuary worker Jack Elder of transporting illegal aliens. When
Stacy Merkt, who was also from Texas and who at the time was the only convicted
sanctuary worker, announced the news from the podium, the more than 1,000
people in attendance stood and cheered (Rothenberg 1985).[7]

A defense attorney identified the three forums in which the ensuing spectacle
took place when he commented, "We lawyers stood with these defendants in the
courtroom after the verdict was returned, then at a prayer service, and finally a
press conference" (*Sequoia* 1986:7). In the courtroom, defendants and their supporters interrupted the trial by reacting vocally and theatrically to proceedings.
Trial spectators (most of whom were the defendants' supporters) cheered a defense attorney's closing arguments (Browning 1986d), protested when the prosecutor said that nothing religious had occurred at sanctuary meetings (U.S. v.
Aguilar 1986: 12960), and laughed when Jesus Cruz, who had spent ten months
working undercover in the movement, said he did not know the word "refugee"
(A.S.D.F. 1986a:4). Occasionally, spectator participation assumed dramatic forms.
On December 3, 1985—the fifth anniversary of the assassination of three American nuns and one layworker by Salvadoran death squads—defendants and their
supporters came to court dressed in black (A.S.D.F. 1985b). Similarly, when three
sanctuary workers were sentenced to house arrest for refusing to testify, defendants, supporters, and defense attorneys stood to honor each as he or she left the
courtroom. The press sometimes magnified the impact of such displays by cover-
ing them in trial-related articles.

In the pulpit, sanctuary workers performed rituals celebrating the justice of
their work. Tucson defendants and their supporters held weekly ecumenical
prayer services, while around the United States, sanctuary communities marked
significant moments (such as opening arguments, verdicts, and sentencing) with
religious ceremonies. Trial-related services featured bilingual prayers, Central

Americans' stories of persecution and flight, biblical readings, songs from Central American Christian base communities, quotations from such figures as Archbishop Oscar Romero and Anne Frank, and traditional hymns whose words took on new meaning in light of the trial. Such religious rituals reaffirmed the defendants' version of reality, defined sanctuary as a religious practice (in contrast to the judge's pretrial ruling), and redefined the trial itself in biblical terms. A modified version of the passage from John 8:32 soon became the defendants' motto: "The truth will set you free ... eventually" (Montini 1986).

Finally, in the press, the defendants, who had not testified during the trial, publicly proclaimed the defenses that had been prohibited.[8] Local sanctuary workers established a trial hotline with the phone number 1–800-LEV-1933, after Leviticus 19:33,[9] the Bible verse that inspired sanctuary work and from which Operation Sojourner derived its name. The defendants held regular press conferences, which, to take advantage of photo opportunities, were often positioned inside a church or in front of a cross. (During his posttrial press conference, prosecutor Reno stood before the seal of the Department of Justice.) The judge found such publicity so offensive that he considered forbidding public statements about evidence that had been declared inadmissible (Turner 1985b). The prosecutor's frustration with the defendants' media success was demonstrated when, after one of the defense's affidavits failed to stand up in court, Reno "stormed over to the press section of the courtroom and said, 'Did you get all that? For one time I hope you guys get it right'" (Browning 1986b:1B). Similarly, after the verdicts were handed down, Reno criticized press coverage, saying, "Thank God for the jury" (Browning 1986e:6A)—in other words, a jury that only heard the knowledge produced in the courtroom.

Publicity became most spectacular at the pinnacles of the trial: verdicts and sentencing. The verdicts that acquitted three and convicted eight defendants initiated a community event that included marches, prayer services, and caravans. Upon receiving word that the verdict was in, defendants reported to the courtroom while a multitude of supporters gathered outside. According to newspaper accounts, "a pall fell over the crowd" as the guilty verdicts were announced. The convicted sanctuary workers, however, redefined the charges, celebrating a "conspiracy of love" and saying they were "guilty of living out the gospel." Defendants and "a hymn-singing congregation of supporters" marched from the Federal Building to a posttrial prayer service along with reporters, photographers, and camera operators (Kreutz 1986:1A, 7A). By the following day, many defendants had dispersed to sanctuary groups around the United States (Montini 1986). In the eight weeks between verdicts and sentencing, sanctuary supporters held a caravan to the border, an all-night vigil at the U.S. Border Patrol Headquarters in Tucson, a march for freedom, and a conference attended by 500 to 600 people where the call and response, "If they are guilty, ... " "SO AM I!!" rang out repeatedly (A.S.D.F. 1986c: 1–2). An Arizona Sanctuary Defense Fund's bulletin described the scene at the sentencing itself:

The courtroom was jammed with supporters and press, with several hundred people waiting outside in the hot Arizona sun, hoping for a seat at the hearing. The walls outside the courthouse were draped with banners, including one with the Emma Lazarus poem from the base of the Statue of Liberty ("Give me your tired, your poor, your huddled masses yearning to breathe free ... "). Across the street from the court, a local sculptor hung a lifesize figure of Jesus Christ on a wooden cross from a traffic light. One of the defendants, Socorro Aguilar, placed a rose in the Christ figure's crown of thorns before entering the courthouse (A.S.D.F. 1986d:1).

Defendants' statements at the July 1–2 sentencing hearings provided an opportunity for convicted sanctuary workers to criticize the process that had constituted them as criminals. The prosecutor had anticipated the political riskiness of the defendants' statements and had cautioned the court not to let the statements become a "final parting harangue." Attempting to restrict the content of convicted sanctuary workers' statements, prosecutor Reno "cited case law that sentencings should not be turned into public forums for attorneys or defendants to express philosophical, religious or political beliefs" (Fimbres 1986a:2A). Despite the prosecution's admonitions, however, defendants used sentencing statements to once again assert their interpretation of sanctuary work and the trial. To give but one example, Sister Darlene Nicgorski, a convicted alien-smuggler, asked the judge why the "truths of terror by victim-witnesses were kept from the jury" (Nicgorski 1986:3). Quoting the oath that witnesses take before testimony, Sister Darlene urged the judge to consider "the whole truth" when he devised her sentence (Nicgorski 1986:10). Sister Darlene questioned the authority of the legal system when she said, "I realize I am treading on delicate ground as I address this court of law, with many officers of the court who hold much power and make their money by debating the law" (Nicgorski 1986: 11). Sister Darlene concluded by situating the judge and the trial within movement discourse. She said:

> You and only you, Judge Carroll, can still make a difference. You have the authority and power. Many have prayed for your conversion, hoping you would see the light of truth and life. You by your sentence can add your YES to the God of Justice and Life and therefore your NO to the Caesar who wants to use his money, power, and law to silence the witnesses of its policies in Central America. I do not ask for myself but ask because it will be a symbol of the change of your heart and herald of hope to Central America (Nicgorski 1986:14).

The spectacle surrounding the sanctuary trial publicized defendants' version of their actions to such an extent that it undermined the truth validated within the courtroom. As one defense attorney whom I interviewed noted, the trial was an anomaly in a system based on punishment, retribution, and deterrence. Rather than punishing the defendants, public spectacle inverted the charges, characterizing the defendants as heroes and the government as criminal. Derisive political cartoons appeared, such as a *Los Angeles Times* drawing that depicted a villainous INS agent arresting Christ and the apostles while warning, "Don't none of you sanctuary people move!" Defendants received widespread support, with forty-seven members of Congress requesting leniency in their sentencing (Fimbres 1986b) and with Amnesty International vowing to declare them prisoners of conscience if they were to be imprisoned. Rather than doing retribution for their crimes, the former defendants continued their sanctuary work. In fact, convicted sanctuary workers persuaded the judge to modify probation conditions that would have prevented them from associating with anyone engaged in smuggling or transporting illegal aliens (Browning and Turner 1986). Rather than deterring sanctuary workers, public prosecution caused the number of sanctuary congregations to double (*Basta* 1986). In the words of one sanctuary worker, the trial challenged people to "fish or cut bait," and many fished, resisting the verdicts through increased sanctuary work. Yet, when the spectacle concluded with probationary sentences for those convicted, the public eye turned elsewhere, though sanctuary workers suspected that the government's eye did not.

### Conscious Visibility

Trial-related publicity not only reproduced movement discourse but also shaped social relations. Just as alienation situated individuals who had never encountered government agents within immigration categories, so too did the 1985–1986 sanctuary trial lead movement members who had not been indicted to define themselves and their actions in legal terms. Such redefinitions took place because, in addition to airing the defendants' version of reality, the 1985–1986 sanctuary trial displayed the state's ability to observe its citizenry. The public—including hundreds of unindicted sanctuary workers—learned of the wiretaps, undercover agents, subpoenas, witnesses, confiscated memos, photographs, tape recordings, fingerprints, and videos that could be amassed to situate individuals within categories of criminality. In essence, members of the sanctuary movement discovered that they were caught in a panoptic network of power relations. According to Foucault, the key feature of panopticism is that authorities can see without being seen. Those within authorities' range of vision know that they can be observed at any moment but are never able to ascertain precisely when surveillance is occurring. This uncertainty gives panopticism its disciplinary force: Even in the absence of actual surveillance, those subject to the gaze of power act as though they are being observed. In effect, panopticism makes discipline unnecessary by compelling individuals to internalize surveillance and become the agents of their own subjection. In his analysis of prison reform, Foucault (1979:201) explained, "The major effect of the Panopticon [was] to induce in the inmate a state of conscious and permanent visibility that assures the automatic functioning of power."

Sanctuary workers' stories about being under surveillance detail the experience of being the subjects of a body of knowledge produced through covert observation. During an interview, one sanctuary worker—named in the indictment as an unindicted coconspirator—told of her shock at realizing how she had been trapped in a web of surveillance. She related that, while helping the defense review the government's evidence in preparation for the trial, a colleague ran across an unidentifiable notebook: "I don't know why I thought I could identify it, but I just walked over and looked over her shoulder and said, 'That's Jesus Cruz's. Look under the G's.' Because I had written my own name and address and phone number in his book. I could have cried right then. But I remember exactly where I was and when I did it." More ominous to sanctuary workers was the surveillance that was not confirmed during the trial and that therefore remained mere suspicion. One sanctuary worker told me, "I'm pretty sure that my mail was also being checked. ... Refugees would get mail here, and it would be addressed to 'Maria, 198 Calle, Tucson, Arizona,' which isn't my address at all. And yet, it would arrive!" Most Tucson sanctuary workers whom I interviewed felt that their phones had been tapped, and a California activist told me that years after she had driven in a sanctuary caravan, she still worried that her license plate number was in an Immigration file.

Like a panopticon, the Tucson trial made sanctuary workers cognizant of their vulnerability to the gaze of authorities. The minutes of a sanctuary meeting immediately following the indictments exemplify this new awareness:

> The INS is using paid informants and are [*sic*] escalating their attack on the movement. Be aware, but don't be paranoid. We should assume that undercover operations are taking place. We should be watchful for agent provocateurs, who usually advocate the most extreme tactics, including violence. Be conscious of what you say on the telephone, and be aware that what you say could be taped (EBSC 1985:5).

Like inmates subjected to a panopticon, sanctuary workers could not determine precisely when they were under observation, so they began to assume that a record of their words and actions was being made by authorities. For example, at one potluck dinner, when a group of border workers met in a participant's bedroom, those present laughed, believing that the government would know of this meeting, and asked, "How's that going to look in a trial? 'The Bedroom Session'?"

Conscious of their own visibility, sanctuary workers began to examine their actions, asking themselves, "*Are* we breaking the law?" They came to internalize the roles of observer and observed, continually attempting to defend themselves against unseen accusers and unspoken accusations. For instance, one of the defendants' colleagues, hoping to substantiate his own lack of criminal intent, formed the habit of frequently stating that sanctuary is legal, like a talisman to protect him on any undercover recordings being made. Another border worker urged his colleagues to prepare for the necessity defense (the argument that the necessity of a particular action outweighed other considerations) by knowing "who they are helping, why they believe they are refugees under the Refugee Act of 1980, and whether the means of assistance are the only and necessary option available." At a 1987 sanctuary meeting that I attended in Tucson, a participant noted approvingly that the group's lobbying efforts would be useful in the event of another trial because these would provide evidence that sanctuary workers *did* pursue change through legal channels.

Such internalized surveillance was imbued with power: It replicated the legal production of knowledge by objectifying people's words and actions as evidence to be measured against legal definitions. In effect, the objects of surveillance, rather than government authorities, were doing the objectifying. Such self-monitoring occasionally deterred potential sanctuary workers, thus entirely relieving the government of the need for surveillance. For example, one Tucson sanctuary worker gave me the following account of an incident that had occurred in New York:

> When I was in New York, there was a caravan that came through with a Guatemalan man, and so I was responsible for organizing a dinner for him with the [Society of] Friends. I called a bunch of people on the phone lists they gave me, and pretty soon I began getting questions from people who were afraid that if they brought a casserole dish to the potluck dinner, that they could be put in jail for aiding and abetting an illegal alien! Just because this one man was there, out of all of the people who were going to be at this dinner. I can see it now, "Mrs. So-and-So, did you or did you not bring a casserole to the potluck dinner, and did that man over there take a bite of it?" ... There were people who actually didn't bring food to the dinner, and that was their reason.

Yet, despite being imbued with power, sanctuary workers' responses to government surveillance demonstrate how particular forms of power create corresponding methods of resistance. In a panoptic society, pervasive yet unverifiable observation disciplines subjects by leading them to internalize authority and become obedient. In reality, this process is limited by subjects' knowledge that complete surveillance is impossible and that the odds of being caught in an act of wrongdoing are sometimes slim. However, if surveillance were indeed complete, then how would one resist a panopticon? Attempting to hide, the most obvious reaction, could actually reinforce the panopticon by inviting observers to extend their powers of surveillance. Therefore, rather than hiding, a panopticon's subjects would have to limit or subvert surveillance itself. There are at least three ways that this could be accomplished: (1) by creating a social space impermeable to authorities' gaze, (2) by manipulating the knowledge produced through observation, or (3) by continuing to act openly, thus robbing the panopticon of its ability to deter.

Sanctuary workers pursued all three of these methods. First, shortly after the 1985 indictments, a group of sanctuary congregations sued the U.S. Attorney General, claiming that infiltrating and tape-recording Bible studies and worship services had infringed upon congregations' constitutional right to practice religion without government interference. In a 1990 ruling that the sanctuary movement hailed as a victory, the court limited (but did not eliminate) the federal government's ability to conduct covert investigations within religious institutions [Presbyterian Church (U.S.A.) v. United States 1990]. Second, once aware of government surveillance, sanctuary workers did not wait for authorities to make a record of their actions; rather, following the principles of civil initiative, they openly and deliberately created a record that they felt defined sanctuary work within their own understanding of the law. Again, the Merkt letters described in the previous chapter provide the best illustration of this process. To recapitulate, during the hearings that preceded the 1985–1986 Tucson sanctuary trial (and which occurred shortly after Stacy Merkt's acquittal), government prosecutor Don Reno conceded that it *was* legal to bring illegal aliens into the United States *if* one then took them to apply for political asylum (U.S. v. Aguilar 1986:885). Shortly after hearing this statement, one of the defendants invited NBC to film him bringing two refugees across the border to apply for political asylum. The defendant increased his own visibility by notifying the INS while this action was under way, yet he encountered no reprisals. Thereafter, before each crossing, border workers sent the INS a letter stating that they were helping refugees reach legal counsel.[10] Third, although the government investigation caused sanctuary workers to internalize surveillance, it failed to deter most participants. During an interview, one of the defendants' colleagues rejected the very system that creates surveillance, saying: "It's unfair, and it's wrong, but it doesn't bother me. I refuse to start acting ... sneakily. I'm not going to sneak around. I'll do what I do in the open." By continuing to act openly, sanctuary workers asserted the truth of their construction of reality and resisted being constituted as criminals.

## Conclusion

The prototypical sanctuary practices and the legal conflicts they engendered demonstrate that the political implications of social movements cannot be assessed solely by evaluating overt accomplishments and setbacks. The type of power that movements engage is not always as tangible as a rent board, a discriminatory policy, a nuclear power plant, or even an armed border patrol agent. Movements—and efforts to repress them—also take shape within and seek to alter the discourses that inform everyday social life. The sanctuary movement confronted not only government authorities and unjust policies but also the cultural categories and practices that constituted individuals (including sanctuary workers themselves) as subjects within immigration discourse. To redefine these categories and practices, sanctuary workers invoked the authority of the law, but in so doing they also created asymmetrical relations between themselves and undocumented Central Americans. Similarly, when government authorities sought to define sanctuary workers within their understanding of legal discourse, they found themselves contending with the embarrassing perception that they were prosecuting religious folk for aiding the persecuted. Moreover, the trial and the publicity surrounding it reinforced that perception and created new opportunities for sanctuary workers to promote the movement. Despite its outcome—the convictions of eight sanctuary workers—the trial process in some ways furthered the very practices that authorities sought to deter.

If one views political action as something that, in the course of pursuing explicit objectives, engages discourses of power in unexpected ways, it then becomes possible to analyze how seemingly superfluous acts are nonetheless a significant part of the resistance enacted by social movements. If creating a means of protest (or repression, for that matter) entails reworking the categories and practices through which protestors live their lives, and if power inheres in these categories and practices, then the cultural forms that protestors create have political implications apart from their strategic effects. Like prototypical movement practices, the jokes, stories, ethics, rituals, and relationships that movement members construct simultaneously critique, reshape, and reproduce the discourses out of which they are made.

## Notes

1. Surveillance of the sanctuary movement was conducted not only with an eye toward possible future indictments of movement participants but also as part of a government investigation of political dissidents (Gelbspan 1991; Select Committee on Intelligence, U.S. Senate 1989). Beginning in 1981, the FBI conducted a six-year probe of 150 groups opposed to the government's Central America policy (*Tucson Citizen* 1988). These groups, including a number of sanctuary churches and offices around the United States, experienced mail-tampering and mysterious break-ins in which files were stolen but valuable office equipment was left behind (Duarte 1986). Members of the Old Cambridge Baptist Church in Massachusetts discovered that they had been infiltrated when the FBI informed them that its files on the church might "reveal the identity of an individual who has furnished information to the F.B.I. under confidential circumstances" (Cox 1986). Even in Tucson, the full extent of the investigation remained unknown, as a female informant who investigated sanctuary work there and in San Diego was never publicly identified (Browning 1987).

2. For analyses of the social constructedness of legal truth in the United States and elsewhere, see Bohannan 1968; Comaroff 1978; Comaroff and Roberts 1981; Geertz 1983; Moore 1986; Clifford 1988; Yngvesson 1988; Merry 1990; and Harding (in press).

3. At a press conference following the verdicts, prosecutor Reno warned sanctuary workers to reexamine their actions if they wanted to avoid being prosecuted (Pittman 1986).

4. The sermon I describe at the beginning of Chapter 1 is an example of how the defendants and their supporters defined the trial as an act of persecution, parallel in kind, though not intensity, to the persecution experienced by Christ.

5. Legal scholar Lawrence Rosen has pointed out that in the United States, the relationships between law and morality and between reason and compassion often creates legal dilemmas. Rosen wrote, "It is part of the western discourse to raise the issue whether reason

diminishes from one's essential humanity if it does not yield to a higher concern for mercy, fairness, or love, particularly when a human life is at stake" (1989:72). By arguing that that which is good ought to be legal, the defense seemed to be attempting to raise this issue in jurors' minds.

6. The verdicts were appealed to the Supreme Court, which, in January 1991, refused to hear the case.

7. The Tucson sanctuary trial was not the only prosecution of sanctuary workers. In addition to Stacy Merkt and Jack Elder, the Rev. Glen Remer-Thamert and Demeria Martinez—a sanctuary worker and a journalist, respectively—were tried in New Mexico in 1988. The Tucson trial, however, had the greatest impact on the movement. Due to the depth and range of the undercover investigation, the number of defendants and unindicted coconspirators, and the detention of some fifty-eight Central Americans around the country, many sanctuary workers perceived the Tucson prosecution as an all-out attack on the movement.

8. The media's role in creating representations of the sanctuary trial deserves further analysis but is beyond the scope of this book. Journalists were not unreflecting conduits for defendants' views; rather, they were situated actors whose portrayals of the movement and trial, although influenced by sanctuary workers' public relations efforts, were shaped by the particular journalist's social position, his or her sense of what makes a good story, the political stance of the newspaper, and numerous other factors. For a study that does analyze media representations of a criminal trial, see Harding (in press).

9. Leviticus 19:33 reads, "When a stranger sojourns with you in your land, you shall do him no wrong."

10. These letters identified Central Americans only by nationality, sex, and age. Tucson sanctuary workers did not turn undocumented Central Americans over to Immigration officials but put them in contact with attorneys who advised them regarding political asylum.

# PART THREE

# THE CULTURE OF PROTEST

# 8

## A Social Critique

Susan: *You were saying earlier that the Christians have learned community from the Central Americans—*[1]

Rabbi: *Not exactly community but* comunidad. *Do you know what that is? Do you know what a* comunidad de base *is?*

Susan: *Yes.*

Rabbi: *I saw one of those in South Texas when I went there, and it's sort of like a shtetl*[2] *... Versus the rugged individualism of North Americans. That's what I meant.*
          —Excerpt of interview with the rabbi of a Tucson sanctuary congregation

In addition to pursuing long-term objectives through explicit strategies, participants in social movements produce practices that, although informed by the movement's social analysis and broader goals, are not explicitly tactics for achieving these goals (Melucci 1989; Evans and Boyte 1986; Touraine 1981; Castells 1983). Creating a method of protest also entails forming a community of protestors, which in turn means devising ways for participants to relate to each other, make sense of their experiences, and connect what they do within the movement to what goes on in the rest of their lives. Although the resulting practices—such as telling jokes or stories, devising ethics to guide relationships between movement members, praying before holding a meeting, and so on—seem incidental to the "real" work of protest, they actually have a great deal in common with prototypical movement practices. Because society is made up of power-laden discourses, almost any social action engages these discourses in some way. To create the organizations, actions, and beliefs that comprise the content of a protest movement, protestors deliberately rework elements of their own practices and categories. Once a movement is founded, participants continue to reexamine their own actions and beliefs in light of the particular cause that they are addressing. This continual reshaping of preexisting cultural discourses provides a commentary on the social context out of which a particular movement arises. Therefore, the cultural constructs created in the process of protest—like the formal strategies of holding sit-ins, boycotting buses, and sheltering undocumented Salvadorans—invoke and reinterpret systems of power.

To analyze how a movement that sought refugee status for Salvadoran and Guatemalan immigrants, an end to U.S. military aid to El Salvador, and peace in Central America also produced a commentary on middle-class U.S. culture, it is necessary to view social criticism as an *implicit* as well as an *explicit* process. The assumption that protestors express their social analysis in clear, political language has led analysts to make having an explicit program for change one of the criteria that distinguishes social movements from other collective actions (Worsley 1968; Gusfield 1968; Hobsbawm 1959; Piven and Cloward 1977; Tilly 1984) and to dismiss the facets of protest that seem irrelevant to movements' agendas (Marwell and Oliver 1984).[3] For example, historian E. J. Hobsbawm defined prepolitical movements as those which "have not yet found, or only begun to find, a specific language in which to express their aspirations about the world" (1959:2). More recently, resource mobilization theorists have assumed that protest consists of "rational actions *oriented towards clearly defined, fixed goals* with centralized organizational control over resources and clearly demarcated outcomes that can be evaluated in terms of tangible gains" (Jenkins 1983:529, emphasis added). Studies of resistance in Third World societies have problematized such definitions of protest by pointing out that social practices—such as requiring purchased commodities to be blessed before they may be used (Comaroff 1985) or believing that successful peasant wage-laborers have sold their souls to the devil (Taussig 1980)—can *implicitly* critique the structures of power in which they occur. Applying this insight to the study of U.S. social movements reveals that the practice and language of protest implicitly comment on facets of society and culture that are not directly related to a movement's stated goals.

As members of the sanctuary movement constituted themselves as a community, they drew on and critiqued middle-class U.S. culture, their own notions of gender, and what Edward Said (1979) has called "Orientalism": the tendency of Western societies to produce authoritative and power-laden images of a non-Western other. Said has argued that academic and literary representations of the Orient are rooted in imperialistic and hierarchical relationships between Europe and Eastern nations. He critiqued these representations less for inaccuracy than for their authors' assumptions of the authority to describe, and even produce, the construct they called "the Orient," a construct that is always defined in contrast to "the West." Thus, according to Said, Orientalists view "the East" as traditional, immature, mystical, dependent, and feminine and "the West" as modern, technologically advanced, rational, independent, and masculine. Though Said employed the term "Orientalism" to refer to Europe's discourse about the East, this discourse is actually broader in scope. Orientalism also applies to dichotomies between Western and non-Western, self and other, North American and Central American. As Clifford noted, "The key theoretical issue raised by *Orientalism* concerns the status of *all* forms of thought and representation for dealing with the alien. Can one ultimately escape procedures of dichotomizing, restructuring, and textualizing in the making of interpretive statements about foreign cultures and traditions? If so, how?" (Clifford 1988:261, emphasis in original). This was the dilemma that sanctuary workers confronted in their relationships with Central Americans.

As they sought to define the legal, cultural, economic, and spiritual significance of Central Americans' lives, sanctuary workers produced images of Salvadoran and Guatemalan peoples that were rooted in Orientalist categories. Well-aware that Orientalist images usually denigrated "non-Western" cultures, sanctuary workers inverted the values ascribed to "Eastern" and "Western" traits, using their representations of Central Americans to expose the shortcomings of U.S. society. The result was a profound critique of the way that middle-class North American notions and practices were connected to repression in Central America. Yet, because its mainstream, middle-class composition was a source of legitimacy for the movement, this critique created a dilemma for sanctuary workers who, for the most part, enjoyed this relatively privileged position. Some participants resolved this dilemma by allowing their social critique to reshape their practices within and outside of the movement—a reshaping that, among other things, involved rejecting sources of power and authority that participants defined as male. Because this commentary was woven into sanctuary work, the anecdotes, jokes, rituals, relationships, and day-to-day actions that comprised sanctuary "culture" implicitly critiqued the social context in which the movement arose.

## Contrasting Anecdotes

Among the practices that made up the culture of the sanctuary movement—and that expressed movement members' social analysis—were the parable-like anecdotes through which sanctuary workers contrasted their own and Central American societies. Such anecdotes were related by sanctuary workers and Central Americans to journalists, public audiences, anthropologists, and most commonly, each other. These stories were told during interviews, meetings, informal conversations, sermons, and presentations. To produce these anecdotes, sanctuary workers, in an Orientalist fashion, studied Central American society and people and defined the significance of this "foreign" culture by contrasting it with that of their own. For example, when I asked sanctuary workers what Central Americans could teach North Americans, participants nodded, as though they'd already given the matter some thought, and launched into their answers. When asked what North Americans could teach Central Americans, however, participants paused to think and were sometimes nonplussed. Responses to the first question included faith, truth, life, spirit, courage, strength, suffering, and so on. Answers to the second question focused on technology, material aid, nutrition, health care, etc.[4] These responses paralleled but revalued the contrasts that Orientalism posited between East and West. Sanctuary workers portrayed Central American culture as *superior,* rather than inferior, to that of their own by valorizing interdependency over independence, faith over secularism, and so forth. The result of such inversions was politically contradictory. The movement created monolithic and idealized images of Central Americans but, in the process, conveyed sanctuary workers' senses that they and their society were deeply complicit in the violence, human rights abuses, and economic deprivation that characterized El Salvador and Guatemala.

By representing the United States as technologically advanced but spiritually starved and Central American culture as less industrialized but more fulfilling, the movement practiced the brand of Orientalism that Renato Rosaldo has termed "imperialist nostalgia":

> "We" (who believe in progress) valorize innovation, and then yearn for more stable worlds, whether these reside in our own past, in other cultures, or in the conflation of the two. Such forms of longing thus appear closely related to secular notions of progress. When the so-called civilizing process destabilizes forms of life, the agents of change experience transformations of other cultures as if they were personal losses (Rosaldo 1989:70).

Sanctuary workers' visions of Central Americans were steeped in such nostalgia. For example, Gail Stewart, an East Bay sanctuary worker, claimed that Central Americans' values were less "adulturated" than those of North Americans. Sandra Trenck, a Tucson sanctuary supporter, stressed that "[Central Americans'] way of life is very much back to the basics," and Arthur Theede, a San Francisco sanctuary activist, commented, "They, it seems, have a more elemental life. ... But our life is so mediated." Merlin Wynn, a member of All Saints, said of Salvadorans and Guatemalans, "They've lived the lives that we read about in the Bible. We have the qualities that they do, but we haven't been put to the test. Our test is to go with them, as far as we can." Linda Allen, an East Bay activist, praised a Guatemalan immigrant who made his children wash their clothes on rocks in a creek. She noted, "They don't want to be *enslaved* by the phony value-system that we have." Although such imperialist nostalgia "licences patronizing attitudes of condescension, such as reverence for a simplicity 'we' have lost" (Rosaldo 1986a:97), the anecdotes generated by this nostalgia nonetheless express sanctuary workers' analyses of the shortcomings of their own society. Constructing images of authenticity critiques that which is felt as inauthentic.

Sanctuary workers' critiques of inauthenticity focused on those aspects of middle-class U.S. life that participants considered causes or products of poverty, injustice, and human rights abuses in El Salvador and Guatemala. These included alienation, consumerism, normalcy, secularism, individualism, materialism, and numbness.[5] Two anecdotes that I heard in Tucson conveyed their tellers' senses that North American notions of buying and selling did violence to the expressiveness of Central American culture.[6] In the Task Force office one day, Teresa Newman, a staff member, told me and several other participants who happened to be present of purchasing handwoven shirts (called *huipiles*) in Guatemala. To quote my notes:

> She said that when she bought the shirts, the man who sold them started beating them, and she thought he'd gone nuts. But then she found out that people there believe that the soul of the woman who makes the shirt is sewn into her weaving, especially if the woman wears the shirt afterwards. So, when they sell the shirts, they have to beat them and hit them against the fences to make sure that the soul leaves the shirt and that they aren't selling the soul of the woman who made it.

A Tucson minister used a similar anecdote to introduce a Guatemalan weaver to his congregation one Sunday morning. The minister told the congregation:

> *Don* _____ has come to us from his cooperative in Mexico, where he, along with other Guatemalan exiles, weaves cloth. He was a catechist in Quiché when the army decided that catechists were a threat to their survival, so they drove them away, killing many of them. *Don* _____ is a survivor, and a martyr. And just to tell you the kind of person he is, he came into my office to show me his weaving. And I was trying to look at it while I was answering the phone and making appointments, and he finally said to me, "I didn't come just to sell this. I want you to take time to look at the colors, to see how they relate to each other, and then, when you have time, I will talk to you." And so I took the time, and I hope that you will later take the time to look at his weaving, to appreciate the colors, and to try to feel what they express to us more than words can about the people and the culture and the suffering that they've experienced.[7]

These two anecdotes portrayed Guatemalan society as a place where people are closely connected, even woven into, the products of their labor; thus, such anecdotes implicitly critiqued "North American" assumptions about economic transactions. The first anecdote depicted exchanging cash for a weaving as an act that threatened the very being of the weaver. In the second anecdote, the speaker belittled his own, North American attitude toward buying goods, noting that because he was busy making appointments, he initially failed to appreciate the beauty and meaning of the weavings. When he told this tale to his congregants, this pastor signaled that purchasing Guatemalan weavings (which were to be sold during coffee hour following the service) was not an ordinary transaction. By taking the time to appreciate the weavings, congregants were to suspend their more businesslike shopping norms and participate in the "Guatemalan" notion of buying. The fact that this anecdote was related by a pastor during a church service gave its admonition religious force.

Sanctuary workers' anecdotes also expressed the notion that the affluence of the U.S. middle class was connected to poverty in Central America. Linda Allen, an East Bay minister, commented:

I was sitting listening on the radio yesterday to something about the ten highest salaries on the stock market. This one guy made 156 million [dollars] in salary. ... See, I
think that is deeply immoral ... because his moving money around didn't provide
any jobs, it didn't put any food in anybody's mouth. In fact, it did just the opposite.
It's making children in the Third World countries die. Because he can take that kind
of money home and they don't get any. At all.

Teresa Newman, the speaker who described the sale of huipiles, also reported that
the Guatemalans she visited only owned two shirts and two skirts, which they
considered quite enough. She said that the Guatemalans laughed at North American visitors who brought suitcases full of clothes for short stays. Joanna Spoakes,
an East Bay participant who had visited Central America, was sickened by the
overabundance of goods in U.S. stores. Joanna told me, "It's always much more
shocking for me to come home than it is to go down there. I'm just *appalled* when
I get home. I go through a supermarket, and I want to throw up! A whole *row* of
detergents! And all they have down there is a bar of soap, if they're lucky, to wash
their clothes with."

In addition to critiquing alienation and affluence, anecdotes conveyed the
sense that, given the degree of violence in El Salvador and Guatemala, the normalcy of sanctuary workers' own lives was callous. When I was in the Task Force
office in Tucson one day, I heard a story about a volunteer who had taken two refugee children to the Tucson Rodeo Parade. After watching the parade, the oldest
child had said to the volunteer, "You know, I've been to a lot of parades in El Salvador, but I've never been to a parade before where there were no soldiers." During interviews, several East Bay sanctuary workers recounted an incident that had
taken place in the viewing balconies above the U.S. Senate after a group of sanctuary workers and refugees had finished a day of lobbying. In contrast to what is often a patriotic moment for U.S. citizens, one of the refugees reportedly looked
down at the Senators and said, "I never thought I would see the men who made
the decision that my family would die." At a Bay Area religious retreat, a speaker
pointed out the abnormality of normalcy[8] by noting that when helicopters had
passed overhead moments earlier no one had run for cover as they would have in
El Salvador. I myself expressed a similar sensation to a Tucson sanctuary worker
during an interview:

Just today, I was at one of the asylum hearings ... and while we were waiting, ... I
was sitting there in the INS office, in the Federal Building, having a conversation
about sanctuary with another woman there. We weren't talking loudly, but we
weren't trying to hide what we were talking about either. And suddenly it hit me; we
were sitting there next to a Salvadoran woman—and she didn't know what we were
talking about, because we were speaking English—but I'm sure that it would be so
far from her experience to sit in a government office and criticize the government.

Participants' anecdotes and observations about El Salvador and Guatemala
also argued that poverty and suffering had deepened Central Americans' faith but

that in the United States, materialism and normalcy had produced a secularism that allowed the U.S. government to act unjustly toward Central Americans. Mark Willows, a San Francisco sanctuary worker, told me, "Religion in Latin America is uncluttered by middle-class accoutrements," while Gail Stewart, an East Bay participant, explained, "Our values are oriented toward guarding our possessions too much, and that always kills religion. ... And of course, *they* [Central Americans] don't have any possessions." Nancy Michaels, one of Gail's colleagues, felt that in the United States, faith had been replaced by such false gods as "television, or consumerism, or materialism. And the drive to get ahead in the world, and get a job, and make money as our new religion." Gustavo Alvarez, a Guatemalan refugee living in Tucson, used an anecdote to explain how risk strengthens faith:

*Susan:* One thing that the North Americans have told me during interviews is that they've noticed that the faith of the Central Americans is deeper and stronger than their own faith. Have you noticed that as well?

*Gustavo:* Yes. We have more faith in the Bible and in God. We have felt these in our own flesh. When you're caught between a rock and a hard place, and you pray to God, and you escape, it's a miracle. Whereas here in the U.S., those who are comfortable in their own homes don't experience this.

*Susan:* So this is because here, people are too comfortable, and they don't face—

*Gustavo:* Death?

*Susan:*—the challenge of—

*Gustavo:* I would say that what it is is this. You have to be in this situation in order to feel that conversion to faith.

I'll give you an example. [Gustavo looked at me intently.] When I was in my country, there were times when I would hear the dogs coming, and then I would hear the National Guard, and I would think, "This is it, the death squads have come to get me." And I would pray, "Please God, don't let them take me away." And then when they didn't, I knew that it was the work of God. This is how it is in my country.

So, here, people have less faith because they haven't had this experience.

Movement members' anecdotes also claimed that, whereas in the United States, people had strong notions of individualism (which permitted the U.S. populace to disregard suffering in Central America) Salvadorans and Guatemalans had a strong sense of community.[9] José Martín, a Salvadoran active in the San Francisco refugee community, said, "Here, what you see is that each person is working towards his own individual salvation. ... And that breeds insensitivity to the pain of others." Felipe Arguelles, a Guatemalan living in Tucson, argued that the community, cooperation, and generosity of Guatemalan society had enabled the poor to survive. Felipe told me:

I was working in a restaurant [in the United States], and if there was a coworker who was busy and I had some free time, I would offer to help. "No," they would say, "I can do it myself." Everybody tried to be better than everyone else. To them, to accept help meant that they were admitting that they were incapable of doing the work themselves. It was at a party once that I asked them, "Why is it that you won't accept help from others? If you are busy and I have some free time, why can't I help you? This is an attitude that stems from egoism and individualism." I told them, "The poor in Latin America survive through *compañarismo* and *comunidad*." Because, if you're in a poor village in Guatemala, and you wake up one morning and find that you have no tortillas, you can go to your neighbor who may be making tortillas and say, "Hey Mrs. So-and-so, can I borrow three tortillas?" And she will say, "Sure." The peasants in Central America wouldn't survive if it wasn't for cooperation.

Anecdotes also expressed movement members' sense that, paradoxically, the Central American poor were more generous than affluent North Americans. This paradox had religious overtones, as shown by a Tucson minister's comment that Central Americans were like the biblical widow whose gift of copper coins was more valuable than all the king's wealth. Joanna Spoakes related a modern-day parable experienced during a trip to Nicaragua:

> The biggest impression that I have is once a week, they would kill an animal in this town of 1,000 people, and everybody would get a half kilo for their family of eight people. And this woman gave us some of their meat! They had done that the day before and she had some left and she gave us some of that. These people had been eating rice and boiled bananas. That's all they had. They didn't even have beans. And yet, whatever was hers was ours too. Totally generous, totally—
>
> I just wondered, if she came knocking on my door here, would I do the same thing? I doubt it! Well, I might. [But] with my neighbors, they'd probably say, "Get out of here!" You know?

Similarly, at a Bay Area religious retreat, a nun told an anecdote that she called, "The Story of the Man with the Bag of Oranges." The story described a trip in El Salvador to visit rural people in a zone of conflict. As the nun and her companions drove to their destination, they passed a man walking on a dirt road and carrying a bag of oranges. After arriving in the rural zone, the nun realized that the children were slowly starving because the military would not allow supplies through. Two hours later, after Mass, the man with the bag of oranges arrived, and subsequently, orange juice appeared as refreshment for the guests. The nun, fearing malaria-infested water, gave her juice to a child. The juice was accompanied by bread, which had been bought in town. The nun concluded: "Which meant that the people had gone to the town, risking their lives—since the army was everywhere—just to buy bread for us. And so, when I ate that bread, for the first time I felt as though I was really sharing bread with the poor, as the scripture says."

All of these contrasts—having only the basics versus technology, expressiveness versus alienation, poverty versus consumerism, suffering versus normalcy, faith versus secularism, community versus individualism, and generosity versus greed—contributed to sanctuary workers' perceptions that life in Central America, like the vivid colors of a Guatemalan weaving, had a greater vitality than that in the United States. For example, after comparing North and Central Americans during an interview, Merlin Wynn of Tucson concluded, "I would rather live a short, difficult, *quality* life than an easy, secure, numb one. I don't want to live in Green Valley [an affluent Tucson community] and play tennis." Gail Stewart, an East Bay sanctuary worker, envied the vitality of Central Americans' religious experience: "It just seems like in the comunidad de base, religion is a much more living, breathing, daily practiced thing than in the churches here. Here it tends to get formalized and structured to the point that it's no longer living and real." Similarly, Anya Fischer of Berkeley told me of a disabled friend who had traveled to El Salvador to design and manufacture wheelchairs:

> He, remember, was wheelchair bound, goes down there, goes among the people, and it was his stories and his reports of the dire poverty in which people live, and how he was welcomed by them, and whatever they had was shared, and by the warmth of the people, and their spirit, and the beauty and a community and closeness in their lives that we don't seem to have. Or we've lost.

Anya's wistful remark that Central Americans still had what "we" had lost typified the romantic images of "traditional" societies that are created by imperialist nostalgia.[10] Said noted that "Orientalism depends for its strategy on this flexible *positional* superiority. ... The scientist, the scholar, the missionary, the trader, or the soldier was in, or thought about, the Orient because he *could be there,* or could think about it, with very little resistance on the Orient's part" (1979:7, emphasis in original). North Americans *could* be there, and therefore had a greater ability to represent Central Americans than vice versa. It was North Americans who could travel on delegations to Central America, question refugees, learn their stories, study their attitudes, vicariously experience their suffering, and produce knowledge about Central Americans. It was because of these abilities that sanctuary workers could make comments like, "We need to *read* their [Central Americans'] people, we need to learn about the political systems, their culture, and their religion," or, "What we need to do here in the U.S. is to personally experience refugees so that we can deal with our own sin of gluttony." In contrast, Central Americans, for the most part, had little opportunity to "read" or "personally experience" North Americans. The movement's inspirational anecdotes about refugees' lives were thus made possible by sanctuary workers' positions as middle-class members of an affluent society. The movement's critique of middle-class U.S. life was in some ways facilitated by the very inequities that it denounced.

Uncomfortably aware that their cultural critique did not change their class position or national identity, sanctuary workers struggled to shed the middle-class North American traits that their involvement in the movement had prob-

lematized. By allowing their social critique to shape their actions within and outside of the movement, participants constituted themselves as a dissident enclave
within the U.S. middle class.


## Refugees from Americanism

The sanctuary movement's critique of middle-class U.S. culture was tempered
by the fact that the movement's roots in middle-class, mainstream congregations
provided a source of legitimacy and material resources. Participants hoped that
because it was composed of what they liked to call "ordinary religious folk," the
sanctuary movement would not be dismissed as radical, fringy, or merely the latest liberal cause. Ernie Tarkington, a Tucson minister, felt that the movement's
mainstream composition distinguished it from what he termed "liberal bandwag-
ons." Ernie explained, "You know the type I mean; they sign onto any antiestab-
lishment cause. They sign on easily. It's very different from a church in Iowa deciding that on this one issue, even though they love their country and may be
conservative, they're going to take a stance in opposition to their government."
Additionally, on a practical level, participants' middle-class status provided the
material resources that made sanctuary work possible. Most sanctuary congregations had meeting rooms, equipment (such as slide projectors), and a budget for
social action. Anita Garvey, a nonchurchgoing sanctuary volunteer, pointed out
that middle-class congregations "have the houses to put people up in. When you
ask, well, couldn't a poor church do that? I think it would really be a strain on a
poor church, to do sanctuary. And the legal sanctions would mean more to a poor
person."

Despite the movement's middle-class roots, sanctuary work set participants
apart from peers who were not involved in the movement. Merlin Wynn, a Tucson sanctuary supporter, recalled that shortly after he began attending All Saints,
"One day after church, the pastor was standing there at the door and shaking everyone's hand, and I told him, 'I'm a refugee. A refugee from Tucson, from Ameri-
canism.' ... I was looking for people with common goals, and people who dealt
with life in a way that I could respect." Larry Hauffen, a Tucson sanctuary worker,
contrasted himself with neighbors in the retirement community where he resided:
"I have a need for social activism and I have to express that somehow. I could be
out playing golf or traveling, or going out and doing things—which is what most
of the people who live around here do all the time." A Tucson pastor found that
because of his work with Salvadoran and Guatemalan refugees:

> There was a period of about four months where I literally couldn't talk to people
> about it [the human rights situation in Central America]. I mean, I could talk to
> other people who were doing the work, but there was such a gap between the world
> that I was living in of crisis on the border and nice, content Tucson that I couldn't
> find the language to describe what I was experiencing.

Flora Grant of Tucson recounted that merely because she belonged to a sanctuary congregation, she had been rejected by a friendly young man she had met at a local church. When the young man had asked her what church she attended, and she had told him that it was All Saints:

> *Immediately,* just like someone had opened and shut a door, he said, "*That's* the church that's involved in *sanctuary,* isn't it?" And I said "Yes!" And he didn't ask me what I did or if I were [involved] or anything, but he, *boy,* he told *me* where to head in! That [it] was the devil working in us, and that we were not only breaking civil laws, we were breaking moral laws, and I finally said, "Well, obviously we don't agree on this subject," and walked on.

Like their anecdotes about Central American society, the differences that sanctuary workers perceived and constructed between themselves and their peers critiqued middle-class U.S. culture. One such difference was that, emulating Central Americans, sanctuary workers sought to create the community that they felt was missing within U.S. society.[11] Through events such as meetings, church services, talks, musical performances, cultural evenings, plays, walk-a-thons, border crossings, and fund-raisers, participants worshiped, worked, and celebrated together. The Tucson trial of eleven sanctuary workers created such close-knit networks that, according to one volunteer, when a flu bug went around, "everyone in the movement came down with it eventually." In the East Bay, when two sanctuary activists got married (and requested donations to sanctuary in lieu of wedding gifts), the wedding became a community event.[12] The bride related:

> We had five clergy performing the ceremony—everyone from the original lectionary group that declared sanctuary[13]—and they broke all kinds of rules to do it. We had Catholics giving Communion to Protestants. And I mean, if you were there to look around the room, some of our friends and family were there, but about half of the people there have to have been sanctuary people. Or at least a significant portion.

Inside jokes also celebrated common knowledge, norms, and experience. At an EBSC Steering Committee meeting, a participant announced that an eighty-five-proof bottle of vodka from the Soviet Union had been found backstage after a recent fund-raising concert. One Steering Committee representative jokingly queried, "Is this an example of Soviet influence on the sanctuary movement?" "No," another answered, "it's an example of alcoholism in the sanctuary movement." At a Tucson sanctuary retreat, when two border workers climbed atop a shaky table to hold out a sanctuary quilt so I could photograph it, another border worker told them, laughing, "I never knew people to take so much risk!"

A second trait that sanctuary workers felt set them apart from wider society was their identity as a religious people. To celebrate this identity—and thus to avoid the secularism that the movement critiqued—participants drew on and constructed a common set of religious rituals (described in Chapter 10), texts, language, and humor. In addition to the Bible, a number of participants had read Robert McAfee-Brown, Ernesto Cardenal, Paulo Freire, and other theologians. Religious language was prevalent, such as one organization's "Paul and Silas bail fund," named after the biblical story in which prison walls shook and doors opened, allowing Paul and Silas to walk away free. Religious humor abounded within the movement. At a December Task Force meeting, one of the clergy present said he had a couple of questions about Christmas that he wanted to put on the agenda. Another participant immediately asked, "What is it? The Virgin Birth?" At the following Task Force meeting, a huge nativity scene—complete with a cradle, dried peppers, shepherd figures, and hay—adorned the room where the meeting would be held. One minister walked into the room and asked in a surprised tone of voice, "What's this?" meaning, how did this get here? "A nativity scene," another participant answered dryly, "Don't you know the Christian symbols?"

Third, as they constructed community and celebrated faith, sanctuary workers sought to elude the materialism that they believed pervaded U.S. life. Many reported forgoing items that they felt typified consumer society—VCRs, a new car, wall-to-wall carpeting, matching drapes, Club Med vacations, filo pans, and the latest clothing fashions. Three Bay Area sanctuary workers went further, buying their families' clothing at flea markets and thrift stores. David Hoffman, a San Francisco sanctuary worker, told me, "When I spend money, I always think about the alternative uses it could be put to." Leanna Vance tithed, giving most of the money to solidarity groups, while Gail Stewart donated money to sanctuary rather than saving it for a trip to Europe. Randy Silbert of Tucson told me that several hours before I had interviewed him, while paying for a bag of grapefruit, he had realized that the fruit probably came from Mexico, from land owned by a U.S. company, where the workers who picked the grapefruits would not have been able to afford the bag he was purchasing. During an interview, Simon Portnoy of Tucson scathingly attacked "Yuppie-ism," saying, "Yuppies are the definition of what the Kingdom of God is not." Finally, antimaterialistic anecdotes occasionally made the rounds within sanctuary communities. One, which I both heard about and witnessed, occurred at All Saints on Thanksgiving Sunday. When the minister asked the congregation what they were grateful for, congregants mentioned things like health, family, good friends, and life. The pastor then said, "Good! No one said they were thankful for the money they have in the bank." A congregant shouted back, "That's because we don't have any!"

Finally, sanctuary workers strove to place their social ethics above the individualistic ambition that they perceived in the U.S. middle class. When looking for a job, Hilary Epstein of Congregation Aron Kodesh deliberately sought out a company that had no connections to the military. After being hired, she was shocked to discover that her coworkers "didn't even seem to care about that. They didn't care what the end product of their work was, and yet this is what they were devoting their life-blood to!" Lindsey Martin, an East Bay sanctuary worker, gave up a career in computer science so that she would not be part of "the acquisition and the rise of the Yuppie movement." Matthew Scott, also of the East Bay, puzzled his boss by valuing vocation over money. Matthew explained:

> I know that my boss can't figure me out. ... If I was willing to work sixty or seventy hours a week, I know I could easily be making $100,000 a year. ... I'm not at all ca-reer-oriented, I'm vocation-oriented, to use the Catholic word. I'm much more in-terested in "what is my place in the Church and where is God calling me?" than "what is my place in the business world, and what should I be doing?"

Such critiques of personal ambition were so strong that they sometimes shaped the way that I presented myself to sanctuary workers. For example, while volun-teering in the EBSC office one day, I told a staff member that my fiancé was con-sidering a move to Los Angeles because teachers' salaries were higher there. I im-mediately felt constrained to add that money would not be the main factor in his decision. Even though in other circles it is acceptable to base job decisions on sal-ary differences, I felt embarrassed saying this to a member of the sanctuary move-ment. On another occasion, which I described in Chapter 1, Simon Portnoy, for-mer pastor of a Tucson sanctuary congregation, contended that my own career choices would either serve or violate the kingdom of God. Simon told me, "If you get your Ph.D., work to be powerful and influential within anthropology, and pursue your career, then you're not serving the kingdom."

The cultural critique expressed through sanctuary workers' anecdotes and through their dissident subculture invoked and reevaluated not only Orientalism and middle-class U.S. culture but also participants' concepts of gender. Examin-ing these concepts (which, it should be noted, varied from individual to individ-ual) reveals that the movement's characterization of the contrasts between Central and North Americans and between sanctuary workers and their peers paralleled participants' notions of male/female differences. The traits that participants la-beled "North American" were, in other contexts, labeled "male"; consequently, sanctuary workers' efforts to enact their critique of middle-class U.S. life simulta-neously commented on their own concepts of gender. The gendered dimension of sanctuary workers' cultural critique emerged when participants discussed male and female involvement in the movement.

## Gendered Notions

The sanctuary movement arose at a time when U.S. religious groups were de-bating the ordination of women, the removal of sexist language from prayers, hymns, and Bible readings, and even God's gender. Generally, the congregations that made up the sanctuary movement were also those that advocated sexual equality; therefore, sexual equality was one of the ideals that participants sought to enact within the movement. Yet, despite this goal, disparities existed. In the East Bay, approximately two-thirds of the participants in congregational sanctuary committees and the EBSC Steering Committee were women, a statistic that some participants felt reflected the composition of U.S. congregations[14] rather than sexism within the movement. East Bay participants were more critical of the fact that men spoke for the local movement more often than did women. A female minister who was a frequent media spokesperson commented, "Even among the men and the women in sanctuary, there's the assumption that men speak better than women." Finally, despite parity within most of the movement's work, the EBSC office was staffed almost entirely by women. Participants considered this fact the most glaring exception to EBSC's sexually egalitarian norms.

In Tucson, unlike the East Bay, I found few sanctuary workers interested in discussing differences between male and female involvement, perhaps because those who were critical of other aspects the local movement—such as its aid to right-wing refugees or its discomfort with the label "political"—had also accused the Tucson sanctuary community of being male dominated.[15] For example, a Tucson minister who had grown frustrated with the movement's antibureaucratic work style told me, "Here in Tucson, sanctuary has largely been white male Anglo dominated. And—it's not an elite exactly—'clique' isn't exactly the right word—but it's closed. By which I mean that there are a few people who seem to think that they're the leaders." A former Tucson defendant, who felt that her colleagues were not political enough, said, "Here, like elsewhere in the U.S., it's the women in sanctuary who've done the most risking, and who've given the most. But in terms of media coverage and leadership, they're not there." In contrast, a nun who was active in crossings at the time of my research commented, "One of the most important things for me personally has been to see how men and women work together in this work."

When I heard East Bay and Tucson sanctuary workers try to explain why more women were involved in the movement than men and why men were spokespeople more often than women, I realized that the characteristics that participants considered "male" were the same ones that they denounced in their critique of middle-class U.S. life. One explanation that sanctuary workers proffered for the differences between male and female involvement was that men had been socialized to pursue power and influence whereas women had been taught to be less ambitious, materialistic, and career-oriented. For example, one male East Bay sanctuary worker said, "Men are conditioned that their lives are really to be spent going out and making a career and stumping up whatever ladders they are on, and leave the housework to the women. ... The women are doing the sanctuary housekeeping." Indeed, one EBSC staff member complained that her job—distributing clothing and other donations to the refugee community—was too much like "housework." Katherine Baerman, a First Church Sanctuary Committee member, argued that sanctuary was inaccurately perceived as "doing good deeds," as apolitical, and therefore as women's work. Katherine said, "I don't think enough men have seen the political aspect of this [sanctuary]. It goes way beyond, 'Oh, isn't that nice, doing nice things for these nice people?' So I think there's condescension there that we haven't yet completely broken through." Lindsey Martin, a Steering Committee representative, said that her own involvement in sanctuary work stemmed from her critique of materialism—a critique that she felt was shared by other women. She explained, "I think there's a real movement [among women] to making the choice to not become so materially oriented, and to become more spiritually oriented." Simon Portnoy, a Tucson minister, said that pursuing power and influence, which he characterized as a male tendency, violated the kingdom of God. Simon gave Rambo and John Wayne, two male figures noted for their macho image, as examples of people who had not served the kingdom of God.

A second explanation that sanctuary workers cited for the differences between men's and women's involvement was the notion that while men talk, women take action. For example, Edward Radtke, who belonged to the border group that split off from Trsg, considered philosophizing a male activity. He told me that the border group with which he worked was "feminine as opposed to masculine. There are few philosophical conversations; we're very intuitive." Anita Garvey, an EBSC office volunteer, would have agreed with this characterization of philosophizing. She said:

> In the Left here in the United States, you see a lot of men. ... And they're all out arguing their little ideological point and struggling for the control of this committee made up of three people. And I think maybe—I'm going to become chauvinistic about my sex maybe—but I think women may tend to get involved [in causes such as sanctuary] because they ... really want to see suffering ended.

Hilary Epstein, a member of Congregation Aron Kodesh, put forth a similar idea. She told me, "Sanctuary has to do with the survival of families—which is something that appeals to women—whereas the men are out there writing the newsletters, giving speeches, and—in Congregation Aron Kodesh at least—serving on the board of directors." Matthew Scott of the East Bay said simply, "Women tend to look at sanctuary more as 'what needs to be done,' as opposed to 'what needs to be said.'"

Third, sanctuary workers argued that because women had been socialized to be nurturers and care-givers, they were more willing to aid refugees than were men. One First Church member felt that men were less capable than women of crossing the "kind of boundaries that you have to cross to care for another person." Joanna Spoakes, also of the East Bay, said that because she didn't have a family, she found sanctuary work an outlet for her own need to nurture others. Lindsey Martin, one of Joanna's colleagues, explained how she had been socialized into a care-giving role. As a child, Lindsey's parents had told her to do volunteer work, while they had encouraged her brothers to get jobs. Lindsey said, "I call it sexism. But now I'm really pleased with the results. ... I really learned the value of having compassion and just doing something for the less fortunate." When women who were mothers felt conflicts between nurturing refugees and nurturing their own children, they used their responsibility to their children as a justification for their sanctuary work.[16] For example, Adele Tilberg, a Jewish sanctuary worker in Tucson, told me, "I used to think of my own child, and I would think, 'What if the situation were reversed? What if it was Germany?'" Sherrie Katz, one of Adele's former colleagues, also found her children a source of inspiration. She told me that one reason she had decided to do sanctuary work had been to have a response when her children grew up and asked her, "Mommy, what were you doing during the sanctuary movement?" Marcia Dalton, a Tucson sanctuary supporter, related the following anecdote about a sanctuary defendant who lived an hour and a half away from Tucson:

> Even though she had children, she had to commute back and forth for the trial four days a week. A lot of people would say to her, "How can you do that, leave your children at home like that? Wouldn't it be better to plead guilty to a lesser charge and be done with it?" She would look people straight in the eye and say, "Wouldn't it be worse for my children if I told them that what I was doing was wrong?"

The overlap between sanctuary workers' notions of gender and their critiques of U.S. culture becomes clear when the contrasts that participants made between Central America and the United States, the sanctuary movement and wider society, and women and men are compared:

| *Central America:* | *United States:* |
|---|---|
| the basics | technology |
| expressiveness | alienation |
| poverty | affluence |
| suffering | normalcy |
| faith | secularism |
| community | individualism |
| generosity | materialism |
| *The Sanctuary Movement:* | *Wider Society:* |
| community-oriented | individualistic |
| religious | secular |
| self-sacrificing | materialistic |
| socially responsible | ambitious |
| *Female:* | *Male:* |
| nurturing | career-oriented |
| spiritual | materialistic |
| action | talk |

This comparison reveals that participants perceived some of the facets of middle-class culture that they felt contributed to repression in Central America—such as pursuing personal ambition and material wealth—as *male* tendencies. Arthur Theede, a San Francisco participant, made this connection explicit. After pointing out that in his marriage, he had had to overcome "the cultural husband-dictates-what-happens-to-the-wife-and-to-the-family kind of thing," Arthur added, "I can see that replicated in, as I say, my relationships with people in Central America. ... As the American, the authority." Moreover, this comparison suggests that when movement members *acted* on their critique of U. S. culture by doing sanctuary work, creating faith-based communities, and placing the social good above individual advancement, participants—both male and female—were acting in ways that they perceived as socially feminine. Movement culture thus not only valorized and emulated traits that participants considered Central American but also constituted an alternative to sources of authority that movement members deemed male.

The comparison between sanctuary workers' notions of gender and their social critique suggests another comparison: Within the sanctuary movement, was the United States to Central America as male was to female? In other words, by defining Central Americans as "other," were sanctuary workers creating feminized images of Salvadorans and Guatemalans? Though this interpretation is possible, I believe that it is inaccurate. If the movement were creating such feminized representations, one would expect them to appear in multiple contexts, not just within participants' commentary regarding culture, gender, and protest. Moreover, such a conclusion would be reductionistic, as some aspects of sanctuary workers' contrasts between North and Central America—such as affluence versus poverty and normalcy versus suffering—did not parallel participants' notions of gender. However, this issue is certainly a fruitful area to explore in future analyses of the sanctuary movement.

The interplay between notions of gender and notions of sanctuary work has complex political implications (see also Alcoff 1988). On the one hand, the view that women are less ambitious, less interested in abstract intellectual discussions, and more compassionate than men parallels traditional gender stereotypes. Valorizing such stereotypes implies that women should continue to act according to these social traits, with the unintended result that women would remain in powerless positions. On the other hand, some women, such as Lindsey Martin and Joanna Spoakes, found their nurturing and antimaterialistic tendencies to be empowering bases for changing society. By attempting to construct a movement that would nurture, take action, and place the social good above personal gain, sanctuary workers promoted social traits that they considered female. Moreover, when Katherine Baerman pointed out that it was condescending to view sanctuary work as apolitical (and hence, according to Katherine, feminine), she was criticizing the same assumptions about "true" social change that have pervaded research on U.S. social movements. By claiming that it was possible for a movement to fuse care-giving and advocacy, religion and politics, and means and ends, male and female sanctuary workers challenged the categories that have defined social protest.

## Conclusion

The cultural critique produced within the sanctuary movement demonstrates that social movements implicitly comment on the contexts out of which they emerge. The sanctuary movement did not form in order to critique Orientalism, middle-class U.S. culture, or "male" sources of power and authority; however, in the course of advocating changes in U.S. immigration and foreign policy, it did just that. This critique was embedded in practices that both produced and re-sulted from the movement. When religious volunteers set out to devise a means of challenging U.S. refugee policy, they almost inevitably drew on Orientalism to make sense of their relationships with Central Americans. As they contrasted their own and Central American societies, movement members critiqued middle-class U.S. social life. Because the movement arose at a time when U.S. religious groups were struggling with questions of sexual equality, participants strove to make their movement sexually egalitarian. Once the movement was founded, it led participants to further reshape these discourses. Sanctuary workers' analyses of political reality led them to invert Orientalist categories and to portray Central American society as an example for North Americans to emulate. Reevaluating their own actions and beliefs in light of Central American reality led participants to devise lifestyles that enacted the movement's critique of middle-class U.S. life. In the process, sanctuary workers rejected traits that participants considered male. Though movement members could and sometimes did explicate their so-cial critiques, this commentary was more often expressed through movement cul-ture. Participants' anecdotes about Central Americans conveyed their sense of cultural inauthenticity. The ways that participants distinguished themselves from their peers critiqued facets of U.S. culture that participants linked to repression in El Salvador and Guatemala. Finally, attributing discrepancies between male and female involvement in the movement to sexism denounced "male" careerism, materialism, and individualism.

If criticism is an implicit as well as an explicit process, then the success of social movements cannot be evaluated solely by comparing outcomes to goals. Not only does movement culture pursue ideals, such as community or sexual equality, that are not among participants' stated goals, but also movements' stated goals are not always as coherent or undisputed as researchers assume.

## Notes

1. This rabbi told me earlier in the interview that Christians were learning community from the Central Americans, while Jews were learning faith.

2. "Shtetl" is the Yiddish term for the Eastern European Jewish villages that were de-stroyed by the Holocaust.

3. The New Social Movement literature, which analyzes the European protest movements that arose during the 1960s and 1970s, does examine the ways that movements enact partici-

pants' social and cultural critiques. See, for example, Touraine 1981; Melucci 1989; Castells 1983; and Pizzorno 1978.

4. For example, when I asked Matthew Scott, an East Bay participant, what North Americans could learn from Central Americans, he described his own conversion to liberation theology, told an anecdote about sharing dinner with an impoverished Mexican family, and described the faith, community, and generosity of the Central American people. (Much of this discussion is quoted during the conversion narrative in Chapter 4.) I then asked the second question:

*Susan:* What do you think, if anything, that Central Americans can learn from North Americans?

*Matthew:* [Long pause] That's an interesting question. Why don't you ask me another question, and I'll answer it maybe after a while.

[After five to ten minutes, I returned to the question:]

*Susan:* Have you thought of anything for the other question? [Long pause] Maybe the answer is "nothing." You can't think of anything?

*Matthew:* I really can't.

*Susan:* A lot of people can't. I mean, it's interesting.

*Matthew:* It's a wonderful question though. I mean, it never occurred to me to think about it, and the fact that I can't think of anything is interesting.

*Susan:* Yeah. Well, many people, their answer is technical knowledge. For many people they say, nutrition, health care, farming, agriculture.

*Matthew:* Oh, I see. That kind of stuff.

*Susan:* But they don't—I mean, that's what most people say if they answer it.

*Matthew:* That's actually a very good answer, although I've seen that stuff in some cases do more damage than good. ... I think it's real important to be sensitive to what they need, and not what you want to give them.

5. This critique of U.S. culture was not limited to the sanctuary movement. Bellah et al. (1985) criticized American character for being utilitarian and individualist, and Merelman (1984) argued that Americans lacked a sense of group-based identities. New Social Movement theorists have pointed out that most movements of the 1960s and 1970s "have broken with the traditional values of capitalistic society. They seek a new relationship to nature, to one's own body, to the opposite sex, to work, and to consumption" (Klandermans and Tarrow 1988:7). Jenkins also noted that the movements of the 1960s were "post-materialist" (1983:535).

6. The critique contained in these anecdotes is similar to that developed by anthropologist Michael Taussig in *The Devil and Commodity Fetishism in South America.* Taussig observed that with the proletarianization of agricultural labor in Colombia came a belief that some workers entered into secret contracts with the devil in order to increase their earnings. He wrote that this devil-contract belief, which was created through colonialism, slavery, missionization, and magic, represented "an adherence by the workers' culture to the principles that underlie the peasant mode of production, even as these principles are being pro-

gressively undermined by the everyday experience of wage labor under capitalist conditions" (1980:38).

7. If sanctuary workers' representations of Central Americans seem anthropological, it is not a coincidence. Like sanctuary workers, anthropologists have often used their knowledge of foreign cultures to expose the cultural basis of their own practices. For example, in *The Devil and Commodity Fetishism in South America*, Michael Taussig used the belief systems of Colombian and Bolivian peasants to reveal that categories and practices associated with Western capitalism are not natural—as members of industrialized societies believe—but rather are socially created. Taussig wrote:

> Rather than ask the standard anthropological question, Why do people in a foreign culture respond in the way they do to, in this case, the development of capitalism? we must ask about the reality associated with our society. ... By turning the question this way we allow the anthropologist's informants the privilege of explicating and publicizing their own criticisms of the forces that are affecting their society—forces which emanate from ours (Taussig 1980:6).

Similarly, in the book *Sex and Temperament in Three Primitive Societies*, Margaret Mead used her knowledge of New Guinea gender roles to critique U.S. views that sexual roles were innate. In the preface to the 1963 edition, Mead wrote, "I would hope that this exploration of the way in which simple primitive cultures have been able to rely upon temperamental clues may be useful in shifting the present extreme emphasis upon sex roles to a new emphasis on human beings as distinct personalities, who, men and women, share many of the same contrasting and differing temperamental approaches to life." Clifford (in Clifford and Marcus 1986) also discussed the ways that anthropologists deploy ethnography to address issues within their own societies.

8. A Tucson participant made a similar point through an anecdote about taking a Central American child to a U.S. doctor. To quote my notes:

> As they were sitting there in the waiting room, the girl started looking around at all of the women sitting there. And finally, she leaned over and whispered to the volunteer, "What's wrong with them?" The volunteer knew that most of them were there to have their skin softened, or their breasts enlarged, or their faces lifted. And here was this little girl with a bullet in her arm! The volunteer didn't have the heart to tell her what the other people were there for so just told her about one woman who was having something fixed about her eye. The little girl leaned forward, squinting and looking at the eye, trying to see what was wrong with it. "If I told her what they were there for, " the volunteer concluded, "then she would really have thought we were crazy!"

9. English-speaking sanctuary workers often added the Spanish term "el pueblo," "the people," to their vocabulary, feeling that these words conveyed a sense of community better than their English equivalents. In the interview excerpt that began this chapter, the rabbi made a point of using the Spanish word "comunidad" to express his notion of community.

10. Sanctuary workers were aware that using images of Central America to critique their own societies risked producing idealized, monolithic representations of refugees. For example, one San Francisco participant told me, "I don't want to romanticize that they're [the refugees are] this or that or the other thing. ... I find that offensive. I find that almost the inverse of racism. Like [saying], 'Oh, you're so natural, happy peasants,' whatever. It's just

obnoxious." One of this woman's colleagues responded to my question about what North Americans can learn from Central Americans by pointing out, "Well, there is no monolithic Central American refugee. … I can tell you, 'I learned this thing from a university professor, I learned this thing from a peasant.' But I can't monolithically say what is to be learned from the Central American refugees." Some sanctuary workers countered romanticized images of refugees by noting that Central Americans, like North Americans, had character flaws. Philip Kaspar, a Tucson participant, pointed out that among the Central Americans he had known, "there are a lot of flakes. Some of them are drunkards, there are child-abusers, some of them steal. There's a real tendency to romanticize the refugees, and actually, most of them have a very tough time here." Nancy Michaels, a First Church member, agreed: "[Within the sanctuary movement] you paint sort of a rosy picture of pastoral peasants who just have a pure faith, and everything's very simple. But I think that there's just as ugly an underside to that as there is in our own culture."

11. In setting this goal, movement members carried on the search for community extolled by Bellah et al. in *Habits of the Heart*: "This is a society in which the individual can only rarely and with difficulty understand himself and his activities as interrelated in morally meaningful ways with those of other, different Americans" (Bellah et al. 1985:50). Unlike Bellah et al., I believe that the description of U.S. culture found in *Habits of the Heart* is limited primarily to the white middle class. As sanctuary workers were, for the most part, white middle-class people, this quotation fits their experience.

12. This wedding was an example of a community-based ritual, similar to the house dedication described in Chapter 10.

13. See Chapter 2 for a description of the role of this lectionary group in the history of sanctuary in the East Bay.

14. Douglas (1977) noted that during the nineteenth century, the membership of U.S. congregations shifted from predominantly male to predominantly female.

15. See Lorentzen 1991 for an analysis of these views.

16. Men, as well as women, discussed the costs of dividing their time between sanctuary work and their own families. For example, Russell Armstrong of Tucson emphasized that "the sons and daughters of sanctuary workers are often under a great deal of stress." Another Arizona sanctuary worker told me he'd had to curtail his sanctuary work after he and his wife had children. However, I did not hear men use fathering as a justification or inspiration for sanctuary work in the way that women talked about mothering.

# 9

## Practicing Change

*We want our country to act justly. And when it is acting unjustly, then in order to live with ourselves, we must act justly as individuals.*
—Randy Silbert, a Tucson border worker

In constructing the movement, sanctuary workers not only formulated a social critique but also used this critique to shape day-to-day sanctuary work. As a result, movement strategies became ends in and of themselves. Sanctuary workers disagreed about the movement's ultimate goals, defining these variously as securing refugee status for Salvadoran and Guatemalan immigrants, ending warfare in El Salvador and Guatemala, and changing the structures that caused both warfare and refugeeism. As they pursued these goals, activists achieved more immediate objectives. First, by acting in solidarity with the oppressed, participants created alternatives to what they considered militaristic and imperialistic relationships between North and Central Americans. Second, participants constructed their volunteer work in opposition to the careerism, materialism, and individualism that they believed characterized wage labor. Third, by grounding their work in the prophetic tradition, sanctuary workers sought to overcome the secularism that they felt made the church accommodationist and the government unjust. Regardless of the ultimate success or failure of movement strategies, enacting these ideals incrementally changed society.

Because they conceptualize protest as an instrumental process, recent social movement theorists have assessed the success of social movements in terms that ignore the kinds of changes enacted by sanctuary practices.[1] To discredit the view, popular within pre-1960s social movement research, that protest is an irrational expression of discontent, resource mobilization theorists have argued that individuals protest to achieve certain ends—usually their own interests (Jenkins 1983; Olson 1968; Oberschall 1973; Zald and McCarthy 1979; Tarrow 1988; Tilly 1984; Klandermans 1984).[2] For example, after reviewing numerous definitions of social movements, sociologists Marwell and Oliver concluded, "Clearly, any theory of how and why people participate in social movements ... must treat the elementary behavioral stuff of a social movement as essentially instrumental, that is, as oriented to the accomplishment of particular ends" (1984:5).[3] Because they assume that protest is a means to an end, researchers have assessed the success of protest movements by comparing their objectives to their outcomes. Thus, to evaluate the effectiveness of various movement strategies,[4] William Gamson (1975) studied the goals, tactics, and outcomes of fifty-three movement organizations. Gamson defined full success as achieving the movement's goals and being accepted as the legitimate spokesperson for the movement's constituency, partial success as garnering either the sought-after benefits *or* legitimacy, and complete failure as obtaining neither. Similarly, Piven and Cloward (1977) judged the efficacy of the 1960s urban riots by assessing whether rioters forced elites to grant concessions that were in rioters' class interests.

Though measuring movements' outcomes against participants' goals facilitates comparative research, it both overestimates researchers' abilities to identify movement goals and outcomes and underestimates the degree to which movement *practices* constitute social change. Setting aside the question of differences between actors' "true" and "perceived" interests (see Lukes 1974), there are difficulties in determining even the *stated* goals of a particular movement. Movement goals vary over time, in different contexts, and from participant to participant (Marwell and Oliver 1984). The difficulty of identifying movement goals makes evaluating the outcomes of social movements even more problematic. Whose goals must be achieved for a movement to be considered successful? And to what degree? Moreover, protestors, like politicians, can retrospectively redefine goals to transform apparent failures into successes (Gerlach and Hine 1970). Similarly, when movements are losing momentum because some of their goals have been achieved, participants sometimes set new objectives of the "what remains to be done" variety. Yet, even if clear-cut goals could be established and outcomes evaluated, protest does not just seek to achieve predetermined objectives. In addition, protestors create practices, institutions, relationships, and systems of meaning— in short, movements—that enact their understanding of truth and their notion of justice (Melucci 1989; Evans and Boyte 1986; Tipton 1982). Even when the costs of action far outweigh the benefits, or when an effort is glaringly futile, individuals sometimes protest simply because this is what they must do in order to live with themselves.[5] People follow their consciences not only in an altruistic sense but also because, as Talal Asad (1983a, 1983b) has noted, particular ways of defining reality authorize and require corresponding courses of action. As a result, the types of actions protestors take are shaped *both* by long-term goals and by participants' notions of justice.

Fully assessing the changes wrought by social movements entails treating movement practices both as strategies and as enactments of participants' ideals. In the course of pursuing long-term objectives, protestors engage discourses of power that may seem only indirectly relevant to the particular grievance a movement addresses. When protestors devise movement actions, they undermine and/ or reinforce the power relations intrinsic to these discourses. As a result, the day-to-day practice of protest gives participants an opportunity to enact the princi-

ples that protestors accept and formulate when they become involved. By select-
ing among and improvising on preexisting practices, protestors reshape and reproduce power-laden discourses on an ongoing basis. Such reshapings
incrementally alter society, thus making movement actions *both* means to ends
and ends in themselves. Therefore, far from being fixed, protestors' goals are im-
provisations, constructed and reconstructed for different times, settings, and audiences.[6] Such, at least, was the case within the sanctuary movement.

### Band-Aids and Root Causes

In interviews, meetings, and private discussions, I encountered widespread
disagreement about whether sanctuary was a refugee rights movement, an
antiwar movement, or a movement to challenge the institutional structures of oppression. Although advocates of each of these perspectives were to be found in
both Tucson and the East Bay, in general, Tucson sanctuary workers saw the
movement's goal as saving refugees' lives, East Bay volunteers compared sanctuary to the anti–Vietnam War protests, and those whom I met at national meetings
argued that to be successful, sanctuary had to challenge institutionalized imperialism. The refugee rights perspective focused on direct services, the structural
change position confronted the root causes of oppression in Central America, and
the antiwar contingent tried to do both. Another way of differentiating these three
positions is to say that the proponents of refugee rights claimed to have primarily
humanitarian motives, those who challenged structures generally characterized
themselves as political, and the antiwar activists said their work pursued both political and humanitarian ends.

Having made these generalizations, I should note that in actuality, the lines de-
marcating these three perspectives were blurred. To some extent, sanctuary workers considered all of these positions somewhat valid, and individual participants
sometimes combined them or prioritized first one then the other. For example,
Marilyn Phillips, a Tucsonan whose border work had been closely linked to refugee rights, told me, "The real issue is how can people of faith work structurally to
change oppression? We can't just do Band-Aid work; we can't just provide shelter
and give people food." Despite sounding like an advocate of challenging structures, Marilyn told me a moment later, "Sanctuary isn't the base from which to
build a large coalition to challenge the structures that cause oppression in the
world." She then concluded that sanctuary was a religious and humanitarian
movement that ought not take political stances about the conflict in Central
America. Clearly, it would be difficult to pigeonhole Marilyn's position in the
schema outlined above.

Participants disagreed not only about the movement's ultimate goals but also
about what would constitute success. When I asked movement members what
would have to happen for the sanctuary movement to have achieved its purpose, a
few said that the movement had already outlived its usefulness, some said that as

long as there were refugees there would be a sanctuary movement, others spoke of the need for peace and justice in Central America, and one woman, reflecting on the kingdom of God, argued that for the movement to be totally successful, Christ would have to come again. Martha Madeira, who volunteered half-time in the EBSC office, did not measure the value of social action by its outcome: "People spend their whole lifetimes at these kinds of things, and things aren't that much different when they're done, but that doesn't mean you shouldn't do it. You just do what you can. It's accomplished small things along the way, but when you consider changing policies, it hasn't been a terrific success, but that doesn't mean you stop trying." Those who brought refugees across the border assessed sanctuary's effectiveness not only by its ultimate objectives but also according to the lives that participants saved on a daily and weekly basis.

Despite blurred distinctions and varied answers, a deeper exploration of the refugee rights, antiwar, and structural change perspectives reveals participants' understandings of movement goals. To order this exploration, I shall use a series of parables that four sanctuary workers told me. These parables were about unidentified bodies floating down a mysterious river, which sometimes was in Africa and sometimes at the U.S.-Mexico border.[7] The tellers of these river parables assumed, in most cases, that I would already be familiar with this story. It was the kind of instructional tale that a church's confirmation class might consider while discussing religious values, that a minister might include in a sermon (in fact, the minister at First Church did begin one of his services with a similar anecdote), or that a church might print on the back of a Sunday morning bulletin.

I heard the first river parable one spring day in Berkeley during an interview with Sam Gersch, pastor of one of the original sanctuary congregations. When I asked him what role the church should play in influencing U.S. refugee and Central American policy, Sam answered:

> You know the story of the people … the bodies that were floating in the river? This is an old African story. And the people would come and pull the bodies out of the river, and finally they realized that it would be better to go up the river and find out who was throwing them in. Or, there's an old anonymous poem, called "The Fence or the Ambulance?" It's about a town at the bottom of a cliff. People keep falling off the cliff, and half the people want to buy an ambulance to put at the bottom of the cliff, and the other half want to put a fence at the top of the cliff so people won't fall off. And then, the whole Good Samaritan story in the New Testament. If the Good Samaritan came the *next* day and found somebody there, and then came the next day and found somebody there, he wouldn't just pick them up and carry them away, he would find out who these people are.
>
> The same thing's true, and that's what's been the genius of the sanctuary movement, is that you can't start necessarily with trying to teach people what's happening in Central America. But you *can* start by introducing them to refugees. And then, once they know them, they say, "But why are they here? Well, they *do* want to go back home! Well, why don't they *go*? Well, this is what's happening down there."

And so, the church begins to realize that it has a responsibility to deal not only with effects but with the causes. And we deal with the cause of refugees who are here, and that is the war. And we deal with the cause of the war, and that's to a great extent the fact that we prop up those dictatorships and we send those military supplies down there.

Sam amassed the weight of an old African story, an anonymous poem, and a biblical parable to support the antiwar position that the church dealt not only with effects but also with causes. The antiwar perspective was grounded not only in this folkloric context but also in a historical analogy whose primacy Sam revealed through a slip of the tongue, saying that his church would give sanctuary "until there's an end to the war in Vietnam—Central America." The Vietnam War had its own morals for sanctuary workers who invoked its memory. Katherine Baerman of First Church, saying she sometimes felt like Sisyphus, told me, "It took nearly ten years before we finally got out of Nam. ... I know change is possible." Those who concluded that ending war was a long-term struggle found the immediacy of sanctuary's hands-on work with refugees both rewarding and powerful—in contrast to the distance between Vietnamese people and anti–Vietnam war protestors. For example, Farrah Roberts told me, "When you get closer to individuals, ... it keeps you in touch with what you're doing the whole thing for." Antiwar sanctuary workers hoped that, through the consciousness-raising described by Sam Gersch, aiding refugees would eventually sway U.S. public opinion against further military aid to Central American governments and thus end the war. Helping refugees was not only a tactic for ending human rights abuses but also an antiwar strategy. According to the antiwar perspective, sanctuary brought participants "up the river" to address both effects and causes.

Having grown used to claims that sanctuary was both applying Band-Aids and addressing root causes, I was surprised when, during my second interview in Tucson, Ernie Tarkington, the minister of a local sanctuary congregation, related the following:

There's a story that Marc [an influential local pastor] tells about pulling babies from the stream, and how after you pull babies from the stream for a while, you decide to go upstream and to find out how the babies are getting into the stream in the first place. Well, here in Tucson, we're largely pulling babies from the stream. We've kept that religious focus.

Unlike Sam Gersch, Ernie ignored the obvious moral of the story and instead used the river parable to *distinguish* the religious (and therefore, in Ernie's eyes, less political) focus of Tucson sanctuary work from approaches that addressed not only effects but causes. Moreover, in Ernie's version of the tale, dead bodies were replaced by (presumably) living—and therefore salvageable—babies. Rather than being represented as an African folktale, Ernie's parable was attributed to a local minister and thus grounded in the Tucson sanctuary community. In addition, Ernie portrayed Tucson's commitment to meeting refugees' immediate needs as an idiosyncrasy and gave no explanation for what he defined as his and his colleagues' decision not to go upstream.

Several months later, I heard a more compelling rendering of the decision to focus on pulling people out of the river. While describing the dilemmas caused by sanctuary work, Marilyn Phillips, a former Tucson border worker, told me:

> I had a dream once back when I was working in Texas. I dreamed that I was crossing a bridge over a river. And I could see that there were all of these people in the river drowning, and so I began to pull them out one by one and to do CPR, but there were always more of them drowning. That was the feeling that I had at the time. How do you choose who to save?

Unlike Ernie's and Sam's quasi-mythical parables, Marilyn's parable, reminding me of grainy newspaper photographs and headlines about drownings in the Rio Grande, emerged from her dreams. In this version, it was Marilyn herself who was confronted with the drowning-yet-salvageable people and who had to decide whether to pull them out or to go upstream.[8] The choice was so obvious to Marilyn that she did not mention an alternative, saying simply, "And so I began to pull them out." The futility of her rescue efforts and the anguish of her question ("How do you choose who to save?") conveyed the urgency of suffering and the overwhelming number of the dying.

It was this sense of urgency that fueled Tucson sanctuary workers' efforts to provide transportation, refuge, food, housing, employment, health care, emotional support, and legal aid to Central Americans who had just fled torture, bombings, death squads, and war. It is important to note that, despite the overwhelming nature of these tasks, members of the Tucson sanctuary community also sought to address the causes of persecution in Central America. Some participants adhered to the antiwar perspective that traditional sanctuary work did just that. Others sought to address root causes through additional activities, such as attending weekly anti-interventionist vigils at the Tucson Federal Building. Within Tucson, however, there was also a contingent of people who, like Ernie Tarkington, believed that due to Tucson's location near the border, Tucson sanctuary workers had a unique responsibility to concentrate on refugee assistance and to leave political advocacy to other regions of the movement. Some of these refugee rights–oriented sanctuary workers argued that helping refugees actually accomplished more than did efforts to institute political change. For example, Flora Grant, a Tucson border worker, told me, "I've never felt that I can change what's going on in Central America; I can only put Band-Aids on some of the wounds and injuries that have occurred. ... I see this as something I can physically do, whereas if I'm out marching or protesting or writing letters, I don't see any end. I don't see anything real in that area." Although refugee rights proponents acknowledged that sanctuary had political implications, they rejected the idea that helping refugees was a political strategy. Alva Armstrong explained, "I've seen that people have been tortured, they have scars, and I've noticed that many of them have memory deficits because of being tortured with electric shock. ... So, to even suggest that people be moved around on the basis of political efficacy is an obscenity."[9] Gina Holmes, noting that there were refugees from both the Left and the Right, told me simply, "I believe in helping people, not causes." For advocates of the refugee rights perspective, the ultimate goal of sanctuary work was helping refugees.

Though they argued that saving refugees' lives accomplished more than did struggling for political change in Central America, refugee rights advocates *did* seek to alter U.S. refugee policy. This aspect of their work became clear to me when, at a Tucson "metamorphosis" retreat, a sanctuary worker invoked the fence and ambulance story to argue that sanctuary should shift from simply picking up the pieces of people's lives to taking proactive steps. This participant asked his coworkers, "Are we going to simply sit at the bottom of the cliff waiting for people to fall off?" In response to this question, Marc Talbot, an influential local minister, disputed the speaker's characterization of sanctuary work, pointing out that civil initiative *was* proactive in that it had led the INS to change some of its immigration policies. Later, during an interview, Marc explained that using traditional sanctuary work to oppose U.S. foreign policy (by, for example, only aiding refugees who were critical of their governments) could *undermine* attempts to force the United States to recognize refugees' rights:

> The problem with refugee policy in the United States is that the Reagan administration has looked at refugee policy and said, "We'd like to politicize that." And there are those in the sanctuary movement who would like to make the sanctuary movement the mirror image of the Reagan administration and simply say, "They're wrong about their politics, but we ought to politicize, or we ought to deal with this as a political issue." And I think both of those are wrong—conceptually, legally, as well as *theologically.*

Now consider two more river parables, both related during an interview with Jerry Alegria, a Tucson Catholic whose church was resettling Ramon Palacios and his family. While arguing that U.S. immigration policy failed to take responsibility for U.S. complicity in the causes of Central American refugeeism, Jerry embarked on a river parable:

> *Jerry:* There's a classic story that's told in—I assume it's in Christian churches—I've only heard it in Catholic churches. About the tribe who lives on the river? Have you heard that story?
>
> *Susan:* And they're throwing—
>
> *Jerry:* They see dead bodies coming down the river?

*Susan:* That's right.

*Jerry:* And they take them out because they're Christians, and they give them burial, and all of that thing. They never look to see what's causing the dead bodies to come down the damn river! And that's been, I think, a *failing* on the part of Christian churches, certainly on the part of Catholic churches, for a long time. We fail to look to the structural causes of pestilence, famine, plague, war, etc. And we do the *charitable* thing. We take the bodies out of the river because we are Christians, we pat ourselves on the back because we give them Christian burial, and we do all of those good things that Christians do! But we never look up the river to see what the heck is going on that's causing those dead bodies to come down the road. Part of the reason—this is my amendment now to that story—part of the reason we don't look up the river is that deep down inside, we realize that we are doing something that's causing those dead bodies to come down the river, and we don't want to look at that.

Jerry's parable recreates the mythical, foreign setting where dead bodies (not salvageable people) float down an unnamed river. Unlike Ernie's and Marilyn's stories, in which those on the shore busily save lives, Jerry's tribe merely provides Christian burial. In Jerry's story, the tribe's refusal to investigate causes cannot be attributed to the urgent need of saving suffering people. Rather, the tribe ignores the causes of suffering to avoid confronting distasteful and horrifying truths about themselves. In Jerry's parable, the tribe/church pats itself on the back for doing charity work instead of truly confronting its own complicity in the killing. Jerry's point in telling this story was the opposite of Sam Gersch's. Where Sam argued that the church *had* realized it must deal with both cause and effect, Jerry contended that the church *had failed* to make this realization. Jerry positioned the church—and thus himself—within the structures of oppression that needed to be changed.

On the heels of this parable, Jerry told another, which, like Marilyn Phillips', moved the river to the U.S.-Mexico border:

The classic example of the thing I'm talking about is a piece on "60 Minutes" about American companies who, because they don't want to abide by the pollution control laws in San Diego, are moving down to Tijuana, and they're dumping their pollution into the river in Tijuana out of the purview of United States law. The *ironic,* the *deliciously ironic* thing about that is that the river flows north! And so all that pollution is coming back again to the United States!

Out of myth and into the world of "60 Minutes," this river parable illustrated Jerry's conviction that the world is interconnected: Just as the structures of oppression extended from the United States into Central America, the suffering—the "pollution"—threatened the United States and Central America alike.

Like refugee rights activists, those who challenged imperialist structures stressed U.S. complicity and attacked systems of injustice in their interconnected entirety. Although its advocates could be found in Tucson and Berkeley, I associate this perspective with the Call to Sanctuary meeting that I attended in Chicago in July 1987.[10] The statement inviting people to attend the meeting declared holistically, "We are confronted by an imperial ideology embedded in structures of violence that dominate the poor and resistant in the name of democracy and national security." On the first day of the three-day meeting, after participating in a group analysis of the current realities in the United States, El Salvador, and Guatemala, I wrote in my notebook, "Basically, the way that this meeting seems to be related to refugee issues is that of cause and effect. People are trying to deal with the *causes* not only of refugeeism but also of [the] oppression that causes war that displaces people." The holistic analysis and the exposure of complicity that Jerry incorporated into his river parables pervaded the meeting. A paper entitled "Analysis of the Sanctuary Movement," which was written by a Chicago participant and distributed at the meeting, denounced "the viciousness of the U.S. government and capitalist system in its slaughter of people around the world."

Although less strongly worded, such denunciations of imperialism were not limited to the structural change perspective. For example, both antiwar and refugee rights advocates sought to counter imperialism by identifying with the poor. Moreover, sanctuary workers' attempts to carry out social ideals in their daily lives were built on holistic analysis.

What differentiated the structural change position from the refugee rights and antiwar perspectives was its conclusion that traditional sanctuary work had *failed* to address the causes of oppression and was therefore insufficient. In sharp contrast to advocates of the refugee rights perspective, the proponents of structural change criticized humanitarian efforts for allowing oppressive structures to remain intact. For example, Gloria Murdock of Tucson wondered, "Is sanctuary the best way to stop the war in Central America? Are we simply draining Central America of its life-blood?"[11] Proponents of structural change were more willing to take political stands than their antiwar and refugee rights counterparts. Echoing Jerry Alegria's notions of church complicity, Gloria Murdock criticized U.S. churches' reluctance to support armed movements such as the FMLN (Frente Farabundo Martí para Liberación Nacional, the Farabundo Martí National Liberation Front) and the EGP (Ejército guerrillero de pobres, Guerrilla Army of the Poor). Similarly, Angel Muñoz, a Salvadoran refugee living in Tucson, told me that the bottom line in his own analysis was whether the sanctuary movement contributed to or worked against revolutionary movements in Central America. Advocates of changing structures argued that when defined primarily as "helping refugees," sanctuary was paternalistic, outdated work that addressed symptoms rather than causes. The "Analysis of the Sanctuary Movement" sheet concluded, "Because we have neither adequately defined nor fully understand the historical depth of these structures of violence we have also failed to plan future directions that might begin to neutralize those structures. ... For the sanctuary movement to simply do more of the same for the next two years will be disastrous for the people of Central America." Proponents of structural change wanted to lay down their trowels, stop providing Christian burial, go upstream, and devise new tactics to end the flow of dead bodies down the river.

The ambiguity of, shifts in, and disagreement about movement goals did not prevent sanctuary workers from devising practices meant to acheive their objectives.[12] Giving sanctuary to undocumented Central Americans, traveling to refugee camps in Honduras, collecting food for refugee groups, sending telegrams to protest human rights abuses, organizing religious services, and performing other movement activities could all be defined as methods of aiding refugees, opposing war, challenging oppressive structures, or some combination of the three. However, movement actions not only pursued these goals but also redefined the discourses that such actions engaged. An examination of the principles guiding sanctuary work reveals that movement activities practiced the movement's critique of Orientalism, careerism, and secularism. This approach to changing society drew on popular theories about the political impact of individual action. Like Southern Baptists who sought to live "a Christian life that is so exemplary that it seems to invite imitation or acceptance without any direct preaching" (Greenhouse 1986:84), sanctuary workers hoped that their actions would serve as examples to others. Sanctuary workers' efforts to practice change were also reminiscent of 1960s counterculture, the feminist movement's contention that "the personal is political," and the more recent political slogan, "Live simply that others might simply live." These religious and political approaches emphasized process as much as result. One young college student and border worker told me that even if he knew that he were going to die the following day, he would still do border work because "there's a way of living your life that's right." Because they were also rooted in power-laden discourses, however, sanctuary workers' efforts to construct just practices, like the critiques that they enacted and engendered, were politically contradictory.

### Solidarity

On March 22, 1987, two days before the anniversary of Archbishop Romero's assassination, a month-long caravan of North and Central American activists returned to San Francisco. At an interfaith service, caravan participants became ritually reintegrated into the community. Carrying banners and posters of the archbishop, we formed a silent processional, walking slowly to the front of a huge Catholic church as two guitarists played and sang:

> *So-li-dari-dad! So-li-dari-dad!*
> *Manos y fuerzas que se funden en una vida y un solo caminat.*
> *So-li-dari-dad! So-li-dari-dad!*[13]

Solidarity. The word that echoed that day in the fairly empty church building represented one of the ideals that movement participants sought to enact within their work. As they reevaluated their own social reality through movement discourse, participants concluded that relationships between the United States and Central America were characterized by imperialism, distance, paternalism, and exploitation—in short, the hierarchical and hegemonic system that generated Orientalism. To counter this system, sanctuary workers strove to act *in solidarity* with the Central Americans they assisted. Volunteers defined solidarity as a relationship in which North Americans abandoned their privileged positions in order to support the struggles of Salvadoran and Guatemalan refugees. Philip Kaspar, a former Tucson border worker, explained, "Sanctuary creates a human bond, a bond that's based on compassion rather than on expediency, legality, etc.," and Gail Stewart, an East Bay participant, pointed out that "you can say no to a political movement that's abstract, but you can't say no to your friends when they're in need." To make their relationships with Salvadorans and Guatemalans collegial rather than hierarchical, sanctuary workers attempted to share the risks that Central Americans confronted. For example, a Tucson congregation loaned money to a Mexican parish in pesos rather than dollars so that the Tucson congregation would share in the vulnerability of the Mexican currency. Though such actions did deconstruct the relationships that Orientalism derived from and authorized, solidarity was also in some ways a *product* of Orientalism. By representing Central Americans, rather than, for example, impoverished U.S. citizens, as "the poor," movement members subjected Central Americans to the quest for knowledge that Orientalism generates.

The principle of solidarity—a principle that did not pertain to one set of sanctuary practices but that rather pervaded movement culture—was constructed *in opposition to* what many participants viewed as military, economic, and cultural imperialism on the part of the U.S. government. A northern California participant's description of the U.S. embassy conveyed his understanding of the government's role in Central America. At a slide show presentation about his trip to El Salvador, the speaker related:

> We walked past the American embassy. To me that was another rather shocking moment of the trip, to be exposed to that atmosphere. It says so much, I think, about the role of the American government in the country, that the embassy is a fortified compound with a ten-foot-high, three-foot-thick concrete wall [that] entirely surrounds the embassy complex. Back at the corner you can see one of the guard towers where the Salvadoran military is constantly stationed with machine guns. These things that look like planters on the left-hand side of the picture are actually intended as antitank defenses. It gives you some idea of the mentality that is held by the people who live inside this place.

Father Thomás Kendrick of Tucson criticized U.S. imperialism by pointing out that in Mexico, Wonder bread had replaced nutritious corn tortillas, while Lydia Crawford, an EBSC Steering Committee representative, denounced "[U.S.] companies that stay fifteen years or more [in Central America] and make all their profits in a little town, and then pull out, and leave it totally devastated." Through solidarity, participants sought to create alternatives to imperialism in their own relationships with Central Americans. At a Task Force meeting, participants stressed that, rather than entering Mexico with a "yankee" attitude, it was important to respect the opinions of Latin Americans. Simon Portnoy and Charles O'Brien, two Tucson participants, abandoned plans to tour Latin American seminaries to teach about sanctuary when they realized, as Simon explained during an interview, that this would look "like Gringos going down to Latin America to tell them what to do there. "

In addition to countering imperialism, solidarity was meant to undermine the isolationism that many participants felt typified middle-class U.S. culture. Although it may appear contradictory to critique the United States for both interventionism and isolationism, sanctuary workers connected the two, arguing that the U.S. populace was insulated from and therefore indifferent to the poverty and suffering caused by the U.S. government's foreign policies. For example, Genevieve Gallegos, an EBSC staff member, said of North Americans, "We're insulated, and we're very middle class. We're very much like licking a lollipop. ... You want to live in your nice little house, all wrapped up in a cocoon, and not know what's going on." Similarly, Gail Stewart, one of Genevieve's colleagues, believed that even when they traveled, most North Americans failed to leave their own world behind. Gail commented, "They live in their suburbs and they don't really go outside them a whole lot. Even if they go to Paris, are they really going outside their suburb mentally or emotionally? And they cannot identify with other peoples of the Third World." By identifying with Central Americans, sanctuary workers sought to connect themselves to events in El Salvador and Guatemala. A Tucson pastor explained that sanctuary entailed "a *removal* from culture and government to a position where they [participants] are associated with refugees. ... It's an act that says, 'I'm not a part of that,' and an entry into a community of faith with the refugees. ... If they kill Archbishop Romero, they kill our archbishop."

Solidarity was an alternative not only to imperialism and isolationism but also to charity, which participants criticized for being paternalistic and accommodationist. Sam Gersch, pastor of one of the original EBSC congregations, told me that originally, East Bay churches conceptualized sanctuary as analogous to sponsoring Vietnamese refugees. They soon concluded, however, that "sponsorship" was paternalistic and moved toward "partnership" with Central Americans. Anya Fischer, member of an East Bay sanctuary synagogue, believed that by listening to refugees rather than instructing them, sanctuary workers had achieved such partnership. Anya said, "The sanctuary movement ... wasn't a bunch of *Norteamericanos* sitting up there deciding what we think is good and what we should do. The clues always come from the refugees themselves. 'How can we help you?' 'What needs doing?'" Participants distinguished sanctuary from charity work on the basis of its political impact as well as its egalitarianism.

For example, José Martín, a Salvadoran community organizer, contended that "sanctuary isn't just giving clothes to the naked or giving water to the thirsty. Rather, sanctuary is working for a future of dignity and of justice." Similarly, Martin Reiner, a Phoenix minister, stated that sanctuary "isn't just caring for individuals; it goes beyond that to structural changes, even just through becoming friends with Latin Americans."

Finally, participants viewed solidarity with the oppressed as a way for North Americans to atone for having exploited Third World peoples. Joanna Spoakes, an East Bay volunteer, commented, "I've spent a lot of time in the Third World, and I think I've suffered from guilt. ... It's hard to be a member of the First World and see the effects of our government's policy." Similarly, Karen Hirsch, one of Joanna's colleagues, told me, "I feel even more responsibility [to act] because our government is perpetuating this horror that's happening. Not that I'm personally responsible, but I'm somewhat responsible. I vote for these people." Linda Allen, an EBSC staff member, lamented:

> This First World society is doomed, and ... the only hope comes from the Third World. I don't know. ... We deserve to be wiped off the face of the world for what we're doing to the rest of the world. We deserve it. And if there was a just God—you read some of the psalms and you hear the people saying, "Kill them, kill them, for what they're doing to me and my children!" And you can see the Third World saying that about the United States! And the Soviet Union! Same thing; different face. And First World Europe.

Linda's comment that hope lay in the Third World was echoed by other participants. After giving his testimony to a northern California sanctuary group, José Martín, a Salvadoran community organizer, was asked by an audience member, "Are there Christian base communities in the United States, and if so, how can I join one?" José answered, "If people here in the United States become in solidarity with the people of Central America, then they can address the sin of sending the bombs that this government sends to El Salvador to kill us. And they can address this social sin by working in this country to stop the actions of their government."

Although solidarity opposed imperialism, isolationism, charitable approaches, and exploitation, it contained a mystification. When participants claimed to be acting in solidarity with "the oppressed," they actually meant "persecuted and impoverished Salvadorans and Guatemalans." The fact that they were passing over the U.S. poor to act in solidarity with the oppressed of other nations was a source of concern for some participants. Rebecca Jonas, an East Bay sanctuary congregation member, wondered, "Consider the situation of the [U.S.] homeless. Why is it that we aren't all rushing out and opening our arms to the homeless?" Similarly, a hunger activist said she would like to tell sanctuary congregations, "*Look!* You're a sanctuary congregation? You're taking these people from 10,000 miles away into your homes, and you won't even look at the person who's hanging around on your church sidewalk." Participants resolved this dilemma in a number of ways. Some argued that, as in the case of the Vietnamese, U.S. atrocities had given U.S. citizens a personal responsibility to assist Central American refugees. Others contended that, due to the severity of human rights violations in Central America, the Salvadoran and Guatemalan poor experienced greater suffering than the U.S. poor. Flora Grant of Tucson pointed out that unlike the U.S. poor, undocumented refugees could not turn to government agencies for assistance. Finally, some noted that congregations and individuals were often involved in more than one cause and that sanctuary work did not preclude assisting the homeless and minorities.

Nonetheless, these arguments only partially explain why Salvadorans and Guatemalans seemed to represent the quintessential "oppressed" to members of the sanctuary movement. In addition, the movement's construction of subjugation was implicated within its Orientalist representation of Central Americans. It was the *Central American* poor who were seen as closer to God, as examples to emulate, as the victims of "our" gluttony, and as representations of the authenticity that "we" once had. Such images of Central Americans were made possible—despite efforts to create personal relationships with Salvadorans and Guatemalans— by the *distance* between sanctuary workers and refugees. To North American sanctuary workers, Central Americans were culturally, linguistically, and ethnically "other." Therefore, they were subject to the West's hegemonic tendency to produce "the Orient" by "making statements about it, authorizing views of it, describing it, by teaching it, settling it, ruling over it" (Said 1979:3). Though their attempts to share the reality of the Central American poor enabled participants to oppose structures of power, this act of resistance simultaneously reproduced culturally ingrained Orientalist tendencies to know, define, and create representations of non-Western peoples.

Sanctuary workers' wishes to act in solidarity with the Central American poor were closely linked to another ideal that participants sought to practice within their work: being of service to others.

## Voluntarism

Sanctuary workers attributed the hierarchical relationships between the United States and Central America to, among other things, an economic system that placed personal ambition above the social good. To counter the individualism, careerism, and materialism that they believed made this system possible, sanctuary workers volunteered with the movement, thus acting for the benefit of others with no (or, in the case of paid staff, little) remuneration in ways that, if anything, detracted from their careers.[14] Because participants considered careerism, materialism, and individualism traits that characterized men more often than women, voluntarism, whether performed by men or women, was a gendered practice. Like solidarity, voluntarism was not one action but rather a principle (and, given the movement's resources, an economic necessity) that was carried out through almost all movement actions. Sanctuary workers volunteered by bringing Central Americans across the border, giving sanctuary, organizing press conferences, translating for refugees during medical appointments, speaking publicly, planning religious services, arranging delegations to Central America, and so on. As acts of service, these activities were alternatives to the (more often than not, participants felt, male) self-interest that movement members believed fueled the U.S. economic system. At the same time, voluntarism in some ways promoted and derived from the power relations that it opposed. Critiquing careerism valorized class-based notions of gender, while sanctuary workers' abilities to volunteer were, to an extent, dependent on their class positions.

Though almost all sanctuary activities constituted volunteer work, my discussion of voluntarism focuses on the EBSC office because it was there that the parallels and contrasts between volunteering and wage-labor were most explicit—and where, not coincidentally, the gap between male and female participation was widest.[15] Though other forms of volunteering were more evenly divided between men and women, approximately 85 percent of EBSC's office volunteers were women. EBSC office volunteers performed secretarial tasks such as answering phones, making copies, filling information packets, making phone calls, receiving visitors, and stuffing envelopes. Much of this work was fairly mundane. Rosemary Graefe, a former office volunteer, observed, "A lot of people … fantasize about volunteering … and doing noble deeds and so on. When they realize that really what we're talking about is paperwork and answering the phone, it really loses people." In contrast to most volunteer work outside the office, office volunteers *filled shifts* rather than *performing specific tasks*. For instance, an office volunteer might work from 1:00–5:00 P.M. every Monday, whereas a health-care translator would accompany a monolingual refugee to a medical appointment and would work until this task was finished. Office volunteers thus participated in the commodification of time characteristic of industrial capitalism (Thompson 1967)—except that, rather than working for an hourly wage, office volunteers *donated* their hours. As a result, office volunteers—like wage-laborers—were somewhat alienated from the results of their labor. During their shifts, office volunteers frequently worked on tasks that were begun during a previous shift and that would be finished by another volunteer the following day. Karen Hirsch, an office volunteer, criticized the "day-to-day drudgery" of office work and commented, "I want more of a sense that I'm really helping people." Similarly, Martha Madeira, one of the most committed office volunteers, felt that, rather than being important in itself, her office work freed other people to do the more important tasks.

Despite the fact that volunteering in the EBSC office closely resembled paid secretarial work, office volunteers felt that the fact that they received no material compensation distinguished the value of their work from labor whose worth was measured in wages. Moreover, volunteers characterized the idea that paid labor was more valuable than volunteer work as a *male* notion. Anita Garvey, an office volunteer, declared that although she did not consider "grunt-work" humiliating, "a man ... might think, 'Boy, these people are really abusing me.' Because they're [men are] not used to donating four hours, and then just collating stuff." Rosemary Graefe found that her volunteer work fulfilled a higher social purpose than her paid work: "A lot of the things that I do on a daily basis at my job are fairly meaningless. ... [But,] doing something like a leaflet for a particular [sanctuary] event, as humble as that may seem, is a very direct kind of act. You disseminate some information." Rosemary added, "If a man who's in my same position, say, who's thirty-two years old, who has a full-time job, is making good money, ... is confronted with the option of giving up some of his work hours to go and sit in an office and answer a phone," he would find it demeaning. Ted Rezier, one of the male office volunteers, agreed, commenting that in the United States, men are more oriented "toward getting ahead in a job" than are women. Farrah Roberts, a retiree and office worker who volunteered full-time for a variety of causes, noted that people "feel that their efforts aren't worth anything unless they're paid for it. They really do. People look down on volunteer work, that it can't be very valuable. The ego is not bolstered by it. ... If society doesn't value it enough to pay you in dollars, that's the criterion." Farrah added, "Men have been taught that if they're worth anything, they have to get dollars for it. Women haven't."

Even the work of *paid* office staff critiqued careerism, as paid staff members had chosen to work for low wages for a social cause rather than pursuing more lucrative career options. In the East Bay, the paid staff (all of whom were women) had volunteered with the movement before they had been hired, so their motives for obtaining these paid positions were not only financial. Similarly, in Tucson, it was generally agreed that the Task Force staff (one man and one woman) were making a financial sacrifice in order to hold these positions. While I was in Tucson, the staff members were being remunerated at half-time wages for full-time work. Because of the low wages, one Task Force staff member needed a second job to pay for rent and transportation. Because funding for paid positions in both Tucson and the East Bay depended on grants and donations, paid staff members lacked job security. In fact, after I left the East Bay, several funding sources were lost and the number of paid staff was cut from six to two. Staff members in both Tucson and the East Bay occupied a more precarious financial position than did volunteers, most of whom had secure sources of income outside the movement. During an interview, one EBSC staff member discussed the dilemma posed by her indeterminate position:

I've realized that I'm not going to be doing sanctuary forever. The money isn't coming in like it used to, plus it just won't last that long. ... We're [my husband and I are] at a point where the two questions, "How can we be happy?" and "How can we be faithful?" are converging and becoming the same question. ... [But,] I have to think about things like, how badly do I want to have security? ... I'm going to want those health benefits that come from an established job. And pensions, and all those other things.

EBSC volunteers and staff enacted their critique of careerism by constructing their office work in opposition to profit-oriented workplaces. Unlike employers, EBSC staff members could exert little authority over office volunteers. Volunteers were free to reschedule their shifts, arrive late, choose which task to work on, and even simply fail to show up (although most volunteers were fairly responsible about keeping their commitments). On one occasion, when a staff member violated this norm by somewhat hierarchically asking an office worker to do her typing, the volunteer complained that the request had been too businesslike and instead worked on another task. Well aware of the optional nature of volunteering, staff members frequently expressed their appreciation of office volunteers. For instance, when I was in the office one afternoon, a staff member greeted a volunteer by exclaiming, "I'm so glad you've come! There's lots to be done here and I can't seem to do it because the phones keep ringing. Aren't our volunteers wonderful!" During interviews, office volunteers stressed that their relationships with coworkers were rewarding. Rosemary Graefe found her work in the office an approximation (though not, she admitted, a close one) of the kind of community that existed in Central America. Martha Madeira, another office volunteer, found it refreshing to work alongside people with similar values. Martha said, "I talk to friends about the jobs they have and the people they work with. They have to listen to racist comments all day long. ... I feel really lucky to be able to work in a place with such nice values and people." One male volunteer found the process of volunteering in the office as important as the end result. He observed:

> Sometimes you can do too much in the desire to be helpful, when actually things have a way of working out. ... Like, being around Ella [a staff member] is just amazing to me, because she's so disorganized. She had old files, new files, and working files, but they were all mixed up. And I could never find anything, so I reorganized it. And there are papers flying around everywhere! But when it comes to Ella, the refugees come first, and she would do anything for them. Sometimes just being there near her is more important than what's being accomplished.

Sanctuary workers, whether they volunteered in the EBSC office or elsewhere, found volunteering an act of *service* that countered the notion that, while off work, money and time were to be used solely for personal pleasure.[16] (When they gathered to bid farewell to a college student who had spent a semester doing border work, Trsg members praised him for "a unique trait among sanctuary workers—knowing enough to take off and get away every so often.") Volunteers whom I interviewed expressed the ethic that each individual ought to contribute in some way to the social good. Judith Bromberg of Congregation Aron Kodesh told me that her sanctuary activities assuaged her liberal guilt. She explained that she could enjoy the financial fruits of her paid labor because sanctuary was her weekly *tzedakah,* her contribution to social justice. Using a euphemism for border work, Gina Holmes of Tucson said that she "give[s] up her vacation days to go 'hiking'—which is terrible, because I *love* my vacation days, and with my job, I only get a few." Martha Madeira delineated the ethic of service that motivated her own volunteer work:

> Everything I ever wanted was given to me. Not every little thing, but in terms of major things. And [I've realized] how totally unjust that is, simply through an accident of birth. I mean, other people born in other circumstances don't have that, and it just doesn't make sense to continue through life in the pursuit of personal happiness. ... Really, the only thing that seems worthwhile is to try to do something to help one's fellow human beings.

Lisa Rothstein, a San Francisco sanctuary worker, told me, "None of us should be going about life as usual. ... We should be devoting our lives in some way, whatever way we can, to making changes." Moreover, several volunteers asserted that donating money (the fruits of wage labor) was not a substitute for doing service. For instance, Janice Propp of the East Bay told me that the meaning of religion was "truly living with and accompanying the meek or the humble or the downtrodden, not just writing a check out and sending it in the mail."

Despite its critique of careerism, materialism, and personal ambition, the volunteer work performed by sanctuary activists was facilitated by their class position. As middle-class people, sanctuary workers had the material resources to create offices, develop programs, and do volunteer work. To function, the EBSC office needed donations of office equipment and funding for phone bills, office supplies, staff salaries, photocopying, and so forth, much of which was supplied by member congregations. Moreover, participants' notions of gender were class-based in that they believed that women were more committed to voluntarism than were men—a relic of the days when housewives and nuclear families were the middle-class ideological, if not statistical, norm. Despite the fact that, apart from students and retirees, most sanctuary volunteers, whether male or female, held paid positions in addition to their volunteer activities, many people whom I interviewed *believed* that women volunteered because they did not work.[17] For example, Anya Fischer of Berkeley told me that two-career families heralded the end of voluntarism, while Farrah Roberts feared that working women would fall prey to the materialist, nonvoluntaristic mentality to which she felt men were already subject. Such views were heir to the history of voluntarism in the United States. In the early 1800s, while lower-class women became factory workers, middle- and upper-class women became "ladies" (Lerner 1979:190) who sometimes formed voluntary associations to eradicate social vices (Smith-Rosenberg 1979). These female philanthropists became a class symbol whose endurance is shown, for example, by the role currently ascribed to First Ladies. By deeming careerism a male tendency, participants unintentionally reinforced the sexual stereotype that women were not interested in pursuing careers. Voluntarism, like other aspects of the sanctuary movement, was politically ambiguous.

A question remains: Is it not the case that volunteering with *any* cause critiques careerism, regardless of the practitioners' political perspectives? In a sense, the volunteer work performed by sanctuary workers did not differ from the philanthropy advocated by President George Bush and other conservatives. Adherents of any political persuasion can volunteer, and when they do, they take action for the social good (as they define it) rather than for financial gain. However, the implications of voluntarism within a broader ideological framework differ for different groups. The Bush administration promoted voluntarism not as an alternative to wage labor but rather as a substitute for government programs.[18] In contrast, sanctuary workers' notion of solidarity opposed volunteer work that did not in some way challenge the status quo. For example, Simon Portnoy, a Tucson pastor, criticized "those who for society's good reasons do good work for the poor. That's the Junior League approach. ... That's the charity approach." Additionally, the sanctuary workers whom I interviewed *explicitly* linked their volunteer activities to social justice and contrasted them with the world of work and pay. Merlin Wynn, a member of All Saints who volunteered with a Mexican squatter community, was not alone when he told me:

> You don't get paid for doing the right thing. ... Now, I believe that if you work growing food, or whatever kind of work, you should get back food or whatever you work for equivalent to the hours that you put in. But not when it comes to helping people. Even though you do get it back, but not in money. And if that [what you get back] is the motivator for helping people, then that's a very watered-down version of what it's supposed to be.

Another ideal that sanctuary workers enacted was a notion of religious activism that critiqued the secularism that participants believed pervaded U.S. society. To create such activism, participants grounded their work in the prophetic tradition.

### The Prophetic Tradition

The sanctuary movement blamed the exploitativeness of U.S.–Central American relations and the injustice of the U.S. economic system, in part, on secularism. Participants who leveled this critique (and not all did) argued that because religious truth had become marginal to the workings of society, the United States as a nation was failing to follow God's commandments to do justice. Moreover, the same individuals contended, the North American church had grown so accommodated to the status quo that it had ceased to fulfill its prophetic role. To counter these effects of secularism, sanctuary workers positioned themselves outside of both secular and religious power structures, questioned authorities, and, like the biblical prophets, warned both church and state to either act justly or face God's wrath. Participants called this prophetic fusion of religion and politics "witnessing."[19] Virginia Quillen, an East Bay participant, explained, "The philosophy [underlying the sanctuary movement] is ... that the refugees are human beings who have been done an immense injustice, and we want both to offer humane alternatives for the refugees in our midst, *and* we wish to have a platform from which to protest and witness in relation to the institutional injustices that have gone on." Like solidarity and voluntarism, witnessing was not a specific practice but rather a principle enacted through all public movement actions. Participants witnessed by declaring their congregations sanctuaries, holding prayer vigils, organizing press conferences, and publicizing refugee testimonies. Though witnessing challenged secularism, it also—like solidarity and voluntarism—in some ways reproduced and derived from that which it critiqued. When indicted Tucson sanctuary workers claimed the protection that the First Amendment affords religious practices, they took advantage of a legal system that separates church and state, religion and politics. Moreover, despite its critiques of the organized church, the movement's roots in mainstream congregations provided a source of legitimacy.

Prophetic-minded sanctuary workers argued that, by failing to grant refugee status to Salvadorans and Guatemalans, by providing military aid to governments that persecuted their own peoples, and by profiting from economic exploitation, the United States had broken its covenant with God.[20] Marc Talbot, an influential Tucson pastor, described the nature of this covenant: "'God will give you [Israel] the land and you will be God's people.' But it was not just a one-way street, the gift of God to Israel. Then Israel had some very clear obligations to care for the poor and the widows and to free the captives and to do justice and to see that covenant was pervasive in the whole life of the people of Israel." Reasoning that the biblical covenant between Israel and God provided a prototype for humanity's relationship with the divine, participants argued that the United States, as a nation, was also required to fulfill the obligations specified in this covenant. Jerry Alegria, whose Tucson church was settling a Salvadoran family, explained, "God calls a *people*. It's like in the Old Testament when God spoke through the prophets to the people. He didn't speak to individuals." Some participants concluded that the United States had so violated its covenant obligations that it could no longer expect to enjoy the prosperity God promised to God's people. Larry Hauffen, a Tucson border worker and minister, believed that the United States had reached that critical point: "I fear that this country is losing its soul—and may have already lost it." Similarly, Linda Allen, an East Bay minister, argued that the United States, the Soviet Union, and First World Europe risked divine sanction because of the injustice they had perpetrated on the Third World.

Those sanctuary workers who invoked this covenant to denounce U.S. policy also criticized U.S. churches for failing to remind the United States of its covenant obligations. Participants contended that, far from ensuring that society followed

God's commandments, U.S. churches had allowed *society's* values to shape their practices and structures. Thus, one First Church member characterized the content of her early church life as "accepting pabulum," while a Tucson minister criticized "the Sunday morning church structure where everything happens at 11:00 A.M." Jamie Porter, a Task Force member, commented, "For most traditional churches in the United States, religion is a one time a week thing, and we recite a lot of words, but we don't put them into practice. But with sanctuary, not only do we put them into practice, but we have to risk our well-being to do so." Larry Hauffen, also of Tucson, argued that since the days of Constantine, the church had been co-opted by structures of power. Larry told me:

> For me, the Sermon on the Mount and especially the Beatitudes are the all-demanding creed of a Christian. That, and the Old Testament traditions. The church should be the church that Micah is talking about when he says, "What does the Lord require of you but to do justice and to walk humbly with God?" That doesn't have a treasury of statements or committees! The church must be called to conversion.

Other participants echoed Larry's contention that the church—by which they referred to all people of faith—was intended to question, rather than become part of, the established social order. Flora Grant, a Tucson border worker, pointed out that Jesus himself sided with the poor: "You never heard of Jesus being at a big banquet and all dressed up and all of that. He was always with the lepers and the prostitutes, or the beggars." Similarly, Virginia Quillen, an East Bay Quaker, concluded that Jesus fought against the "institutional injustices in his time—both the Roman occupation, as well as the Jewish society itself. ... But also the church, also the temple."

To counter both the United States's covenant violations and U.S. churches' accommodationism, sanctuary workers sought to follow the example set by the Old Testament prophets. To participants, the prophets were ordinary people who had been called by God to denounce social injustice even at the risk of persecution and martyrdom. In a speech before a Bay Area ecumenical gathering, Congregation Aron Kodesh's rabbi termed this prophetic calling "a choosing not of our own." During an interview in Tucson, Jennie Haight, the pastor of a sanctuary congregation, described experiencing such a choosing. Jennie recounted:

> At the time, I was angry over the calling, because I'd recently become engaged, and I felt that [because I was living in Michigan,] in order to work with sanctuary I would have to move. ... I was angry at having to choose between getting married and fulfilling my calling. Then, about a month later, we found out that my husband—who hadn't anticipated leaving his church in East Lansing—was being offered a position in Tucson. It was providential.

Linda Allen, an East Bay minister, declared that denouncing injustice in El Salvador and Guatemala followed the example of the prophets. Preaching at First

Church one Sunday morning in the absence of the regular minister, Linda gave a gruesome description of how the phosphorous bombs exported to El Salvador burned through skin and bone. She then exhorted the congregation to "announce the truth from the rooftops, screaming it out." Similarly, Marc Talbot, a Tucson pastor, argued that sanctuary was grounded in the prophetic tradition: "A part of that prophetic tradition is the reminder that you are to care about the refugee in your midst, because you were all once refugees yourselves."

By following the prophetic tradition, sanctuary workers constructed a form of activism that they believed was shaped by religious values. Though a minority felt there was no difference between sanctuary and traditional political activism,[21] the majority of those whom I interviewed sharply distinguished between the two. For example, Flora Grant, a Tucson border worker, told me emphatically, "I *never, never* want to be classified as a political activist. ... I work with them, and love them, but I don't—I can't be one. It's just not my make-up." Even some of the movement's nonreligious participants said that they'd chosen to work with sanctuary—rather than a secular group such as the Committee in Solidarity with the People of El Salvador (CISPES)—because of the movement's religious character. Sanctuary workers did not actually *oppose* secular activism (which many practiced in addition to their sanctuary work); rather, they sought to avoid the dogmatism and factionalism that they associated with traditional politics. Linda Allen, an EBSC staff member, told me that unlike secular activism, "Our faith challenges us not to make idols out of what we're doing and always to challenge ourselves. Not to say, 'This is the way, the truth, the light,' but rather to *question* what it is that we're doing." Frustrated with debates about Marxism versus socialism, Terri Sieger was pleased to find the Congregation Aron Kodesh Sanctuary Committee a group whose "work comes from their heart rather than from their intellect." One EBSC staff member told me, "I was very turned off by the political groups because they seemed to be so fanatical. And I really liked sanctuary because it seemed to be sincere." Participants also felt that relationships within the movement were more harmonious than those found in secular groups.[22] For example, one First Church Sanctuary Committee member characterized political activists as having an " 'as it affects me as an American' perspective," whereas faith-based perspectives transcended national divisions. She explained, "It's something I feel real deeply, because we're all part of God's family. ... We all have this right to share in God's kingdom." Marty Finn, an East Bay volunteer who was not religious, chose to work with the sanctuary movement rather than secular activists because

> in the organized Left, it's always "us" and "them." And it's always about things like power. Winning power, keeping power from other people, jockeying for position— what E. P. Thompson called "instrumentalism." ... And I think that a wonderful thing about religious people in general, ... [is] there's none of that sectarianism that goes on. It's more broad than that. There's a basic humanity here in the sense that

working in sanctuary is an affirmation of the human spirit, and that all people are welcome in God's house.

By denouncing injustices perpetrated by the U.S. government and by constructing a religious, justice-oriented praxis, prophetic-minded sanctuary workers sought to create a society that fulfilled God's covenant with humanity. Participants referred to this truly just society as the kingdom of God.[23] For example, at a Covenant for Compassion gathering in Berkeley, Linda Allen, an East Bay minister and EBSC staff member, held aloft a brightly painted Salvadoran carving that depicted villages and people emerging out of a cracked egg. Linda told the audience, "When we asked Central Americans what this meant, they said it was the kingdom of God hatching." When asked to describe the kingdom of God, most sanctuary workers spoke of peace, shared resources, land reform, and the absence of hunger. Marilyn Phillips of Tucson, who said she had dedicated her life to serving the kingdom of God, depicted the kingdom as an agricultural paradise in which farmers would have enough land and enjoy the fruits of their labor. Marilyn told me, "If you read Isaiah and Amos, you will see that there's a vision of the kingdom of God where there will be no more hunger and where people will have the necessities of life. Whereas now, the Third World is producing for other countries." Similarly, Linda Allen contended that unbeknownst to most Christians, the year of jubilee announced by Jesus and celebrated "blithely in our Sunday morning churches" actually would be the year when landholders redistributed the land. Linda explained, "It's [jubilee is] an economic term, and it means, 'this is like the beginning of God's kingdom, this is what God's kingdom is all about, it's justice.' ... That's really radical stuff ... about empowering, enfranchising the radically poor, the *marginales,* the scum of our society, as we're wont to put it."

Despite such millenarian efforts to bring the kingdom of God into fruition, the prophecy practiced by sanctuary workers, like solidarity vis à vis Orientalism and voluntarism vis à vis careerism, in some ways derived from and reinforced the church-state divisions that it critiqued. This contradiction was most apparent during the 1985–1986 Tucson sanctuary trial when defendants tried to situate their work within categories that would establish its legality. During pretrial hearings, defense attorneys argued that because sanctuary was a *religious* activity, the constitution prohibited the state from infringing on sanctuary practices. Placing the sanctuary movement outside government jurisdiction on religious grounds reinforced the political/religious dichotomy that constructed the U.S. government as a *secular* institution—party to no covenant with the God of any faith[24]—and the church as a *sacred* body whose work constituted "ministry" rather than "political action."[25] Moreover, to buttress this argument, defense attorneys used testimonies from religious experts and cited prosanctuary statements affirmed by the governing bodies of defendants' faiths—the very institutional structures denounced by some participants' critique of accommodationism. Though the movement's invocation of the First Amendment was largely limited to legal contexts, its use of the movement's roots in mainstream congregations as a source of legitimacy was more widespread. For example, Marty Finn, a nonreligious East Bay participant, commented, "If you want to reach out to Mr. and Mrs. Middle America, you don't do it by having a demonstration. ... Whereas church organizations, bowling clubs, health clubs, those kinds of places, are where people really are." To reach "middle America," church groups had to be the kinds of institutions that the prophetic tradition opposed. Within the movement, witnessing coexisted uncomfortably with the accommodationism and church-state divisions that this witnessing critiqued.

## Conclusion

Sanctuary workers' efforts to bring about the kingdom of God would be difficult to analyze using the interest-based, goal-oriented notion of action that has guided much social movement research. Yet this and the other ideals that participants practiced within the movement enacted alternatives to Orientalism, individualism, careerism, sexism, secularism, accommodationism, and so forth and therefore were a significant portion of the social changes produced by sanctuary work. It is true that movement practices pursued long-term changes in U.S. foreign and immigration policy, such as the recognition of Central Americans' refugee status and an end to U.S. military aid to El Salvador; yet, giving sanctuary to undocumented Salvadoran and Guatemalan refugees also created a community that, however partially, temporarily, and contradictorily, *lived* according to its notions of justice. Assessing the impact of a movement's actions therefore entails not only evaluating its success in achieving the various and contested goals set by participants but also entering into the system of truth through which movement members define reality (Gerlach and Hine 1970). Only if one understands the ethics of solidarity, service, and prophecy that inform sanctuary practices does it become clear that movement actions not only seek to prevent human rights abuses but also create relationships that transcend national boundaries, place the social good above participants' personal ambitions, and work to bring the kingdom of God into fruition.

The rituals that the sanctuary movement created to celebrate its religious, social, and political vision challenged instrumental notions of action from yet a different angle. By creating a community of religious folk who were committed to social justice, movement rituals defied analytical distinctions between expressive and pragmatic action.

## Notes

1. Melucci has criticized such approaches. He argued that focusing exclusively on measurable political action "ignores the way in which the visible action of contemporary move-

ments depends upon their production of new cultural codes within submerged networks" (1989:44).

2. A solidarity model has been proposed as an alternative explanation for participation in social movements (Fireman and Gamson 1979). According to this model, "activists contribute their efforts to social movement organizations because they believe in the goals and methods of the organization" rather than out of self-interest (Hirsch 1986:373).

3. This view of human action derives from interest theory and has influenced more than social movement research (Ortner 1984). For example, Bourdieu's theory of practice assumes that individuals are rational strategists who pursue their own interest (1977). Foucault's theory of power critiques interest-based notions of political action (1980a, 1980b).

4. Research mobilization theorists are interested not only in internal factors, such as strategies that affect movement success, but also in external factors, such as "the physical and environmental requirements and restrictions that affected the development and behavior of movements" (Pichardo 1988:98).

5. In making this point, I am not referring to distinctions between "altruistic" and "self-benefiting" groups. On the one hand, even self-benefiting groups aid free riders (Gamson 1975), while on the other, once actors have altruistically adopted the cause of, say, Central American refugees, furthering this cause *is* in their interest. Rather, I am claiming that protest is more than the calculating pursuit of an objective; it is also a creative effort to realize participants' notions of justice.

6. I do not mean that goals are not genuine or that they in no way motivate protestors. For example, sanctuary workers *did* seek to end human rights abuses in El Salvador and Guatemala, save lives, prevent the deportation of legitimate refugees, and so on.

7. One sanctuary worker who read this section drew my attention to the parallels between these river parables and the Rio Sumpul massacres along the Honduras–El Salvador border. On May 30, 1982, some 2,000 Salvadorans who were trying to cross the Sumpul River into Honduras were attacked by Salvadoran and Honduran military units. For accounts of this and previous massacres, see Camarda 1985 and Dilling 1984.

8. Sam's parable might have had a different moral if the dead bodies floating down the river had been alive and suffering. In his fence and ambulance story, those in danger of falling off the cliff were still alive and well. If they had instead been in mid-fall, then the town might have opted for an ambulance instead of a wall. In Sam's third story, the Good Samaritan found living, suffering people, but only one per day, thus giving him free time to search for their assailants. Sam chose his analogies well. In the Bay Area, the sanctuary movement housed small numbers of refugees, most of whom had been screened and deemed "mentally stable in spite of the persecution and dislocation they had suffered" (EBSC 1983). Moreover, unlike their counterparts south of the border, Bay Area Central Americans had reached relative safety.

9. Alva Armstrong's critique of individuals being "moved around on the basis of political efficacy" is a reference to disputes between Tucson and Chicago participants regarding the purpose of sanctuary. According to Tucson members of the movement, Chicago activists refused to shelter Central Americans who either were unwilling to give public testimonies or who sided with the Salvadoran and Guatemalan governments rather than with opposition movements. See Corbett 1986, Bau 1985, and Lorentzen 1991 for further details of this controversy.

10. See the "Institutionalization" section of Chapter 2 for a history of this meeting and a discussion of its role in national organizing efforts.

11. Gloria Murdock's question shows that issues of Band-Aids versus root causes were debated both within and between regions.

12. Because it allows actors to reinterpret the past in light of subsequent events and to reshape meanings for different contexts, ambiguity can be an advantage as well as a shortcoming (Rosaldo 1989; Gilbert 1989; Comaroff 1978).

13. Loosely translated, these words mean: Solidarity! Solidarity!/Hands and efforts born of one life and one single journey./Solidarity! Solidarity!

14. The benefits that social movement theory terms "purposive incentives" (see Hirsch 1986) would seem to be a low priority for sanctuary workers.

15. In Tucson, the Task Force office was not as critical to volunteer efforts as the EBSC office was in the East Bay because most Tucson volunteer work occurred outside the office itself. Few Tucson volunteers devoted the bulk of their time to making phone calls and doing paperwork, as did EBSC office volunteers.

16. One of the major constraints confronting volunteers was a conflict between volunteering and those other forms of unpaid labor: child care, housework, and family responsibilities. Both men and women found it difficult to balance commitments to sanctuary and to their families, and some encountered opposition from their spouses. Rosemary Graefe, an office volunteer, told me of a married couple that had conflicts because the husband was more involved in sanctuary than the wife. Rosemary said, "His wife is sick of him donating all his time to everybody *except* the household." Similarly, Jamie Porter of Tucson told me that he didn't do border crossings because "my family is scared to death of my being arrested or the car being confiscated. … I was ready to do it; I had reached that point. But I wasn't able to, because of my family being scared." Adele Tilberg, a Tucson housewife, student, and border worker, encountered opposition from her husband when volunteering superseded housework. She related, "He didn't like it when I stopped going to classes, when I stopped working, when dinner wasn't ready, when the laundry would pile up. The house used to be complete chaos, because I was gone all the time. And if I was here, I was on the phone." Despite this conflict, she felt compelled to do the work. "If it was a question of whether to wash the underwear or to do sanctuary," she told me, "then the answer was clear." One of Adele's colleagues encountered a more difficult dilemma:

> The main dilemma that I had was, was I sacrificing my own kids for other people's kids? And that was a very difficult question for me. I didn't feel it when I was carrying someone's kid in my backpack or when I was holding a child's hand. But then, when I had finished, I would get back in my car, and I would rush back to my kids, and I would hug them, and I was so happy to see them again! Because I kept asking myself, "What if I had to go to prison?"

This woman eventually had to quit volunteering because her husband—whom she was divorcing—threatened to argue in court that her sanctuary work made her an unfit mother.

17. One man whom I interviewed told me that he'd been willing to turn down a job offer so that he could volunteer. When he got the job offer, he called the EBSC office to find out how badly they needed volunteers. The need did not seem urgent, so he took the job.

18. The Bush administration's proposal that government programs be replaced by private efforts is different from the civil initiative practiced by sanctuary workers. Tucson sanctuary workers created a substitute for the immigration system because they believed the government had *failed* to fulfill its responsibility to do so. In contrast, the Bush administration ar-

gued that social services ought to be the responsibility of private citizens rather than the government.

19. "Witnessing" refers not only to the fusion of religion and politics but also to an evangelical practice by which Christians seek to convert others by living an exemplary life and recounting their own religious experiences. See Greenhouse 1986.

20. See Bellah (1975) and Bercovitch (1978) for analyses of the notion of covenant within U. S. Protestantism.

21. For example, Farrah Roberts felt that "standing in the rain on a rainy Christmas Eve afternoon, trying to [en] circle the [U.C. Berkeley] campus" with peace activists created "the same good feeling of support" as did sanctuary work.

22. I am drawing attention to participants' *belief* in avoidance of factionalism rather than their *actual* avoidance of factionalism. On a national level, factionalism abounded, as shown by movement-wide debates over organizational structures and the nature of social change. On a local level, divisions sometimes occurred, such as the split between Trsg and the other Tucson border group. In the East Bay, the few overt conflicts that I observed took place "behind the scenes" and were over such issues as whether to divide northern California into two regions—a debate that became irrelevant once the National Sanctuary Communications Council gave way to national groups, which dispensed with regional representation.

23. The social gospel movement, one of sanctuary's predecessors, also sought to bring about the kingdom of God. For analyses of the social gospel movement, see Coleman 1972, White and Hopkins 1976, Hopkins 1940, Dombrowski 1936, Carter 1971, and King 1982.

24. Robert Bellah (1975) has argued that the United States practices what he terms "civil religion," the faith that defines the United States as "a nation under God."

25. Indicted sanctuary workers also claimed that they, unlike employers and others who brought individuals across the border for humanitarian purposes, had been singled out for prosecution because of their criticisms of government officials. This argument did not define "religion" as "apolitical."

# 10

## Rituals of Resistance

*There's a certain kind of interplay, almost a sort of a contradictory dynamic, in between this concept of social-political action and spiritual action. And I think that when done together, the political action becomes more effective and the spiritual action becomes more spiritual. For me, the sanctuary movement was the first place in which I really got to experience that in a really full way.*

—Yosef Meyer, member of Congregation Aron Kodesh

Members of the sanctuary movement sometimes gathered in churches, synagogues, meeting halls, and homes to perform rituals that celebrated the truth of their work. These worship services, prayer vigils, and other ceremonies creatively reinterpreted sanctuary workers' religious traditions in ways that focused on Central American issues. As a result, Christian prayers, Protestant hymns, Quaker silences, Catholic Communion, Salvadoran *¡presentes!,* and Jewish Seders became part of the praxis of the movement. To devise religious rituals that opposed U.S. foreign and immigration policy, sanctuary workers invoked and constructed a tradition of religious activism, drew on and developed methods of ritual improvisation, and called forth and created an ecumenical, social justice–oriented community. Movement rituals thus not only resisted imperialism, human rights abuses, and unjust refugee policies but also defied the separation of politics and religion, the marginalized role of religious truth in the United States, and the boundaries that divided denominations and faiths. By creating rituals, developing methods of improvisation, and celebrating unique forms of religious community, sanctuary workers practiced change.

What is one to make of the presence of rituals within a social movement such as sanctuary? Would not the time, energy, and expense of organizing worship services be better spent assisting refugees or opposing U.S. military aid to El Salvador? The reason that rituals seem out of place within a protest movement is that social scientists have frequently posited an opposition between instrumental and expressive action, placing protest in the former category and ritual in the latter. Some researchers who view protest as instrumental action have simply ignored facets of protest deemed expressive. For example, sociologists Marwell and Oliver defined social movements as "essentially instrumental" and noted, "This is not to

deny that emotions and expressiveness are also important" (1984:5). Other analysts have developed instrumental explanations for seemingly expressive actions.
For instance, Bert Klandermans listed "symbolic public acts such as prayer and
worship" as one possible means of mobilizing consensus around a movement's
goals (1988:184), and E. J. Hobsbawm contended that rituals within social movements serve to foster social cohesion (1959). Although such instrumentalist interpretations of "expressive" action are certainly partially correct, to end one's analysis here would reduce faith practices, such as worship and prayer, to strategic
actions. But to take the opposite view and assume that expressiveness is apolitical
is just as problematic. The previous chapter showed that strategic actions, like
volunteering in a sanctuary office or traveling on a delegation to Central America,
can express and enact participants' social ideals. Similarly, within rituals, there is
an intertwining of process and strategy, faith and protest, and meaning and action. Rituals can define participants' political and religious identities (Geertz
1980; Sahlins 1981); dispute and overturn the social order (Sahlins 1981); contest
political relationships (Comaroff 1978; Cohen and Comaroff 1976); and shape and
reconstruct history (Sahlins 1981, 1985; Gilbert 1989). The production of meaning
is itself a political process (Harding 1984; Comaroff 1978; Melucci 1989; Yngvesson
1988; Foucault 1980b; Kapferer 1976; Williams 1977).

If protest consists of process as well as strategy, meaning as well as action, and
mysticism as well as pragmatics, then the political implications of rituals are not
all that different from those of other movement activities. Rituals, like other
movement practices, are created by reinterpreting preexisting cultural discourses
in light of particular social and political issues. As protestors construct these reinterpretations, they address systems that are not directly related to the movement's
explicit goals. Sanctuary rituals, not surprisingly, not only engaged the Orientalism, sexism, materialism, and so forth that other movement actions confronted;
they also reworked the religious praxis of movement participants. Rituals, like
other protest activities, gave participants the opportunity to practice their social,
religious, and political ideals. As they prayed, sang, and worshiped, sanctuary
workers connected faith to social action, celebrated the movement's understanding of sociopolitical reality, and acted on the notion that religious obligations to
do justice transcend denominational divisions. These by-products of ritual action
were as politically significant as the policy changes that sanctuary work was designed to achieve. For, power lies not only in formal political and legal systems
but also in the cultural and religious discourses that construct social reality.

## Inventing Tradition

Sanctuary rituals defied the assumption, common within anthropology, that
rituals repeat fixed forms.[1] Each sanctuary ritual was historically unique, an improvisation constructed for a specific occasion, audience, and context and to be
added to participants' ritual repertoires as a source of future improvisation. To

create rituals, movement members "invented tradition" (Hobsbawm and Ranger 1983) by reinterpreting their ritual knowledge in light of Central American issues and the ethics that guided sanctuary work. Participants *produced* rituals, almost in the sense that one produces a play or a film. The fact that they were deliberate constructions did not mean that sanctuary rituals were experienced as "inauthentic" by their authors and other participants. On the contrary, many participants found that linking worship to political action *deepened* ritual experience. Sam Gersch, pastor of one of the original EBSC churches, explained:

> [Sanctuary] draws on ... tradition, but it's not traditionalism. Jaroslav Pelikan says that the difference between tradition and traditionalism is that tradition is the living faith of the dead, and traditionalism is the dead faith of the living. Sanctuary is tradition. It's the living faith; it's not just drawing on the dead faith, but the living faith. It's something that is evolving always.

The view that connecting religious and social action enlivened tradition was shared by a Tucson rabbi who told me, "Sanctuary is going to be a footnote to American history. It's alive and it's pulsating, and that's what's important."

The rituals devised by sanctuary workers can be divided into four general types: meeting-related, intracongregational, intercongregational, and community-based. First, meeting-related rituals usually consisted of prayers, meditations, songs, or reflections given at a sanctuary meeting, conference, potluck, retreat, or fund-raiser. Because they were not the purpose of the gathering, meeting-related rituals were often short. The participants were sanctuary workers from multiple congregations who had come together for the event rather than for the ritual. Second, intracongregational rituals consisted either of references to sanctuary during a congregation's regular services or of an entire service focused on the congregation's sanctuary work. In addition to the congregation's active sanctuary workers, participants in intracongregational rituals included congregation members who were not active in the movement. Third, local sanctuary workers organized intercongregational services focusing on events (such as the beginning of the Tucson trial), religious holidays (such as Passover or Christmas), or significant dates (such as the anniversary of the death of Archbishop Romero). Intercongregational services brought together sanctuary workers from a variety of congregations for the explicit purpose of ritual action. Finally, community-based rituals related a life event, such as a wedding, to sanctuary work. These rituals drew on a sanctuary worker's particular network of friends, relatives, and coworkers both within and outside of the movement.

Other than meeting-related rituals and brief references to sanctuary during congregations' regular services, most sanctuary rituals were patterned after a church service and included the same elements: processionals, prayers, reflections, responsive readings, scripture readings, liturgies, songs, offerings, testimonies, Communion, recessionals, and so forth. Exceptions to this format included synagogues that performed sanctuary Seders and, in Tucson, a network of sanctuary congregations that took turns hosting a graveyard of crosses bearing names of those killed in Central America. (When Benjamin Linder was killed in Nicaragua, a Star of David was added to the graveyard.) While the elements of a church service generally provided the ritual "slots" that participants could fill, the *content* of these slots was created by invoking and reinterpreting religious practices in ways that established the *justice* of sanctuary work and the *in*justice of U.S. foreign and immigration policy. By expressing this critique in the form of a religious service, sanctuary workers staked out a moral ground from which to speak. Moreover, defining immigration and foreign policy in religious terms asserted that, far from being a separate sphere of action marginal to the workings of society, religion had everything to do with politics.

To fill the slots provided by the church service format, sanctuary workers perused their ritual knowledge for items that could be made relevant to sanctuary, Central America, human rights, peace, and social justice. For example, "O God of Every Nation," a Protestant hymn about universal humanity, was sung during EBSC's Archbishop Romero commemoration in 1987. This hymn, which was written in 1923, decades before refugees began fleeing El Salvador and Guatemala, took on new meaning within the context of sanctuary work. The first verse ended, "Where hate and fear divide us/And bitter threats are hurled,/In love and mercy guide us/And heal our strife-torn world." The divisive "hate and fear" could be the attitudes of U.S. citizens toward undocumented immigrants. The "strife" could be the armed conflict in El Salvador and Guatemala. By singing this hymn, the Protestants, Jews, Unitarians, and Catholics who participated in the commemoration denounced governments that were not guided by "love and mercy" but that instead deported people and financed armies. Similarly, during a regular Sunday service at All Saints Church, Charles O'Brien (a Tucson intellectual and sanctuary participant) reinterpreted the Lord's Prayer in a way that stressed U.S. responsibility for the plight of Latin American debtor nations. Charles told the congregation that "forgive us our debts as we forgive our debtors" applied not only to personal but to national sin. In Charles's reinterpretation, the prayer meant something along the lines of, "forgive us for perpetrating injustice and indebtedness as we *do* justice by forgiving the debts of other nations." When Charles reinterpreted what is probably the most sacred of all Christian prayers, he applied the religious doctrine of forgiveness to a sociopolitical problem.

Sanctuary workers' reinterpretations of religious traditions were part of a broader ritual experimentation occurring in the theologically liberal congregations out of which the movement arose. To construct their regular worship services, congregants consciously reshaped religious symbols, rejecting those dissonant with their own beliefs, using those they found appropriate, and creating new symbols. For example, First Church rejected male-gendered terms of address for God as sexist, and experimentally began the Lord's Prayer with, "Our Mother," "Our Father and Mother," and "Our Parent" before settling on "Our Creator."

Congregation Aron Kodesh sometimes used alternative liturgy that balanced "Adonai," a male term for God, with "Shechina," a female alternative. Congregations sometimes revised entire services in search of renewed meaning. During a dramatic Palm Sunday service at First Church, congregation members ritualistically placed branches and leaves on the aisle to the altar. Instead of giving a sermon, the assistant minister sat on the path of branches, pretending to be a disciple recollecting her ride into Jerusalem with Jesus. Instead of singing the doxology, church members acted out a narrative of Jesus' betrayal and crucifixion, with the entire congregation taking the role of the crowds who condemned Jesus to death. The service concluded when the choir sang, "Alas, they have taken Jesus, my Master, and whither they have borne Him surely I know not" and then silently filed out of church, heads downward, eyes meeting no one.

Within the sanctuary movement, participants drew on four sources to construct rituals: the religious practices of member congregations, scripture, Central American traditions, and the history of religious activism. First, participants incorporated practices from diverse congregations into ecumenical services by *reaching into* different religious traditions to uncover common commitments to social justice. Through joint ritual and social action, religious groups recovered and created a ritual discourse that challenged human rights abuses and injustice. This reaching into religious traditions made diverse religious practices authoritative to movement members, thus enabling sanctuary workers to participate in each others' traditions without resolving theological differences. For example, a Quaker woman responsible for the closing meditation at an EBSC Steering Committee meeting asked those present to observe the Quaker tradition of silent meditation. Yosef Meyer of Congregation Aron Kodesh explained the rationale behind such ecumenicism:

> To have all these traditions basically mean something about the affirmation of the value of human life and of our common destiny together—and not just in abstract terms, but united by a particular action that we were doing together—to me was an extremely spiritual and uplifting moment. ... In short, when done purely as a point of spiritual uplift, it [an ecumenical service] had nothing in it. But when it was done as part of social action, its spiritual component became the most important component in it.

By reaching into participants' traditions, sanctuary rituals celebrated religious diversity while affirming the religious—and therefore morally compelling—nature of sanctuary's claim to truth. For instance, a staff member urged EBSC members to attend a peace procession at the Concord Naval Weapons Station—each dressed in his or her own religious garb. (A Unitarian later told me that it would have to be a cold day in hell—or at least in Concord—before she'd march down the street wearing her choir robe.)

Second, sanctuary rituals reinterpreted scripture in ways that reflected and constructed a religious mandate for social action. The most frequently cited verses were Leviticus 19:33–34: "When a stranger sojourns with you in your land, you shall do him no wrong. The stranger who sojourns with you shall be as the native among you, and you shall love him as yourself; for you were strangers in the land of Egypt."[2] Another oft-cited passage was the biblical story of Herod and the baby Jesus. During a sermon shortly after Christmas, a Tucson minister used this story to reveal his involvement in sanctuary work to his congregation. The minister announced that two days before Christmas, he had crossed two Central American refugees, one of whom was due to give birth on December 25. He explained that, like the baby Jesus, these Central Americans were "refugees fleeing their country and homeland into a foreign and alien country; people, hunted and haunted by political oppression, fleeing cruel human behavior and unjust laws." Similarly, in an article for an ecumenical newsletter, a Tucson sanctuary worker described a painting he had noticed during one of the intercongregational services performed during the sanctuary trial:

> I looked more closely at it to discover the subject. To my amazed growing awareness I saw that it was a painting of Mary, Joseph, and the baby Jesus on their flight to Egypt. You remember the story: King Herod, concerned about the security of his throne because of the story that a king had been born, dispatched his soldiers to Bethlehem to slaughter all the babies under two years old. Joseph, warned by a messenger of God, takes his wife and child and flees into Egypt, escaping the slaughter of the innocents.
>
> How ironic I thought. How ironic that it should be this picture that looked down on sanctuary workers and worshipers all those Tuesday mornings of the sanctuary trial in Tucson: looked down on Methodists and Catholics, Baptists and Presbyterians, UCC's and Disciples, Jews and Unitarians, Mennonites and Episcopalians, Luthers and Quakers, and assorted others. What a reminder to all of us who prayed together there. Mary and Joseph, with their newborn in their arms, fled persecution and death in their homeland and found sanctuary in the land of Egypt. If they hadn't, where would we be today? (Kennon 1987: 1)

Third—and consonant with participants' ethic of solidarity—sanctuary rituals drew not only on U.S. religious traditions but also on Central American customs and theology. Gatherings mostly composed of monolingual North Americans practiced solidarity by lunching on Salvadoran and Guatemalan food, praying in Spanish, and singing songs from the Central American base community movement. Services often featured a Central American ritual in which participants shouted the names of martyrs and all present responded, *"¡Presente!"* ("Here!")[3] Central American liberation theology entered services through references to Archbishop Romero and through songs with titles like *"Vos sos el dios de los pobres"* ("You are the God of the poor"), *"Paz y libertad"* ("Peace and liberty"), and *"Cuando el pobre crea en el pobre"* ("When the poor believe in the poor").[4] Central Americans were often invited to give the spiritual reflections that were the central elements of services. A liturgical celebration at the 1986 national sanctuary gathering in Washington, D.C., honored Central Americans by inviting refugees (along with sanctuary workers who had been indicted or convicted) to walk in the processional that began the service.

Finally, in constructing rituals, sanctuary workers redefined the past,[5] thus invoking and creating a tradition of religious activism. By noting parallels between sanctuary and previous religious movements, participants established precedents for their actions. Paul Dedona of First Church found the Apostle Paul's community organizing "sort of an inspiration for the way I see the sanctuary movement. And I've heard refugees talk about—like when a priest from El Salvador comes and talks to groups all over the place and kind of gets everybody enthused, they sort of see that [as similar to] the way the early Christian apostles were keeping the communities going." Peter Lockhart, an EBSC volunteer, traced religious commitments to social action to "the tradition of sanctuary, like in Notre Dame, when the hunchback swung down, grabbed the maiden about to be guillotined, and landed in the church, crying, 'Sanctuary!' *That's* the tradition that comes close to what the church is actually about." Claude Grimshaw of First Church found a precedent for sanctuary in pre–Civil War abolitionism:

> When the sanctuary movement is compared to the underground railway, 100–130 years ago, it's a fairly apt comparison, because I think that the helping [of] people whose skins were black to a different kind of lifestyle had an influence on how we feel about ourselves 130 years later. It's part of our tradition. And we're trying to use that tradition in the sanctuary movement.

Sanctuary rituals drew on these and other examples of religious activism by including protest songs from the civil rights movement, readings from figures such as Martin Luther King and Anne Frank, and political theater, such as using a black coffin to symbolize the Salvadoran dead.

Though it drew on the ritual experimentation taking place in mainstream congregations, the sanctuary movement's ritual practices created and celebrated an ecumenical community that existed *alongside* organized religious institutions. The sanctuary movement called forth a justice-oriented slice of the membership of a variety of congregations, denominations, and faiths. Many of these individuals considered sanctuary a more authentic religious practice than that of their own religious organizations. For example, at a June 1987 analysis workshop, one EBSC staff member told her colleagues, "Movements like sanctuary are what keep the church alive," and Ernie Tarkington, minister of a Tucson sanctuary congregation, told me, "Sanctuary is giving aid and succor to someone who is escaping persecution and death. What else is the church called to do but that? How can you not do that and still be the church?" The inclusive way that sanctuary workers spoke of "the church" presumed a unity among people of faith who struggled against injustice. Katherine Baerman, a First Church Sanctuary Committee member, told me that during a protest rally at the Concord Naval Weapons Station, when she found herself concentrating on the crucifix held by a Catholic woman who was being arrested, the distinctions between Presbyterians, Episcopalians, and Catholics faded. In Tucson, several Catholic and Quaker sanctuary workers developed a running joke about the "Quakolic religion" and its "popesa." (Such "Quakolic" ecumenicism is even more significant considering that institutionally, Catholics and Quakers represent two extremes of hierarchy and egalitarianism, respectively.) But perhaps the most profound ecumenicism within the sanctuary movement was that between Christians and Jews. During a presentation to the Borderlinks group, a Tucson rabbi quoted two ecumenical sayings that he attributed to a Tucson pastor: "We're all Jews, except some of us are Christians," and "There are not two covenants. There is either one or none."[6] Samuel Durand, a Protestant Task Force member, told me during an interview:

> Although I've been ecumenically minded throughout my ministry, the best times of that have come through this experience and this common commitment. I've learned about the Jewish community, and now I regard them as my sisters and brothers. I've worshiped with them, and I've shared a ministry with them. I've been especially moved for the past two years by their remembrance service, where they remember the Holocaust. In spite of our diversity, we have a commitment together.

Connecting ritual to social action was both a strategy to legitimize sanctuary work and an expression of deeply felt claims to truth. At times, performing rituals seemed more a tactic than a demonstration of faith. For example, I attended two EBSC Steering Committee meetings at which no one volunteered to do the next meeting's opening meditation. The first time that this happened, Linda Allen—the only minister present—admonished the group, "Come on, somebody volunteer. This is important, because we have to remember that we are a faith-based movement and that we should celebrate the richness of our traditions." A woman volunteered and, at the May meeting, read a poem that contrasted a Salvadoran woman's hope, faith, and vitality with herself, out of shape and overburdened by possessions. In June, there was no opening meditation because at the May meeting, participants had forgotten to select a volunteer. When no one wanted to take responsibility for July, Linda's reaction was stronger: "It grieves me that there's no meditation, because we're a faith-based movement, and we need to express that. I'll do it every time if I have to, but it's important that it be done." Sister Ella McNealy, a nun, agreed to do the July meditation. The fact that Linda found it necessary to remind participants of sanctuary's religious underpinnings suggested that opening and closing meditations primarily legitimized the movement's claim to *be* faith-based. Like saying grace before dinner, these meeting-related rituals were not integrated into the course of the event. Once performed, meditations were rarely referred to again.

When connected to significant moments, however, ritual experience *was* intense. For example, Lindsey Martin, an East Bay sanctuary worker, found the September 1986 National Sanctuary Celebration a turning point in her own political and spiritual development. Until the issue of sanctuary arose within her church, Lindsey had been "skeptical that anything wrong was going on in Central America or that I had anything to do with it." Lindsey then began reading about Central America, volunteered in the EBSC office, and visited El Salvador. Two months after this trip, she attended the National Sanctuary Celebration. Lindsey explained, "That was the first time that I started to open my eyes up to the real cultural issues of really starting to embrace more of what I had learned when I had been there [El Salvador]." Similarly, Samuel Durand, a minister who had initially been reluctant to get involved in sanctuary, was deeply moved by a Mass held in 1981 immediately after the first group of Central Americans was bonded out of detention by church workers. Sam recalled:

> Something else that was a strong symbol for me at the time was that we held a Mass at the blacktop parking lot there in front of the ... hotel where we'd been staying. ... It had been 100 or 112 degrees that day, and Father _____ and Father _____ came to give the Mass. And they asked me to join them, and I was asked to select scripture readings for the Mass. So I chose Romans 8:31–39, which goes, "We are regarded as sheep to be led to the slaughter." First I read the passage, and then we had a catechist from El Salvador come and read it in Spanish. And he had known and worked with Archbishop Romero. And that was *incredibly* powerful for me. I remember passing the peace,[7] which must have been thirty minutes to an hour after the first forty-five were released from detention.

To fully understand how sanctuary rituals sometimes put forward powerful claims to truth, it is necessary to link rituals more closely to the contexts in which they were performed. To do so, I shall examine two sanctuary services that I attended in 1987. These two services have not been selected because one is typical of the East Bay and the other of Tucson. Rather, the two services illustrate two types of rituals that occurred in *both* locations. The first, an intercongregational ecumenical service in the East Bay, observed the anniversary of the original sanctuary declarations and Archbishop Romero's assassination. The second, a community-based service, dedicated a house that Arizona sanctuary workers had built for a sanctuary defendant whose home had been destroyed by arson after the trial. Each of these events demonstrate how ritual performance is linked to the context in which it occurs.

## Sanctuary: A Remembrance

On March 24, 1987, EBSC commemorated the fifth anniversary of the original sanctuary declarations and the seventh anniversary of the assassination of Archbishop Oscar Romero. When the Sanctuary Remembrance ceremony took place, interest in sanctuary and Central American issues was waning. Several months before the service, Ralph Lieber, First Church's pastor, had told me that whereas he used to attend programs on Central America whenever possible, more recently, other causes and interests had become priorities. Ralph regretfully acknowledged, "I think that sanctuary is at a plateau right now. . . . Some of the initial enthusiasm is draining, and less churches are declaring, while some are even reconsidering or just letting it rest." Because of this lull in sanctuary work, much of the Remembrance service basked in the 1982 declarations, which had generated a public procession, press coverage, volunteers, donations, and fears of immediate imprisonment for those involved. However, although it did reflect the decreasing enthusiasm of member congregations, the Remembrance service also celebrated the movement's growth from a half dozen congregations into an established movement with its own traditions, key figures (such as Archbishop Romero), and sacred texts (such as Leviticus 19:33–34).

I had spent the early part of the evening of the commemoration with ten other sanctuary workers at a potluck dinner for EBSC office volunteers and staff. As our dinner ended, three individuals who were participating in the service rushed off, another three of us leisurely drove to the service, and the other volunteers went home instead of attending. As we walked into the Protestant church where, on March 24, 1982, five East Bay churches had declared themselves sanctuaries for Central American refugees, the other sanctuary volunteers reminisced about the 1982 service. The sparse attendance at the 1987 event—some forty-five individuals, including five or six Central Americans who sat together in a pew—presented a sharp contrast to the excitement of the original declarations.

The officiants at the Remembrance service included Ralph Lieber, First Church's pastor; Linda Allen, a Protestant minister and EBSC staff member; Yosef Meyer, a cantor at Congregation Aron Kodesh; Erica Castillo, a Salvadoran refugee organizer; Marie Walters, a member of the church where the commemoration was being held; Ted Rezier, an EBSC Steering Committee representative; and Karen Durant, an EBSC congregation member. Each of these individuals represented important moments in the local movement's history. Ralph Lieber and Linda Allen had belonged to the lectionary Bible study out of which the East Bay sanctuary movement arose; Yosef Meyer was from one of the first Jewish sanctuary congregations; Erica Castillo had lived in sanctuary in San Francisco for many years and was a leader of a local refugee organization; Marie Walters was filling in for her pastor, the East Bay participant credited with thinking of sanctuary; Ted Rezier was a member of the first congregation to shelter a refugee family; and Karen Durant had written the original sanctuary declaration. The officiants were fairly evenly divided between men and women (three and four, respectively) and between clergy and laypeople (again, three and four, respectively). The only glaring imbalance was the single Salvadoran among the seven officiants.

The first hint of the service's commencement was the sound of an organist playing a hymn. Participants continued to talk until the hymn ended and the service proper began. Marie Walters welcomed those present, apologizing that the church's pastor was out of town. Marie then read a speech that stressed that at the time of the original declarations, no one had imagined that in five years, this handful of congregations would be a movement. She asked, "Who would have foreseen all these years of hard work, of achievement, and of dedication?" Following Marie's welcome, an interpreter read a written translation for the Central Americans present. Such translations, which occurred throughout the service, followed the ethic of solidarity by emphasizing communication across language barriers.

Following Marie's welcome, Ralph Lieber gave an opening prayer, then Linda Allen invited the La Peña Community Chorus to enter the church and to sing. (La Peña—not a pseudonym—was a political, cultural, and community center in Berkeley, California.) As some fifteen chorus members entered, a volunteer leaned over to me and whispered, "There are almost more of them than there are us." The chorus's selections included music from both Latin America and the United States, and songs were introduced both in Spanish and in English.

Following the first selection—a Chilean song about the impossibility of extinguishing a light that has been lit—one of the clergy announced that Yosef Meyer of Congregation Aron Kodesh would be doing the Old Testament reading. Yosef told those assembled that his synagogue had been one of the first to declare sanctuary and that he had helped write the Jewish version of the sanctuary covenant. He then explained that when Jews read from the Torah it was customary to chant, and that he would be chanting in English, Spanish, and Hebrew. During an interview two months after this service, Yosef (who was a cantor) told me how he had designed this trilingual chanting of the Torah for an earlier sanctuary service:

I was called ... to do the, what is it? The reading from scripture. And when it was phrased to me that way, "reading from scripture," I immediately had a feeling of what I was going to do that was different. Because just the concept of reading from scripture to me sounded so Christian when, in fact, we "read from scripture" every Saturday. But we don't "read" from scripture, we "chant" from scripture. ...

And so I said, "Okay, let me do the scripture reading from Leviticus 19:33," which is sort of the seminal biblical statement that all the sanctuary movement refers to. "Remember that you were a stranger, and do justice by the stranger, for remember you were strangers in the Land of Egypt. When a stranger resides with you in your land, do him no wrong. Treat him as you would treat yourself, for remember you were strangers in the land of Egypt."

So I said, "I'm just going to read Leviticus 19:33 and 34." And they said, "Oh! It's just two sentences." And I said, "Yeah, but I'm going to be singing it in Hebrew, English, and in Spanish." And they said, "You're going to be singing scripture?" And I said, "Yes, this is what we do in synagogue. We sing scripture, we chant it."

So I came, and it came to my time in the service, and I got up, and I had my English with the notation, my Hebrew with the notation, my Spanish with the notation. And I was in [_____] Church with crucifixes all around me, but great acoustics. And to have my voice go out and do the chanting in the traditional melody, and it be something that could then be heard by Jews and recognized as Torah, heard by

Christians and recognized as the Bible, and even be heard by Salvadoran refugees and recognized as the Word by them. I felt that we can all be united in this particular melody such that when twenty minutes down the ceremony, we were singing a Prot-estant hymn—one that was chosen that didn't have references to Christ specifically, so it could be interfaith, but it was done in ... the style of a Protestant church—I could make it my own. Because everybody else there had made the Torah their own by me chanting it the way I did from my tradition.


The way that Yosef Meyer redefined the requested "scripture reading" exempli-fied the form of ecumenicism created within the sanctuary movement. Yosef's tri-lingual chanting of the Torah translated not only *languages* but *religions*. When Yosef translated the Leviticus verses, he expected the Jewish practice of chanting scripture to be recognized as truth by Jews and Christians, North Americans and Central Americans. As he chanted in a church sanctuary, surrounded by crucifixes, the unity of struggle and the sharing of traditions transcended divi-sions such that a Protestant hymn was later "translated" and made into truth for him. Such sharing of traditions argued that, although faith takes different forms, when "translated" for those of another religion, all can participate. Through such "translations of faith," sanctuary rituals asserted a common commitment to "Re-ligion" while proclaiming equality among "religions."

After Yosef finished chanting, Linda Allen stepped forward and said, "I just want to apologize for asking that you do an Old Testament reading. To you, it isn't the Old Testament. We have so much to learn!" This comment, like the chanting itself, reflected participants' respect for religious diversity. (Later, during an inter-view, Yosef told me, "I've already come to accept over a long period of time that people in the East Bay Sanctuary Covenant are going to think, 'Ooo! This might be offensive to somebody who's Jewish.' Like referring to the Torah as the Old Tes-tament. Which for me, is not such a [big deal].")

The chorus then sang its second selection, a rousing song dedicated to Arch-bishop Romero entitled, "The Voice of All." A choir member explained that this song, based on a poem by Pablo Neruda, was written by Paul Robeson and put to music by a former chorus director. Next, Karen Durant read the original press re-lease for the 1982 sanctuary declarations, which was followed by a Spanish transla-tion. Following this reading, those present sang a Protestant hymn, "O God of Ev-ery Nation," a song of universal humanity. As was the case throughout this service, there was no sexist language within the song, with the exception of the word "Lord" for God. Out of respect for the non-Christians present, in the copy of the hymn distributed in the program, the word "Christ" had been whited out and replaced by "peace."

Following the hymn, Erica Castillo read words from Archbishop Romero about picking up the cross, going forward, and not conforming. This reading, which was given in Spanish then translated into English, filled the slot normally devoted to a sermon. After Erica's reflection, an offering was taken for accompaniment, which speakers announced was EBSC's new emphasis. Ted Rezier then led the group in a responsive reading of the Jewish and Christian sanctuary covenant statements. These statements (which were the closest thing to a doctrinal statement within the service) were divided into sections to be read by the leader, the Christians, the Jews, and everyone present. To respect the Unitarians, who were neither Christians nor Jews, Ted invited them to read the Jewish or Christian portion as they preferred.

The service moved toward its conclusion when Linda Allen asked everyone to join hands while bearing in mind that they might be standing next to someone from a religious tradition about which they would have known nothing only a few years earlier. The officiants, who were themselves a religiously diverse group, also joined hands, standing in the front of the church and facing the congregation. First Linda prayed, translating as she went. Her prayer stressed the unity of the group, the work that they had done, and the need to stay together five years, fifty years, or however long it took to achieve justice and peace in Central America. Linda's call for perseverance confronted not so much government persecution of sanctuary workers as the fatigue resulting from long-term struggle.

After the prayer, Linda performed a ¡presente!, a custom she said she had learned from Central Americans. Within the sanctuary movement, this rite, which invoked the presence of martyrs, was sometimes used in place of or as part of Communion. Linda explained that when she'd first been asked to do a ¡presente! five years earlier, she had somewhat ignorantly done so in the subdued style typical of her Protestant denomination. This time, she announced, she wanted to do a *real* ¡presente!. She began, "Holy One, we call on you to be in our midst tonight as we remember those who have died as a result of working for peace and justice in Central America. Tonight, we wish to remember the spirits of those people among us now. Oscar Romero!" The gathering, which was familiar with this ritual, responded by shouting, "¡Presente!" "Rutilio Grande!" Linda continued. "¡Presente!" "The four religious sisters!" "¡Presente!" "All of the dead of El Salvador!" "¡Presente!" "Reverend Martin Luther King!" "¡Presente!" "Anne Frank!" "¡Presente!" Linda continued listing names of activists from around the world.

Linda's ¡presente! demonstrated how sanctuary rituals fused politics and religion, innovation and tradition, process and strategy. The ¡presente! opposed injustice in Central America by invoking Archbishop Romero and other Central American martyrs, whose deaths served as reminders of the fate that could await Salvadoran and Guatemalan immigrants if they were deported. Honoring these martyrs valorized commitment and risk-taking and thus encouraged participants to continue the struggles for which others had died. By naming not only Central American but also other martyrs, this ritual linked sanctuary to civil rights, the Holocaust, and other struggles. Such linkages constructed and invoked a tradition of religious activism by portraying sanctuary as the latest manifestation of a force that was moving throughout history. Connecting sanctuary to this force implied that, like Anne Frank, Archbishop Romero, and Martin Luther King, who were condemned during their time but later recognized as heroes, so too would sanctuary workers be appreciated by history. By addressing God as "Holy One," Linda deliberately employed inclusive, nonsexist language. Moreover, the ¡presente! enacted solidarity by enabling North Americans to perform a Central American custom and by honoring martyrs from around the world. When Linda included "all of the dead of El Salvador" on her list of those who had died for peace and justice, however, she presented a monolithic and idealized vision of the Salvadoran people.

Linda concluded the commemoration service with a benediction, explaining that this was how services concluded in Protestant churches. This explanation revealed a weakness within the ecumenicism of this ritual. Though participants in the service sang a Protestant hymn, honored a Catholic Archbishop, listened to a chanting of the Torah, and shouted ¡presente!, the Remembrance was essentially a Protestant rite with spots for other religious practices. Organizers had assumed that participants would understand the service's elements and format. No one had found it necessary to explain what a hymn was, or what a responsive reading was, and yet Yosef Meyer had felt that he had to explain chanting the Torah to the group. According to what Yosef told me during the interview, the organizers basically found a place in the service where they could work in something Jewish. Only at the end of the service, when Linda explained that Protestants concluded with benedictions, was the Protestant character of the event acknowledged and "translated" for participants.

As the organ played, participants gradually walked out and gathered in the hallway to chat. The office volunteers with whom I had attended commented that the event should have been better publicized.

## House Dedication Ceremony

On October 31, 1987, sanctuary workers from Tucson and other towns in southern Arizona had a party and prayer service to dedicate the newly constructed residence of Sharon Martinez (pseudonym), a sanctuary defendant whose house had been destroyed by arsonists shortly after she was acquitted. Within the local movement, it was rumored that a right-wing group was responsible and that the neighbors who had witnessed the arson were afraid to report it. To rebuild Sharon's house, Arizona sanctuary workers mounted a fund-raising and construction effort that generated donations from around the United States and volunteers from local communities. During an interview, John Fisher, the Tucsonan who had organized this effort, explained: "The slogan is 'In Solidarity.' I felt that those who've put their lives and their reputations on the line should stick together. If one of us gets in trouble, then the others should be supportive of that person." When sanctuary workers finished rebuilding the house, Sharon and her family invited the community to celebrate an achievement that was a metaphor for the movement itself. The completion of the house meant that Sharon and her family would be able to resume the life they had had before the arson attack. It meant that those who had rebuilt the house had successfully supported a colleague in need. And it demonstrated that the local movement could respond to repression. Thus the dedication celebrated not only rebuilding a house but also reconstructing border work in the face of chilling undercover surveillance, a draining months-long trial, and felony convictions on alien-smuggling charges.

Even more than EBSC's Remembrance service, the house dedication defied anthropological assumptions that rituals repeat socially and culturally significant forms. The participants in the dedication ceremony combined and reinterpreted diverse ritual practices, including Communion services, prayer requests, and protest actions, in unique ways. Like the EBSC Remembrance ceremony, the dedication roughly followed the format of a church service; however, it also resembled an awards ceremony and a political protest. Unlike the Remembrance and other public services, the dedication was a private party that was not designed to be politically and religiously correct. The dedication ceremony had no printed program, and much of its content seemed to be created spontaneously. Participants felt free to add speeches to the agenda, chime in with their own jokes and comments, and improvise. The fact that the ceremony occurred at a private home rather than a religious institution enhanced its informality and flexibility.

On the Halloween morning that the dedication service was to be held, some fifty to sixty people gathered at Sharon's house, greeting each other with hugs and kisses then catching up on each others' lives. Those who attended the dedication were Sharon's friends, colleagues, and friends of friends. These were the individuals who had rebuilt the house and rebuilt border work, and they had come to celebrate their commitment not only to the poor and oppressed but also to each other. As I had not worked on the house, engaged in border work, met Sharon, or even been formally invited, I felt somewhat awkward attending this event. I concluded it would be appropriate for me to attend when I learned that a Task Force staff member who also belonged to Trsg and was very active in local sanctuary networks simply assumed I would be going. A few days before the dedication, I arranged a ride with a couple of sanctuary workers, and when we arrived, Sharon greeted me, like everyone else, with a warm hug. As this was a private party rather than a public event, however, I was uncomfortably aware of the tension between researching and participating, particularly given that the government agents who had testified against Sharon and her colleagues had, while under cover, visited this house only three years earlier. The ambiguities in my identity came to the fore as people socialized and participants whom I did not know asked who I was and why I was there. When I explained that I was in Tucson doing research about the sanctuary movement, one man asked pointedly, "So, is this a clinical study for you, or are you in sympathy?" I answered that I was in sympathy. Later, when I gave the spouse of one of the convicted sanctuary workers a similar explanation for my presence, he commented, "Oh, so you're here living among the natives." I immediately repositioned myself, saying, "I guess I *am* one of the natives, so this is an introspective study." At the end of the day, I was pleased to be seen catching a ride home to Tucson with one of the individuals who had stood trial with Sharon.

After gathering at Sharon's house, participants continued socializing until the time came to eat—well after 2:30 P.M. when prayer service had been scheduled to begin. Those present squeezed into a mostly unfurnished living room in front of a large table as a Mexican priest—who was also one of the Tucson defendants— gave a blessing in Spanish, thanking God for the food and asking that the hungry might find bread and the full might hunger for God. The lunch was a delicious spread of beans, tortillas, chips, sodas, salsa, tomatoes, potato salad, Mexican cheese, and more. Appropriately enough for a house only a few yards from the border, U.S. foods were interspersed with Mexican dishes. Even the cake—a gigantic, delicious-looking concoction—came with a border-crossing story. Sharon said that she had bought it in Mexico and brought it back across the border, much to the suspicion of the Immigration agents who scrutinized it. "I have yet to meet a Salvadoran who could fit in the cake," Sharon joked.

Following lunch, the prayer service began. There wasn't space indoors, so participants went outside to sit in folding chairs or to stand around the edges of the group. The service began with several Bible readings, including a passage about "the hills of oppression." Readers pointed across the border to a hill where broken down houses were clearly visible. Next a Catholic priest and a Protestant minister announced that Sharon, who was a devout Catholic, had requested that they have Communion. The two clergy performed the ceremony, proclaiming that God was present wherever two or more gathered in God's name. Participants passed around a loaf of bread, breaking off pieces and repeating Christ's words, "This is my body, broken for you." The bread was followed by a cup of wine, from which (to my knowledge) everyone drank and which had to be refilled because it almost ran out. The ecumenicism of this Communion derived not only from translating faiths but also from shared struggle in the face of persecution and from the fact that it was performed by a priest and a minister, representatives of faiths whose understandings of Communion differ.

After Communion, there were a number of speeches praising Sharon's generosity and self-sacrifice. In addition to Sharon Martinez and John Fisher, speakers included Marc Talbot, an influential Tucson pastor; Father Thomás Kendrick, the Tucson priest who had initiated public prayer services for the Central American people; Samuel Durand and Teresa Newman, two Task Force staff members; and Merlin Wynn, a young member of All Saints Church. Speeches were given half seriously, half jokingly. One Task Force staff member began his speech by holding up the Communion cup and saying, "Here is a symbol of sanctuary." The cup had "Budweiser" written on the side of it. As participants laughed at the irreverence of using a Budweiser glass as a Communion cup, an audience member called out, "At least it wasn't Coors!"—a reference to labor, minority, and women's groups' call for a boycott of Coors products due to the company's hiring practices. Other speakers began by commenting that, despite being behind schedule, they were going to go beyond their allotted ten minutes. Between speeches, one audience member stood to announce, "Because I'm a revolutionary and I believe in social change, I'm going to change the agenda and do something that isn't on it." He then began a speech of his own. Speakers' disregard for agendas and schedules exemplified Tucson sanctuary workers' antibureaucratic attitudes, while their inside jokes emphasized the importance of personal networks to the local sanctuary community.

To give an example of one of the many speeches, I will describe Father Thomás's presentation in depth. Father Thomás made the house dedication's symbolism explicit by equating the rebuilding effort, the reconstruction of the local movement, and the Resurrection. He began by saying that although he'd been asked to talk about sanctuary's future, he didn't know what the future would be. He noted optimistically, however, that the existence of the newly constructed house showed that even when people tried to destroy God's earthly temples, the temples would be rebuilt. The reason that God's temples were destroyed, Father Thomás explained, was that sanctuary workers were doing things that bothered someone. And, he added, sanctuary workers ought to go on doing those things, not in order to bother people, but rather in order to do God's will. Calling for greater commitment on the part of participants, Father Thomás pointed out that in contrast to the torture, death, and disappearance experienced by Central Americans, the worst that sanctuary workers would experience would be the destruction of their homes. Father Thomás concluded that the sanctuary movement could not be destroyed because the kingdom of God could not be destroyed and because God's temple would always be resurrected. Father Thomás thus expressed the empowerment, elation, optimism, and determination engendered by the successful rebuilding effort.

During one of these speeches, a border patrol car drove down the street and stopped near the house. Participants reacted to this sign that they were under observation by urging everyone present to wave at the surveillance cameras posted along the border. This sight of the "enemy" made speakers' references to persecution more concrete.

The final speech was given by John Fisher, the man who had organized the rebuilding effort and who had been chosen to officially deliver the key of the house to Sharon and her family. He called for the *"dueña de la casa,"* ("mistress of the house"). This and other Spanish phrases during the service reflected the bicultural nature of the border, Sharon's own bilingualism and roots in the border region, and participants' solidarity with their Salvadoran, Guatemalan, and Mexican colleagues. Sharon came forward, asking her children to stand with her. At first one child was missing, but just as his absence was noted, he reappeared holding a helium balloon bearing the words "I love you" that had blown away during an earlier speech. The perfect timing of the boy's and balloon's reappearance won applause from the gathering. John presented the key to Sharon and her children, saying, "These kids are the *real* keys to this household."

Sharon took the key, and it became her turn to address those present. She began by telling several stories about herself, her family, border work, and the trial. One of the stories was about taking her youngest daughter—who was born in Mexico—to her First Communion. The official who blessed the child had not been supportive of sanctuary during the trial, so Sharon had told him, "This is my daughter. She's a *mojadita*" ("little wetback"). The official had asked the girl, "What's your name?" "Mojadita," the girl had replied. "But don't worry," Sharon had told him, "She's not an illegal alien, just a mojadita like some people we know." This was a reference to the official himself, who presumably had immigrated from Mexico or elsewhere. By telling this anecdote, Sharon criticized the official church structure for failing to commit itself to righteousness as had this portion of its membership.

Sharon was obviously moved by this gathering and by the effort to rebuild her house. She called sanctuary a wonderful and powerful community, noting that she had experienced that community. She thanked everyone and repeated, "My house is your house, and I mean that." In the midst of these strong emotions, she also told jokes. She said that one of the ministers who had been preparing the prayer service had called to ask her if she had any folding chairs. She said that she'd answered, "No, all we have is Catholic chairs." (In fact, like Catholic pews, the chairs in which we were sitting folded down in back so that people could kneel in prayer.)

As Sharon had been talking, she'd been holding the balloon string in her hand. A participant yelled out, "Don't let go of it," implying that if she did, they would have to search for the balloon again. Then another joked, "Tie the key to it." As Sharon continued trying to express what this group of people meant to her and what her work meant to her, she actually did tie the key to the balloon string. She said, "I love all of you, and your names are in this balloon, because I love you. And I'm going to send this balloon to God, and hopefully, someone who needs shelter will find this key, and will find their way to this house. Because I really mean it when I say that this house is your house, it's everyone's house." She then let go of the balloon, and it floated off into the sky. Participants watched it disappear, then started joking again. "Was that the only key?" one called out. "It doesn't matter," Sharon replied nonchalantly, "We'll just change the locks." Sending the key to Sharon's house to the poor via a helium balloon was an entirely spontaneous and improvised portion of the dedication ritual.

Mistaking the balloon incident for the dedication's conclusion, participants began to leave, but Merlin Wynn came forward and said, "Wait, we're not through yet." Merlin announced that there would be a prayer session, during which participants could share their thoughts or request a prayer. Merlin began, "I don't know if I dare do this, if I have the blood in me to do this, but I want us to say these prayers in the names of those who have shed their blood for us, who couldn't be here, and who have died for liberty." The phrasing of this prayer imbued Central American martyrs with Christ-like qualities, as Christians often pray "in Jesus' name" or "in Christ's name." Saying that Central Americans died "for us" gave Central Americans a redemptive quality similar to Christ's martyrdom. Such examples of martyrdom encouraged commitment and made the sacrifices endured by sanctuary workers seem pale by comparison.

Participants began requesting prayers of thanksgiving for Sharon, her work, her spirit, and the successful rebuilding effort. A sense that "anything is possible" pervaded their requests. In a conciliatory mood, one participant asked that God might so move the hearts and minds of those who had burned down the house that they might now feel joy at its reconstruction. Another added, "I pray that the likes of Jesus Cruz and company never come to this house." At first Merlin questioned this request because it contradicted the prevailing mood of reconciliation. He then said, "Well, okay, that the *likes* of Jesus Cruz not come here, because if they don't change, then they shouldn't come here." Another man asked God to remove the word "alien" from the English vocabulary.

As the service approached its conclusion, several young musicians led the group in "Love Has No Borders," a song that rejects national boundaries and affirms religious notions of universal humanity. The chorus went, "Love has no borders, love knows no bound, love has no borders, love can tear the tallest mountains down." As they sang about tearing down mountains, participants motioned to the aforementioned "hills of oppression" across the border.

Following this song, Teresa Newman announced the last event of the day. Although it had been planned, much of this final action, like the balloon incident, seemed improvised. Teresa asked those present to write a message on a piece of crepe paper—red crepe paper, for the blood of the Central American people. Teresa explained, "If you get in a car that works [a reference to border workers' difficulty acquiring cars that run well] and drive south of here, you'll get to Guatemala. And on your way, you'll pass tens of millions of suffering souls whose suffering has gotten worse due to the new immigration law. So what we are going to do now is to send a message to the Latin American people." Sharon and the speakers passed out crepe paper and pens, and participants wrote messages like, "Bienvenidos" or "Welcome." I wrote, "May there be peace." Then the musicians started playing "When the Saints Go Marching In," and participants sang and marched down to the fence that separated Mexico and the United States. In an act that was reminiscent of protest tactics devised by antinuclear protestors at Greenham Commons and elsewhere, we tied our ribbons around a hole in the fence, setting off, I was told, buzzers in an Immigration office with each touch. Participants joked that they were giving Immigration agents something interesting to watch on their surveillance cameras. As each participant tied his or her ribbon, the musicians played spirituals such as "Swing Low Sweet Chariot" and other participants clapped to the beat and sang along. These songs proclaimed the religious character of the action.

After all of the ribbons had been tied to the fence, participants joined hands, formed a circle that filled the road, and once again sang, "Love Knows No Borders." Although the decision to do this seemed spontaneous, it made ritual sense that participants would end the service this way. Many sanctuary-related meetings, gatherings, and services concluded with participants holding hands, standing in a circle, and praying. By this time, it was 5:00 or 6:00 P.M., and local children wearing Halloween costumes were beginning to trick-or-treat. A car came along, and participants broke the circle so that the car could pass, motioning it on through. But the driver parked, so they closed the circle again. Finally, after the song ended, everyone applauded enthusiastically and Sharon shouted, "Who wants cake?" Participants headed back to her house for cake and more socializing before heading home. Later that night, when I got home, I wrote in my journal, "Being around people like this in a gathering like this, it's hard to understand why everyone isn't out doing sanctuary work."

Despite its affirmations of sanctuary work, the house dedication was not a protest in the sense of a public demonstration. Except for the neighbors and, presumably, the border patrol, no one watched this event. The only newspaper article that referred to participants' actions misinterpreted their significance. The November 1, 1987, issue of the *Arizona Daily Star* featured a photograph of two Mexican trick-or-treaters crossing through a fence hole that had been "decked with festive orange crepe paper, adding a Halloween touch." The dedication's organizers neither invited the press nor sought publicity. Yet, the entire event was imbued with resistance and confrontation. The border patrol car and the surveillance cameras gave participants a sense of being observed. After the ceremony, as I rode back to Tucson, the sanctuary worker who gave me a ride suggested that we were being tailed. Despite participants' consciousness of their visibility to authorities, the house dedication defied the deterrence that is supposed to result from surveillance. By waving at the border patrol, deliberately setting off buzzers in an INS office, and singing "Love Knows No Borders" in full view of surveillance cameras, participants asserted that repression would not destroy sanctuary work. The house dedication was directed not only toward the INS but also inward, with messages of optimism and community empowerment. Through socializing, through their work, and through this service, participants celebrated the community that performed sanctuary work.

## Conclusion

The rituals performed by sanctuary workers were neither "merely expressive" and therefore superfluous nor solely strategies for garnering support or claiming moral legitimacy. Rather, by putting forth powerful claims to truth, prayer, worship, Communion, *¡presentes!*, and reflections challenged U.S. immigration policy, international imperialism, human rights violations, the separation of religion and politics, and the boundaries that divide faiths. Ritual improvisation fused re-

ligion and politics by bringing religious knowledge to bear on participants' interpretations of sociopolitical reality and vice versa. By creatively combining and reconstructing religious practices, scriptural passages, Central American liberation
theology, and past instances of religious activism, sanctuary workers strategically
invoked the authority of religious truth while also celebrating their own understanding of the sacred. Sanctuary rituals practiced change by constructing unique
religious services, innovative methods of improvisation, and a justice-oriented
community that transcended the bounds of religious institutions. Rituals were
also powerful and often public statements regarding U.S. treatment of refugees,
U.S.–Latin American relations, the immorality of war, oppression in Central
America, and religious obligations to do justice. Ritual was integral to the sanctuary movement.

The practices, meanings, and relationships that composed the culture of the
sanctuary movement demonstrate that social movements engage the discourses
in which protestors' lives are embedded. Members of the sanctuary movement
critiqued not only U.S. foreign and refugee policy but also the Orientalism, individualism, materialism, secularism, consumerism, comfort, and greed that participants felt derived from and contributed to unjust government practices. By
*acting* on this critique, sanctuary workers constructed alternatives to the facets of
U.S. social life that they denounced. Creating, reproducing, and embracing
movement culture reshaped social relations, categories, and institutions to produce actions that, though politically contradictory, nonetheless incrementally altered society. The cultural constructs created within the sanctuary movement
were among the political acts that shape social life on an ongoing basis.

## Notes

1. See Gluckman 1965 and Lewis 1980 for discussions of anthropological notions of ritual.
Rosaldo 1989, Gilbert 1989, and Taussig 1987 critique the assumption that rituals are invari-
ant in form.

2. This passage was quoted in both the original and the Jewish versions of EBSC's Covenant of Sanctuary and served as the basis for the name of the undercover investigation of the
movement—"Operation Sojourner"—as well as for the hotline that Tucson sanctuary supporters established for trial updates (1–800-LEV-1933).

3. The word "presente" also connotes commitment and a readiness to struggle. For example, during a political demonstration that I attended in Argentina in 1985, a speaker told
the gathering of approximately 50,000 people, *"Pidamos, compañeros, la libertad de los
compañeros presos políticos, y gritemos,* '¡Presente compañeros!'" ("Let us ask, comrades, for
the freedom of our comrades the political prisoners, and let us shout, 'Ready, comrades!'")
Thus when participants shout "¡presente!" during a ¡presente! ritual, they are both invoking
the presence of the dead and committing themselves to be present in the struggle for which
the dead perished.

4. During a workshop at a Northern California Sanctuary Covenant gathering, a Salvadoran catechist led the group in a Christian base communities version of "Simon Says"

called "El pueblo dice" ("The People Say").

5. For other discussions of ways that communities and individuals have redefined their notions of history, see Yanagisako 1985, Appadurai 1981, Hobsbawm and Ranger 1983, Clifford 1988, Blu 1980, Comaroff 1978, and Moore 1986.

6. The second saying refers to the covenant between God and humanity.

7. Passing the peace is a practice in which participants in a service greet each other with handshakes, hugs, and the words, "Peace be with you."

# 11

## Conclusion

*As far as the conversion goes, sanctuary is only the current one. There will be another Kairos. History repeats itself.*
—Simon Portnoy, former pastor of a Tucson sanctuary congregation

In March 1992, as I was completing revisions of this manuscript, the East Bay Sanctuary Covenant celebrated the tenth anniversary of the declarations that initiated the movement.[1] Those who led some 300 members of the local movement in song, responsive readings, prayer, and other rites included people whose words fill these pages as well as individuals whose names and voices I did not recognize. Unlike the 1987 Sanctuary Remembrance service, which took place at a time when participants' enthusiasm was waning, public interest had ebbed, EBSC's growth had slowed, and the struggle to achieve peace in Central America seemed interminable, the 1992 commemoration celebrated a number of successes. In 1990, following the assassination of six Jesuit priests, their housekeeper, and her daughter, the U.S. government had cut military aid to El Salvador.[2] In the same year, the U.S. Congress had passed legislation granting Temporary Protected Status (TPS) to Salvadorans,[3] and, facing a lawsuit filed by the American Baptist Church and other religious and refugee rights groups, the INS had improved its asylum procedures and agreed to reopen the cases of some 150,000 Salvadorans and Guatemalans. Perhaps most significantly, in 1991 the Salvadoran government and the guerrilla forces had signed peace accords that officially ended more than a decade of civil war. Despite the accomplishment of a number of movement goals, the commemoration's tone was not one of finalization but rather recommitment. Speakers stressed that in El Salvador, war-ravaged communities needed rebuilding, continuing human rights abuses needed to be denounced, and the peace accords needed to be implemented. In Guatemala, human rights work and efforts to end the violence needed support. And in the United States, TPS needed to be extended past its June 30, 1992, expiration date. Moreover, newly arrived Salvadorans and Guatemalans, who were not eligible for TPS, needed sanctuary and social services. The movement, speakers emphasized, had not ended.[4]

I cannot predict the movement's future course, but I *can* delineate some of the ways that, to date, sanctuary has changed participating individuals, congregations, communities, and thus, incrementally, society as a whole. To assist and advocate for undocumented Salvadoran and Guatemalan refugees, religious volunteers created close-knit formal and informal networks of individuals and congregations that crossed borders, sheltered Central Americans, and publicized refugee testimonies. To construct these practices, movement members manipulated the procedures and concepts that made up U.S. immigration law, arguing that, because they met the legal definition of "refugee," Central Americans *were* refugees, regardless of court rulings to the contrary. To substantiate this claim, participants incorporated legal processes into movement practices. Sanctuary workers assessed immigrants' asylum claims, aided those immigrants judged to be refugees, and publicized the accounts of persecution and flight on which participants' interpretations of the law were based. Sanctuary workers defined this partial substitute for the U.S. immigration system as civil *initiative,* rather than civil *disobedience,* contending that because the U.S. government had failed to fulfill its legal obligations, citizens were obliged to do so. By practicing civil initiative, movement members not only authorized citizens to interpret and enforce the law but also sought to *validate* such interpretations on a societal level. By acting on their understanding of the law, sanctuary workers challenged the government to either tacitly accept their legal notions or indict movement members and thus give them the opportunity to prove their claims in court. When the government *did* indict and convict sanctuary workers, defendants used the trial to publicize the movement, question the validity of the verdicts, and defy the deterrence that was supposed to result from being subjects of a government investigation.

The border crossings and other activities devised to carry out participants' understanding of law not only produced novel legal notions but also led movement members to reevaluate their own culture and faith from what they believed was the perspective of the Central American poor. Participants experienced crossing international borders as traversing boundaries between First and Third Worlds, affluence and poverty, apathy and commitment, security and risk, and secularism and faith. From across these borders, movement members reexamined social reality and concluded not only that their values, assumptions, and theologies had been developed in a middle-class North American context, but also that the practices in which these were embedded were connected to violence and injustice in El Salvador and Guatemala. Participants incorporated this critique, which was largely expressed through anecdotes contrasting Central and North America, into sanctuary practices, attempting, within the movement at least, to live according to the principles that they espoused. By striving to create egalitarian, personal, committed relationships with Salvadorans and Guatemalans, sanctuary workers tried to counter the imperialism and exploitation that they felt typified U.S.–Central American relations. By, without remuneration, performing acts for the benefit of others, movement members opposed the pursuit of self-interest that they perceived as a cause of unequal international distribution of wealth. In addition, by fusing religion and politics, participants opposed the secularism that they blamed for the United States's failure to truly be a "nation under God."

As they critiqued U.S. culture and devised unique legal practices, sanctuary workers also reexamined their own religious traditions. For some Christian participants, reinterpreting their faith from the perspective of Central American refugees produced a conversion to liberation theology's risk-filled commitment to social action. Some Jewish sanctuary workers made sense of Central Americans' suffering by constructing parallels between Jewish and Central American experiences of persecution and exile. Such reinterpretations of faith not only informed movement practices, which thus became methods of religious witness as well as political action, but also led movement members to invoke, recombine, and redefine elements of their ritual repertoires in light of Central American issues. The rituals that resulted united religion and politics, content and context, worship and protest. By coming together to work and to worship, Jews, Catholics, Protestants, Unitarians, and even, after the conclusion of my research, Buddhists reached into their diverse traditions to uncover common commitments to social action. Through such interconnected legal, cultural, and religious innovations, members of the sanctuary movement *created* culture and changed society.

The innovations created within movements such as sanctuary shed light on how culture is produced within society at large. Societies, like social movements, are continually transformed and reproduced; individuals, like protestors, continually shape and are shaped by society; and, because these processes unfold over time, societies and individuals are simultaneously products and agents of history. Sanctuary workers reproduced both the movement and wider culture by acting on their understanding of reality in ways that reauthorized that understanding. For example, when sanctuary workers constructed their relationships with Central Americans, they acted on the preexisting Orientalist notion[5] that technology and faith are inversely related (Said 1979; Clifford 1988; Taussig 1987). This notion, along with other considerations, encouraged sanctuary workers to make "pilgrimages" to Central America, seek knowledge of refugees' lives, and regard Central Americans' words as sources of wisdom. These actions in turn defined Central Americans as more faithful than North Americans, an interpretation that was further reproduced through sanctuary workers' anecdotes about Central Americans. These anecdotes, and the interpretations they conveyed, encouraged additional crossings. Society and culture were thus continually recreated as movement members realized their notions of reality.

At the same time as the mutually constructing relationship between meaning and action reproduces society and culture, it also transforms them. In the case of the sanctuary movement, for example, the notion that less technologically advanced peoples are more religious than more technologically developed ones took on new meaning when it was applied to a new context: the relationship between religious volunteers and undocumented Salvadoran and Guatemalan immigrants. After this initial modification, further revisions ensued. Because culture is not homogenous (Sahlins 1981), not all sanctuary workers shared the view that Central American peasants were more spiritual than North American profession- als. Some found this characterization offensive, the "inverse of racism," to quote one participant. As these dissenters interacted with other movement members, they challenged the "dominant" movement interpretation of Central American reality. Moreover, individuals sometimes simultaneously held contradictory cul- tural concepts. For example, a Tucson pastor whom I interviewed insisted that Central Americans could teach North Americans about faith even as he warned against "romanticizing" refugees. Such ambiguity infused events with multiple significances and allowed movement members to reframe their analyses for dif- ferent contexts and to revise their initial conclusions in light of subsequent expe- riences. Finally, actions take place in historical rather than structural time, and therefore no two actions are ever identical. Because actions differ from one in- stance to the next, the interpretations of similar actions can also differ, either minimally or dramatically. Thus, for example, one border crosser might experi- ence confronting death in El Salvador as an encounter with religious truth, while another might resort to therapy to interpret an equally harrowing incident.

Not only is society continually reproduced and transformed, but the individu- als who perform these processes continually shape and are shaped by society. Cu- mulatively, society is a product of individual and collective actions. Not only do "ordinary people, pursuing subjective ends, realize the structures of inequality that constrain their own possibilities" (Collier 1988:2); in addition, individuals create new social opportunities. Individuals improvise by making sense of unex- pected events, combining preexisting ideas and practices in novel ways, applying cultural constructs to new situations, interacting with others who hold conflicting beliefs, and so on. (Note that all this creativity is not necessarily beneficial. Fas- cists and torturers are as good at it as artists and activists. ) Yet, paradoxically, the individuals who, on an ongoing basis, produce the social order *are themselves* products of society. Society (which is an amalgam of conflicting and coalescing ideas, traditions, strains, cultures, and histories) provides the cultural clay, the raw material, out of which people construct the conditions of their existence. When sanctuary workers devised legal arguments, they manipulated preexisting cultural constructs, such as the distinction between "natural" and "official" law (Greenhouse 1989), the separation between juridical and physical existences, and the view, expounded during the sanctuary trial, that, when lives are at stake, abso- lutist interpretations of the law must be tempered by mercy (Rosen 1989). Though individuals can create, they do so in contexts and using materials that, to an ex- tent, have predetermined significances.

Both social constructs and the individuals they create are products and agents of history. Reproduction and transformation, innovation and imposition occur over time through forces, trends, effects, and causes that are larger than the indi- viduals and communities involved. When individuals act in the ways that simul- taneously perpetuate and alter the social order, they do so because of a conjuncture (to borrow a term favored by Marshall Sahlins) of circumstances. In the case of the sanctuary movement, these circumstances included the development of liberation theology, the assassination of the Salvadoran Archbishop, and a coyote's decision to abandon his charges in an Arizona desert. Such conjunctures shape individuals' actions and the social conditions that these actions create. Moreover, the traditions, practices, notions, and institutions that individuals rely upon to improvise are endowed by history. To some extent, it was inevitable that, given the conjuncture that acquainted them with Central American reality, the particular network of relationships in which they were embedded, and the traditions of activism that were woven into their theologies, religious volunteers would protest the deportation of Salvadoran and Guatemalan immigrants (see also Piven and Cloward 1977). At the same time, even within the constraints set by social and historical circumstances, the course of events is *never* wholly (or even mostly) determined. In responding to (and playing a part in producing) a socially and historically created opportunity, religious volunteers did not *have* to resort to declaring their congregations sanctuaries, nor did they *have* to define this act as legal. They could have filed class action suits against the INS (which they, in fact, did), organized marches and sit-ins, or offered sanctuary but construed this as civil disobedience. In acting as they did, sanctuary workers became agents of history. Though the practices and meanings (such as the underground railroad, sanctuary, covenant, and so forth) that participants drew on and redefined to create the movement were products of history, the movement itself was historically unique. Even if sanctuary had not succeeded (as it at least partially has, with the help of historical circumstances and the actions of other solidarity groups) in affecting the decisions of lawmakers, by its very existence, the sanctuary movement would have "made history."

To analyze the political implications of producing social movements (which also means producing culture and history), I have followed Foucault in contending that power and resistance inhere in discourses, the systems of meaning and practices that construct social reality. These discourses are imbued with power in that they constitute individuals as beings (patients, deviants, criminals, illegal aliens, etc.) within particular systems of knowledge. Resistance then consists of questioning, subverting, deconstructing, and reconstructing the identities and constructs that are produced, authenticated, and validated through daily life. Particular discourses create opportunities to define and question, to subject and resist, *at the same time.* For example, as the enforcement of U.S. immigration law was increasingly displaced from government officials to private citizens, surveillance became more deeply embedded in daily life; at the same time, however, individuals acquired greater opportunity to redefine immigration categories through social action. If society is composed of discourses that constitute reality while undermining these constructions, then the reproduction and transformation, imposition and innovation, determinism and agency that produce social movements are all imbued with both power and resistance. For example, when they applied the legal category "refugee" to undocumented individuals, sanctuary workers simultaneously challenged the exclusivity of the government's authority over immigration matters and placed themselves in a position of power vis-à-vis Central Americans.

If social action is inherently contradictory, then how is one to assess the political content of movements such as sanctuary? To try to weigh the amount of resistance within movement actions against the degree to which they are power-laden would be the wrong approach. Crossing, sheltering, and publicizing the stories of undocumented Central Americans were unquestionably acts of resistance. They were contradictory because *all* actions, including the repressive measures taken by authorities, engage multiple discourses, have unintended consequences, and occur under circumstances and manipulate constructs whose implications actors cannot entirely control. Rather than attempting to envision a "purely counterhegemonic act" and then measuring actual incidents against this ideal, the task confronting analysts is to delve deeper into the multifaceted and often conflicting implications of actions. Such an endeavor would both expose the systems of power in which people operate (Abu-Lughod 1990) and reveal the ways that people *do*, sometimes against tremendous odds, seek to create more just societies. Acknowledging that, mediated as they are by the contexts in which they occur, such efforts will necessarily be imperfect does not imply that they are not worthwhile.

This analysis of the production of culture suggests that far from being a rare event, resistance is an ongoing part of social life. The myriad and minute ways that individuals and communities subvert, contest, and redefine the practices that situate individuals within power-laden categories are difficult to discern, but, just as sanctuary workers found themselves addressing careerism as they sought to change U.S. refugee policy, so too do the actions that make up daily life both intentionally and unintentionally engage multiple cultural discourses. If society is continually constructed through human action (which is itself a product of society), and if these actions have the potential to reinforce or deconstruct particular power relations, then acts that are as seemingly trivial as furnishing proof of work authorization to an employer or not requiring identity documents of one's babysitter have political implications. Like their implications, the effects of such actions may not be immediately apparent. However, because transformation is implicated within reproduction, because innovation is part of imposition, and because history is both determined and determining, such actions continually remake society. Social change is process as well as result, the ongoing state of affairs more than the exception to the rule. When individuals make and remake society, they may not level grandiose challenges to immigration discourse, structural racism, or the inequities of capitalism, but they do, inevitably, address such systems. Daily acts of resistance—and of power—continually and incrementally reshape society.

## Notes

1. I was living in Los Angeles at the time and, owing to other commitments, was not able to attend the commemoration. However, EBSC members sent me a tape recording of the event.

2. Aid resumed in 1991.

3. Salvadorans who had been present in the United States since September 19, 1990, were eligible to register for Temporary Protected Status (TPS). TPS was not the same thing as asylum. Asylees were permitted to stay in the United States indefinitely and to apply for Permanent Legal Resident Status (which would eventually make them eligible for citizenship) after one year. In contrast, TPS expired on June 30, 1992, at which time those who had been granted TPS became eligible for a new status, Deferred Enforced Departure (DED). DED delayed the deportation of these immigrants by one year and provided that the U.S. president could extend this period if desired. After DED expires, DED recipients will once more be subject to deportation, unless they are able to obtain asylum or another form of legal relief.

4. In addition, though this was not mentioned at the commemoration service, some participating congregations were considering extending sanctuary to Haitian refugees. One exciting facet of such a project, in participants' eyes, was that it would forge alliances between sanctuary groups and members of the African-American community.

5. Of course, the opposition between "science" and "religion" is not limited to Orientalism.

# Appendix

## East Bay Sanctuary Covenant:
## Original Covenant of Sanctuary

*When a stranger sojourns with you in your land, you shall not do him wrong. The stranger who sojourns with you shall be to you as the native among you, and you shall love him as yourself; for you were strangers in the land of Egypt; I am the Lord your God.*

—Leviticus 19:33–34

*... for I was hungry and you gave me food, I was thirsty and you gave me to drink, I was a stranger and you welcomed me, I was sick and you visited me, I was in prison and you came to me.*

—Matthew 25:35–36

The Bay Area has become a place of uncertain refuge for men, women and children who are fleeing for their lives from the vicious and devastating conflict in Central America. Many of these refugees have chosen to leave their country only after witnessing the murder of close friends and relatives.

The United Nations has declared these people legitimate refugees of war; by every moral and legal standard, they ought to be received as such by the government of the United States. The 1951 United Nations Convention and the 1967 Protocol Agreements on refugees—both signed by the U.S.—established the rights of refugees *not* to be sent back to their countries of origin. Thus far, however, our government has been unwilling to meet it's [*sic*] obligations under these agreements. The refugees among us are consequently threatened with the prospect of deportation back to El Salvador and Guatemala, where they face the likelihood of severe reprisals, perhaps including death.

This is not the first time religious people have been called to bear witness to our faith in providing sanctuary to refugees branded "illegal" in their flight from persecution. The slaves who fled north in our own country and the Jews who fled Nazi Germany are but two examples from recent history. We believe the religious community is now being called again to provide sanctuary to the refugees among us.

Therefore, we join in covenant to provide sanctuary—support, protection, and advocacy—to El Salvadoran and Guatemalan refugees who request safe haven out of fear of persecution upon return to their homeland. We do this out of concern for the welfare of these refugees, regardless of their official immigrant status. We acknowledge that legal consequences may result from our action. We enter this covenant as an act of religious commitment.

## East Bay Sanctuary Covenant:
## Jewish Covenant of Sanctuary

For the past several years the United States has become a place of uncertain refuge for men, women and children who are fleeing for their lives from the vicious and devastating wars in Central America. Many of these refugees have chosen to leave their country only after witnessing the murder of close friends and relatives.

The United Nations has declared these people legitimate refugees of war; by every moral and legal standard, they ought to be received as such by the government of the United States. The 1951 United Nations Convention and the 1967 Protocol Agreements on refugees—both signed by the U.S.—established the rights of refugees *not* to be sent back to their countries of origin. Thus far, however, our government has been unwilling to meet it's [*sic*] obligations under these agreements. The refugees among us are consequently threatened with the prospect of deportation back to El Salvador and Guatemala, where they face the likelihood of severe reprisals, perhaps including death.

The plight of these refugees powerfully reminds us of our own history. Hundreds of thousands of whom could have been saved from Hitler's ovens did not meet the U.S. immigration nor those of virtually any other land. With all sanctuary denied them, our people were forced to wander as illegal aliens. Their return to Hitler's Europe almost always meant their death. Against this denial of safety there were a few courageous voices—the righteous gentiles—who followed their consciences and provided safe haven.

Our historical experience of the Diaspora has given us a profound appreciation for the exiled and the homeless among all people: black slaves who fled north to freedom, all the immigrants who fled desperate oppression. In their name we now seek to answer the call from our own tradition.

"When a stranger sojourns with you in your land, you shall do him no wrong. The stranger who sojourns with you shall be as the native among you, and you shall love him as yourself; for you were strangers in the land of Egypt." (Lev. 19: 33–34)

"Give council, grant justice; make your shade like night at the height of noon; hide the outcasts, betray not the fugitive. Let the outcasts of Moab sojourn among you; be a refuge to them from the destroyer." (Isaiah 16:3–4)

The words of the Torah, the demands of the prophets, the ethics of the Talmud and the centuries of Jewish response are clear. Therefore we join in covenant to provide sanctuary—support, protection, and advocacy—to Central American refugees who request safe haven out of fear of persecution upon return to their homeland. We do this out of concern for the welfare of these refugees, regardless of their official immigrant status. We understand that sanctuary is a serious responsibility for all persons involved. Although we recognize that legal consequences may result from our action, we do not acknowledge that the provision of sanctuary is an illegal act. We enter this covenant as an act of conscience and moral imperative.

# References

Abrahams, Roger D. 1986. "Ordinary and Extraordinary Experience." In Victor Turner and Edward Bruner, eds., *The Anthropology of Experience*, 45–72. Urbana, Ill.: University of Illinois Press.

Abu-Lughod, Lila. 1986. *Veiled Sentiments: Honor and Poetry in a Bedouin Society.* Berkeley: University of California Press.

————. 1990. "The Romance of Resistance: Tracing Transformations of Power Through Bedouin Women." *American Ethnologist* 17(1):41–55.

Alcoff, Linda. 1988. "Cultural Feminism Versus Post-Structuralism: The Identity Crisis in Feminist Theory." *Signs* 13(3):405–436.

Althusser, Louis. 1971. "Ideology and Ideological State Apparatuses (Notes Towards an Investigation)." In *Lenin and Philosophy, and Other Essays,* Ben Brewster, trans., 127–186. New York: Monthly Review Press.

Appadurai, Arjun. 1981. "The Past as a Scarce Resource." *Man* 16:201–219.

Arax, Mark. 1988. "INS Scoops Up 51 Alien Ice Cream Vendors." *Los Angeles Times,* 24 March, sec. 2, 7.

Asad, Talal, ed. 1973. *Anthropology and the Colonial Encounter.* London: Ithaca Press.

Asad, Talal. 1983a. "Anthropological Conceptions of Religion: Reflections on Geertz." *Man* 18(2): 237–259.

————. 1983b. "Notes on Body Pain and Truth in Medieval Christian Ritual." *Economy and Society* 12: 287–327.

A.S.D.F. (Arizona Sanctuary Defense Fund). 1985a. "Phoenix Sanctuary Trial: The First Week of Hearings." Unpublished bulletin, 7 June. On file at American Friends Service Committee office, Tucson, Ariz.

————. 1985b. "Update for the Sanctuary Trial for the Week of Dec. 3–6, 1985." Unpublished bulletin. On file at American Friends Service Committee office, Tucson, Ariz.

————. 1985c. "Update for the Sanctuary Trial for the Week of Dec. 10–13." Unpublished bulletin. On file at American Friends Service Committee office, Tucson, Ariz.

————. 1985d. "Weekly Update for the Sanctuary Trial, December 17–19, 1985." Unpublished bulletin. On file at American Friends Service Committee office, Tucson, Ariz.

————. 1986a "Weekly Update for the Sanctuary Trial, January 7–10, 1986." Unpublished bulletin. On file at American Friends Service Committee office, Tucson, Ariz.

————. 1986b. "Sanctuary Trial Update for the Week of April 8–11, 1986." Unpublished bulletin. On file at American Friends Service Committee office, Tucson, Ariz.

————. 1986c. Arizona "Sanctuary Defense Update." Unpublished bulletin, circa 20 May. On file at American Friends Service Committee office, Tucson, Ariz.

————. 1986d. "Sanctuary Defendants Sentenced to Probation: Vow to Continue Work with Refugees." Unpublished bulletin, 3 July. On file at American Friends Service Committee office, Tucson, Ariz.

Bach, Robert L. 1990. "Immigration and U.S. Foreign Policy in Latin America and the Caribbean." In Robert W. Tucker et al., eds., *Immigration and U.S. Foreign Policy*, 123–149. Boulder, Colo.: Westview Press.

Bailey, Eric, and H. G. Reza. 1988. "An Alien Presence." *Los Angeles Times*, 5 June, sec. 1, 36.

Barrios de Chungara, Domitila, and Moema Viezzer. 1978. *Let Me Speak: Testimony of Domitila, a Woman of the Bolivian Tin Mines*. Victoria Ortiz, trans. New York: Monthly Review Press.

*Basta*. 1986. "Total Number of Sanctuaries, 7/82 to 10/86." December issue, 35.

Bau, Ignatius. 1985. *This Ground Is Holy: Church Sanctuary and Central American Refugees*. New York: Paulist Press.

Bellah, Robert N. 1975. *The Broken Covenant: American Civil Religion in Time of Trial*. New York: Seabury.

Bellah, Robert N., et al. 1985. *Habits of the Heart: Individualism and Commitment in American Life*. New York: Harper and Row.

Bercovitch, Sacvan. 1978. *The American Jeremiad*. Madison: University of the First World Warf Wisconsin Press.

Blu, Karen. 1980. *The Lumbee Problem: The Making of an American Indian People*. Cambridge: Cambridge University Press.

Bohannan, Paul. 1968. *Justice and Judgment Among the Tiv*. London: Oxford University Press.

Bourdieu, Pierre. 1977. *Outline of a Theory of Practice*. Richard Nice, trans. Cambridge: Cambridge University Press.

————. 1987. "The Force of Law: Toward a Sociology of the Juridical Field." Richard Terdiman, trans. *The Hastings Law Journal* 38:805–853.

Browning, Daniel R. 1986a. "Hints of Atrocities Enter Testimony in Sanctuary Trial." *Arizona Daily Star*, 11 January, 1B, 7B.

————. 1986b. "Salvadoran Witness Contradicts His Affidavit." *Arizona Daily Star*, 7 February, 1B.

————. 1986c. "Defense Attorneys Find Carroll's Rulings Inconsistent and Confusing." *Arizona Daily Star*, 9 February, 1B, 7B.

————. 1986d. "Sanctuary Jury Asked to Give INS Message to Leave Churches Alone." *Arizona Daily Star*, 11 April, C7.

————. 1986e. "Reno Pleased that American Justice System Works." *Arizona Daily Star*, 2 May, 6A.

————. 1987. "Sanctuary Lawyers to Use FBI-Spying Allegation." *Arizona Daily Star*, 13 February.

Browning, Daniel R., and Mark Turner. 1986. "5 Sanctuary Defendants Receive Suspended Sentences, Probation." *Arizona Daily Star*, 2 July, 1A, 10A.

Camarda, Renato. 1985. *Forced to Move*. San Francisco: Solidarity Publications.

Carter, Paul Allen. 1971. *The Spiritual Crisis of the Gilded Age*. Dekalb, Ill.: Northern Illinois University Press.

Castells, Manuel. 1983. *The City and the Grassroots: A Cross-Cultural Theory of Urban Social Movements*. London: Edward Arnold.

Clifford, James. 1988. *The Predicament of Culture: Twentieth-Century Ethnography, Literature, and Art*. Cambridge: Harvard University Press.

Clifford, James, and George E. Marcus, eds. 1986. *Writing Culture: The Poetics and Politics of Ethnography*. Berkeley: University of California Press.

Cohen, A. P., and J. L. Comaroff. 1976. "The Management of Meaning: On the Phenomenology of Political Transactions." In Bruce Kapferer, ed., *Transaction and Meaning: Directions in the Anthropology of Exchange and Symbolic Behavior,* 87–107. Philadelphia: Institute for the Study of Human Issues.

Coleman, Richard J. 1972. *Issues of Theological Conflict: Evangelicals and Liberals.* Grand Rapids: Wm. B. Eerdmans.

Collier, Jane Fishburne. 1988. *Marriage and Inequality in Classless Societies.* Stanford: Stanford University Press.

Comaroff, Jean. 1985. *Body of Power, Spirit of Resistance: The Culture and History of a South African Chiefdom.* Chicago: University of Chicago Press.

Comaroff, John L. 1978. "Rules and Rulers: Political Processes in a Tswana Chiefdom." *Man* 13: 1–20.

Comaroff, John L., and Simon Roberts. 1981. *Rules and Processes: The Cultural Logic of Dispute in an African Context.* Chicago: University of Chicago Press.

Corbett, Jim. 1986. *Borders and Crossings.* Vol. 1, *Some Sanctuary Papers,* 1981–1986. April edition. Tucson: Tucson refugee support group.

Coutin, Susan. 1990. *The Culture of Protest: Religious Activism and the U.S. Sanctuary Movement.* Doctoral Dissertation, Stanford University.

Cox, Harvey. 1986. "The Spy in the Pew." *New York Times,* 3 March.

Deloria, Vine. 1969. *Custer Died for Your Sins.* New York: Macmillan.

Dilling, Yvonne. 1984. *In Search of Refuge.* Scottdale, Penn.: Herald Press.

Dombrowski, James. 1936. *The Early Days of Christian Socialism in America.* New York: Columbia University Press.

Dominguez, Jorge I. 1990. "Immigration as Foreign Policy in U.S.–Latin American Relations." In Robert W. Tucker et al., eds., *Immigration and U.S. Foreign Policy,* 150–166. Boulder, Colo.: Westview Press.

Douglas, Ann. 1977. *The Feminization of American Culture.* New York: Alfred A. Knopf.

Duarte, Carmen. 1986. "FBI Inquiry Sought in Burglaries at Sanctuary Centers." *Arizona Daily Star,* 31 January, 1A.

Durazo, Armando. 1986. "Sanctuary Witness Says He Came to U.S. for Economic Gain." *Tucson Citizen,* 5 February, 8B.

Durkheim, Emile. 1933. *On the Division of Labor in Society.* George Simpson, trans. New York: Macmillan.

Earl, John E. 1986. "Taking Care of U.S. First." *Arizona Daily Star,* 1 February, 14A.

EBSC (East Bay Sanctuary Covenant). 1983. "Minutes of EBSC Steering Committee Meeting." 4 December.

————. 1985. "Minutes of EBSC Steering Committee Meeting." 3 February.

Esper, George. 1987. "Aliens Canada Refused Await Fate in N.Y. Town." *Arizona Daily Star,* 1 March, B13.

Evans, Sara M., and Harry C. Boyte. 1986. *Free Spaces: The Sources of Democratic Change in America.* New York: Harper and Row.

Favret-Saada, Jeanne. 1980. *Deadly Words: Witchcraft in the Bocage.* Cambridge: Cambridge University Press.

Fimbres, Gabrielle. 1986a. "Sanctuary 8 Will Get to Speak." *Tucson Citizen,* 30 June, 1A–2A.

————. 1986b. "Leniency Asked for Sanctuary 8." *Tucson Citizen,* 1 July, 1A–2A.

Fireman, Bruce, and William Gamson. 1979. "Utilitarian Logic in the Resource Mobilization Perspective." In Mayer N. Zald and John D. McCarthy, eds., *The Dynamics of Social Movements: Resource Mobilization, Social Control, and Tactics,* 8–44. Cambridge: Winthrop.

Fischer, Howard. 1986. "Panel OKs INS Trace for Welfare." *Arizona Daily Star,* 2 April, 1C.

Foucault, Michel. 1979. *Discipline and Punish: The Birth of the Prison.* Alan Sheridan, trans. New York: Vintage Books.

_____. 1980a. *The History of Sexuality.* Vol. 1, *An Introduction.* Robert Hurley, trans. New York: Vintage Books.

_____. 1980b. *Power/Knowledge.* Colin Gordon, ed. New York: Pantheon.

Fuchs, Lawrence H. 1985. "The Search for a Sound Immigration Policy: A Personal View." In Nathan Glazer, ed., *Clamor at the Gates: The New American Immigration,* 17–48. San Francisco: Institute for Contemporary Studies.

Gamson, William. 1975. *The Strategy of Social Protest.* Homewood, Ill.: Dorsey Press.

Garner, Roberta, and Mayer N. Zald. 1985. "The Political Economy of Social Movement Sectors." In Gerald D. Suttles and Mayer N. Zald, eds., *The Challenge of Social Control: Citizenship and Institution Building in Modern Society,* 119–149. Norwood, N.J.: Ablex.

Geertz, Clifford. 1973. "Religion as a Cultural System." In *The Interpretation of Cultures: Selected Essays,* 87–125. New York: Basic Books, Inc.

_____. 1980. *Negara: The Theatre State in Nineteenth Century Bali.* Princeton: Princeton University Press.

_____. 1983. "Local Knowledge: Fact and Law in Comparative Perspective." In *Local Knowledge: Further Essays in Interpretive Anthropology,* 167–234. New York: Basic Books.

Gelbspan, Ross. 1991. *Break-ins, Death Threats and the FBI: The Covert War Against the Central America Movement.* Boston: South End Press.

Gerlach, Luther P., and Virginia Hine. 1970. *People, Power, Change: Movements of Social Protest.* Indianapolis: The Bobbs-Merrill Co., Inc.

Giddens, Anthony. 1976. *New Rules of Sociological Method: A Positive Critique of Interpretative Sociologies.* London: Hutchinson.

Gilbert, Michelle. 1989. "The Cracked Pot and the Missing Sheep." *American Ethnologist* 16(2):213–229.

Gluckman, Max. 1965. *Politics, Law and Ritual in Tribal Society.* Oxford: Basil Blackwell.

Godelier, Maurice. 1977. *Perspectives in Marxist Anthropology.* Robert Brain, trans. Cambridge: Cambridge University Press.

Greenhouse, Carol J. 1986. *Praying for Justice: Faith, Order, and Community in an American Town.* Ithaca: Cornell University Press.

_____. 1989. "Interpreting American Litigiousness." In June Starr and Jane F. Collier, eds., *History and Power in the Study of Law: New Directions in Legal Anthropology,* 252–276. Ithaca: Cornell University Press.

Gusfield, Joseph R. 1968. "The Study of Social Movements." *International Encyclopedia of the Social Sciences* 14:445–452. New York: Macmillan.

_____. 1970. *Reform and Revolt: A Reader in Social Movements.* New York: John Wiley and Sons, Inc.

Hannigan, John A. 1985. "Alain Touraine, Manuel Castells and Social Movement Theory: A Critical Appraisal." *The Sociological Quarterly* 26(4): 435–454.

Harding, Susan. 1984. "Reconstructing Order Through Action: Jim Crow and the Southern Civil Rights Movement." In Charles Bright and Susan Harding, eds., *Statemaking and Social Movements: Essays in History and Theory,* 378–402. Ann Arbor: University of Michigan Press.

_____. 1993. "Epilogue: Observing the Observers." In Nancy Tatom Ammerman, ed., *Southern Baptists Observed,* 318–337. Knoxville: University of Tennessee Press.

Harwood, Edwin. 1984. "Arrests Without Warrant: The Legal and Organizational Environment of Immigration Law Enforcement." *University of California, Davis, Law Review* 17:505–548.

————. 1986. *In Liberty's Shadow: Illegal Aliens and Immigration Law Enforcement.* Stanford: Stanford University Press.

Hirsch, Eric L. 1986. "The Creation of Political Solidarity in Social Movement Organizations." *The Sociological Quarterly* 27(3):373–387.

Hobsbawm, E. J. 1959. *Primitive Rebels: Studies in Archaic Forms of Social Movement in the* 19th and 20th Centuries. New York: W. W. Norton and Co.

Hobsbawm, E. J., and Terrence Ranger, eds. 1983. *The Invention of Tradition.* Cambridge: Cambridge University Press.

Hopkins, Charles Howard. 1940. *The Rise of the Social Gospel in American Protestantism,* 1865–1915. New Haven: Yale University Press.

Hull, Elizabeth. 1985. *Without Justice for All: The Constitutional Rights of Aliens.* Westport, Conn.: Greenwood Press.

James, Bob. 1988. "Boy Is Denied Place on List for New Liver." *Los Angeles Times,* 25 March, sec. 2, 3.

Jenkins, J. Craig. 1983. "Resource Mobilization Theory and the Study of Social Movements." *Annual Review of Sociology* 9:527–553.

Jensen, R. 1988. "Letters to the Times." *Los Angeles Times,* 6 June, sec. 2, 8.

Kapferer, Bruce, ed. 1976. *Transaction and Meaning: Directions in the Anthropology of Exchange and Symbolic Behavior.* Philadelphia: Institute for the Study of Human Issues.

Kaplan, Temma. 1977. *Anarchists: 1868–1903.* Princeton: Princeton University Press.

Kendall, John. 1988. "Probe into Death of Youth Seized in INS Raid Urged." *Los Angeles Times,* 3 March, sec. 1, 24.

Kennedy, Edward M. 1981. "Refugee Act of 1980." *International Migration Review* 15(1–2):141–156.

Kennon, Ken. 1987. "Worship Nurtures Sanctuary." *Corletter* 2(5):1.

King, William McGuire. 1982. "The Biblical Base of the Social Gospel." In Ernest R. Sandeen, ed., *The Bible and Social Reform,* 59–84. Philadelphia: Fortress Press.

Kingston, Maxine Hong. 1980. *China Men.* New York: Alfred A. Knopf.

Klandermans, Bert. 1984. "Mobilization and Participation: Social-Psychological Expansions of Resource Mobilization Theory." *American Sociological Review* 49:583–600.

————. 1988. "The Formation and Mobilization of Consensus." *International Social Movement Research* 1:173–196.

Klandermans, Bert, and Sidney Tarrow. 1988. "Mobilization into Social Movements: Synthesizing European and American Approaches." *International Social Movement Research* 1:1–38.

Kreutz, Douglas. 1986. "Verdict Makes 8 Criminals." *Tucson Citizen,* 2 May, 1A,7A.

Labov, William. 1972. *Language in the Inner City: Studies in the Black English Vernacular.* Philadelphia: University of Pennsylvania Press.

LaFeber, Walter. 1984. *Inevitable Revolutions: The United States in Central America.* New York: W. W. Norton and Co.

Lerner, Gerda. 1979. "The Lady and the Mill Girl: Changes in the Status of Women in the Age of Jackson, 1800–1840." In Nancy F. Cott and Elizabeth H. Pleck, eds., *A Heritage of Her Own: Toward a New Social History of American Women,* 182–196. New York: Simon and Schuster.

Lewis, Gilbert. 1980. *Day of Shining Red: An Essay on Understanding Ritual.* Cambridge: Cambridge University Press.

Limon, Jose E. 1983. "Western Marxism and Folklore: A Critical Introduction." *Journal of American Folklore* 96(379):34–52.

Lorentzen, Robin. 1991. *Women in the Sanctuary Movement.* Philadelphia: Temple University Press.

Lukes, Steven. 1974. *Power: A Radical View.* London: Macmillan.

Malkki, Liisa. 1992. "National Geographic: The Rooting of Peoples and the Territorialization of National Identity Among Scholars and Refugees." *Cultural Anthropology* 7(1): 24–44.

Marrus, Michael R. 1985. *The Unwanted: European Refugees in the Twentieth Century.* New York: Oxford University Press.

Marwell, Gerald, and Pamela Oliver. 1984. "Collective Action Theory and Social Movements Research." *Research in Social Movements, Conflict and Change* 7: 1–27.

Marx, Gary T. 1988. *Undercover: Police Surveillance in America.* Berkeley: University of California Press.

McAdam, Doug. 1982. *Political Process and the Development of Black Insurgency.* Chicago: University of Chicago Press.

McCarthy, John D., and Mayer N. Zald. 1973. *The Trend of Social Movements in America.* Morristown, N.J.: General Learning Press.

———. 1977. "Resource Mobilization and Social Movements: A Partial Theory." *American Journal of Sociology* 82:1212–1241.

McDonnell, Patrick. 1988. "Owners Show Zero Tolerance for Border Car Seizures." *Los Angeles Times,* 19 September, sec. 1, 3.

McLeod, Ramon G. 1987. "1.7 Million Aliens in State May Be Eligible for Amnesty." *San Francisco Chronicle,* 7 July, 8.

Mead, Margaret. 1963. *Sex and Temperament in Three Primitive Societies.* New York: Morrow Quill Paperbacks.

Melucci, Alberto. 1989. *Nomads of the Present: Social Movements and Individual Needs in Contemporary Society.* John Keane and Paul Mier, eds. London: Hutchinson Radius.

Merelman, Richard M. 1984. *Making Something of Ourselves: On Culture and Politics in the United States.* Berkeley: University of California Press.

Merry, Sally Engle. 1990. *Getting Justice and Getting Even: Legal Consciousness Among Working-Class Americans.* Chicago: University of Chicago Press.

Miller, Frederick D. 1983. "The End of SDS and the Emergence of Weatherman: Demise Through Success." In Jo Freeman, ed., *Social Movements of the Sixties and Seventies,* 279–297. New York: Longman.

Montini, E. J. 1986. "Tucson Congregation Wondering When Truth Will Do Its Job." *Arizona Republic,* 4 May.

Moore, Sally Falk. 1986. *Social Facts and Fabrications: "Customary" Law on Kilimanjaro, 1880–1980.* Cambridge: Cambridge University Press.

Narayan, Kirin. 1989. *Storytellers, Saints, and Scoundrels: Folk Narrative in Hindu Religious Teaching.* Philadelphia: University of Pennsylvania Press.

Nash, June. 1979. *We Eat the Mines and the Mines Eat Us: Dependency and Exploitation in Bolivian Tin Mines.* New York: Columbia University Press.

Nicgorski, Darlene. 1986. "Statement Before Sentencing to the Court and Public." Text of sentencing statement, 1 July. On file at American Friends Service Committee office, Tucson, Ariz.

Oberschall, Anthony. 1973. *Social Conflict and Social Movements.* Englewood Cliffs, N.J.: Prentice-Hall.

O'Laughlin, Bridget. 1975. "Marxist Approaches in Anthropology." *Annual Review of Anthropology* 4:341–370.

Olson, Mancur. 1968. *The Logic of Collective Action: Public Goods and the Theory of Groups.* Cambridge: Harvard University Press.

Ong, Aihwa. 1987. *Spirits of Resistance and Capitalist Discipline: Factory Women in Malaysia.* Albany: State University of New York Press.

Ortner, Sherry B. 1984. "Theory in Anthropology Since the Sixties." *Comparative Studies in Society and History* 26:126–166.

Pichardo, Nelson A. 1988. "Resource Mobilization: An Analysis of Conflicting Theoretical Variations." *The Sociological Quarterly* 29(1):97–110.

Pittman, David. 1986. "Warning: U.S. Will Continue Prosecuting Smugglers." *Tucson Citizen,* 2 May, 1A, 6A.

Piven, Frances Fox, and Richard A. Cloward. 1977. *Poor People's Movements: Why They Succeed, How They Fail.* New York: Pantheon Books.

Pizzorno, Alessandro. 1978. "Political Exchange and Collective Identity in Industrial Conflict." In Colin Crouch and Alessandro Pizzorno, eds., *The Resurgence of Class Conflict in Western Europe Since* 1968, vol. 2, 277–298. London: Macmillan.

Pratt, Mary Louise. 1977. *Toward a Speech Act Theory of Literary Discourse.* Bloomington: Indiana University Press.

———. 1986. "Fieldwork in Common Places." In James Clifford and George E. Marcus, eds., *Writing Culture: The Poetics and Politics of Ethnography,* 27–50. Berkeley: University of California Press.

Presbyterian Church (U.S.A.) v. United States. 1990. 752 F. Supp. 1505 (D. Ariz.).

Price, Richard. 1983. *First-Time: The Historical Vision of an Afro-American People.* Baltimore: Johns Hopkins University Press.

Reiter, Rayna R. 1975. *Toward an Anthropology of Women.* New York: Monthly Review Press.

Rosaldo, Michelle Z., and Louise Lamphere, eds. 1974. *Woman, Culture, and Society.* Stanford: Stanford University Press.

Rosaldo, Renato. 1986a. "From the Door of His Tent: The Fieldworker and the Inquisitor." In James Clifford and George E. Marcus, eds., *Writing Culture: The Poetics and Politics of Ethnography,* 77–97. Berkeley: University of California Press.

———. 1986b. "Ilongot Hunting as Story and Experience." In Victor Turner and Edward Bruner, eds., *The Anthropology of Experience,* 97–137. Urbana, Ill.: University of Illinois Press.

———. 1989. *Culture and Truth: The Remaking of Social Analysis.* Boston: Beacon Press.

Rosen, Lawrence. 1989. *The Anthropology of Justice: Law as Culture in Islamic Society.* Cambridge: Cambridge University Press.

Rothenberg, Jackie. 1985. "Tucson Show of Solidarity Supports Sanctuary Workers." *Arizona Daily Star,* 25 January, 2A.

Sahlins, Marshall. 1981. *Historical Metaphors and Mythical Realities: Structure in the Early History of the Sandwich Islands Kingdom.* Ann Arbor: University of Michigan Press.

———. 1985. *Islands of History.* Chicago: University of Chicago Press.

Said, Edward. 1979. *Orientalism.* New York: Vintage Books.

*San Francisco Chronicle.* 1987. "Heat Suffocates Illegal Aliens on Texas Track." 3 July, 1.

*San Jose Mercury News.* 1986. "Two Cuban Refugees Survive 8 Days at Sea in Inner Tubes." 22 April, 9A.

Schmidt, Herb. 1985. "Preface." In Gary MacEoin, ed., *Sanctuary: A Resource Guide for Understanding and Participating in the Central American Refugees' Struggle*, 1–6. San Francisco: Harper and Row.

Schwartz, Bob. 1988. "Group Advises Day Laborers Targeted in Sweeps for Illegals." *Los Angeles Times*, 3 March, sec.1, 24.

Scott, James C. 1985. *Weapons of the Weak: Everyday Forms of Peasant Resistance.* New Haven: Yale University Press.

Select Committee on Intelligence, United States Senate. 1989. *The FBI and CISPES.* Washington, D.C.: U. S. Government Printing Office.

*Sequoia.* 1986. "Here's Brosnahan on America: Tucson Sanctuary Trial Lawyer Speaks Out." June issue, 3, 7.

Shields, Tom, and Julie Morris. 1987. "Million Immigrants Beat Fear." *Tucson Citizen*, 25 November, 1A.

Sklar, Helen, et al. 1985. *Salvadoran and Guatemalan Asylum Cases: A Practitioner's Guide to Representing Clients in Deportation Proceedings.* San Francisco: Immigrant and Legal Resource Center.

Smith-Rosenberg, Carroll. 1979. "Beauty, the Beast and the Militant Woman: A Case Study in Sex Roles and Social Stress in Jacksonian America." In Nancy F. Cott and Elizabeth H. Pleck, eds., *A Heritage of Her Own: Toward a New Social History of American Women*, 197–222. New York: Simon and Schuster.

Subcommittee on Immigration and Refugee Policy, Committee on the Judiciary, United States Senate. 1984. *Refugee Problems in Central America.* Washington, D.C.: U.S. Government Printing Office.

Tarrow, Sidney. 1988. "National Politics and Collective Action: Recent Theory and Research in Western Europe and the United States." *Annual Review of Sociology* 14:421–440.

Taussig, Michael T. 1980. *The Devil and Commodity Fetishism in South America.* Chapel Hill: University of North Carolina Press.

―――――. 1987. *Shamanism, Colonialism, and the Wild Man: A Study in Terror and Healing.* Chicago: University of Chicago Press.

Thompson, E. P. 1963. *The Making of the English Working Class.* New York: Vintage Books.

―――――. 1967. "Time, Work-Discipline, and Industrial Capitalism." *Past and Present* 38: 56–97.

Tilly, Charles. 1978. *From Mobilization to Revolution.* Reading, Mass.: Addison-Wesley.

―――――. 1984. "Social Movements and National Politics." In Charles Bright and Susan Harding, eds., *Statemaking and Social Movements: Essays in History and Theory*, 297–317. Ann Arbor: University of Michigan Press.

Tipton, Steve. 1982. *Getting Saved from the Sixties: Moral Meaning in Conversion and Cultural Change.* Berkeley: University of California Press.

Touraine, Alain. 1981. *The Voice and the Eye: An Analysis of Social Movements.* Alan Duff, trans. London: Cambridge University Press.

*Tucson Citizen.* 1987a. "Amnesty: At 1 Million." 23 November, 1A.

―――――. 1987b. "Inmates Are Men Without Hope, Without a Country." 27 November, 2A.

―――――. 1988. "FBI Dissent Probe 'Took on Life of Its Own,' Lawmaker Says." 28 January. 8A.

Turner, Mark. 1985a. "Sanctuary Evidence Suppression Sought." *Arizona Daily Star*, 29 March, 1B.

_____. 1985b. "U.S. Judge Tightens Media Restrictions for Sanctuary Trial." *Arizona Daily Star,* 22 October, 1B.

Tyler, Alice Felt. 1944. *Freedom's Ferment: Phases of American Social History to* 1860. Minneapolis: University of Minnesota Press.

U.S. v. Aguilar. 1986. *Official Trial Transcripts.* No. CR-85–008-PHX-EHC (D. Ariz.).

U.S.C.R. (United States Committee on Refugees). 1986. *Despite a Generous Spirit.* Washington, D.C.: American Council for Nationalities Service.

Varn, Gene. 1986. "Sanctuary Judge Accused of Racial Prejudice." *Arizona Republic,* 16 January.

Waskow, Arthur. 1983. *These Holy Sparks: The Rebirth of the Jewish People.* San Francisco: Harper and Row.

White, Ronald C., Jr., and C. Howard Hopkins. 1976. *The Social Gospel: Religion and Reform in Changing America.* Philadelphia: Temple University Press.

Williams, Nick B., Jr. 1988. "Cambodian Refugees: Life in Limbo." *Los Angeles Times,* 19 March, sec. 1, 1.

Williams, Raymond. 1977. *Marxism and Literature.* Oxford: Oxford University Press.

Willis, Paul. 1981. *Learning to Labour: How Working Class Kids Get Working Class Jobs.* New York: Columbia University Press.

Worsley, Peter. 1968. *The Trumpet Shall Sound: A Study of "Cargo" Cults in Melanesia,* 2nd ed. New York: Schocken Books.

Yanagisako, Sylvia. 1985. *Transforming the Past: Tradition and Kinship Among Japanese Americans.* Stanford: Stanford University Press.

Yngvesson, Barbara. 1988. "Making Law at the Doorway: The Clerk, the Court, and the Construction of Community in a New England Town." *Law and Society Review* 22(4):409–447.

Zald, Mayer N., and John D. McCarthy, eds. 1979. *The Dynamics of Social Movements: Resource Mobilization, Social Control, and Tactics.* Cambridge: Winthrop.

Zolberg, Aristide R. 1990. "The Roots of U.S. Refugee Policy." In Robert W. Tucker et al., eds., *Immigration and U.S. Foreign Policy,* 99–122. Boulder, Colo.: Westview Press.

# About the Book and Author

*The Culture of Protest* explores how religious activists and Central American immigrants by protesting U.S. policy, create practices, meanings, and relationships that are, themselves, a form of social change. By viewing change as an ongoing, incremental process the author shows how the movement's reinterpretations of legal, religious, and social practices produce cultural forms that help bring participants' visions of a more just social order into practice.

Unlike recent studies that view U.S. social movements primarily as strategies for achieving political objectives, this book analyzes what goes on in the midst of protest—the conversions that some North Americans experience as they come to know Central American reality, the relationships between refugees and sanctuary workers, the jokes and stories told by volunteers, and the religious rituals devised by participants. This rich ethnography reveals facets of change that would be missed by focusing exclusively on explicit goals and long-term strategies. As they assist refugees, sanctuary workers develop international notions of citizenship, create ecumenical interpretations of faith, form egalitarian communities, and cross a border between First and Third worlds to view their own society through the eyes of the poor. Sanctuary is thus not only a practical effort to aid refugees and affect U.S. policy but also a cultural and religious movement with profound implications for U.S. society.

Susan Bibler Coutin received her Ph.D. in anthropology from Stanford University in 1990. In addition to her study of the U.S. sanctuary movement, she has analyzed state terrorism, human rights, and the mothers of the "disappeared" in Argentina. Her central research question concerns the ways that seemingly apolitical cultural practices critique injustice, help create a more equitable social order, and, in some cases, become the basis of protest movements. She has taught at the University of New Mexico and California State University, Fullerton, and is now assistant professor of anthropology at North Adams State College in Massachusetts.

# Index

Abrahams, Roger, 63(n6)
Accommodationism, 193–197
Accompaniment, 47–48, 63–64(n8)
   East Bay work in, 38, 43
   tales of, 52–56, 57–59
Activism. *See* Political/social action;
   Religious activism
Alienation, 87–88, 91–98, 102. *See also*
   Illegal aliens
Alliance of Sanctuary Communities (ASC),
   41–42
All Saints Church, 1–2, 8–9, 29–30, 132–
   133
   sanctuary arrangements, 117
   sanctuary declaration, 34, 109–110
American Baptist Church, 223
Amnesty International, 100, 145
Antiwar objectives, 176, 177–178, 182
*Arizona Daily Star*, 96, 220
Arizona Sanctuary Defense Fund, 143–144
Asad, Talal, 175
ASC. *See* Alliance of Sanctuary
   Communities
Asylum. *See* Political asylum

Bail bonding, 26–28, 44(n6)
Barrios de Chungara, Domitila, 124–125
Bau, Ignatius, 105(n15)
Berkeley, 5
Border crossings
   effects on identity, 53(n7), 56–62, 76
   "Merkt" letters, 111, 148, 150(n10)
   in reproducing sanctuary movement,
      43, 45–46, 83, 224
   sanctuary screening procedures, 113–
      116

   tales of, 46–60, 63(n4)
   by Tucson sanctuary workers, 33–34, 36
Borderlinks, 61
Border patrol, 96
Brosnahan, James, 139
Bush administration, 192, 199–200(n18)

Call to Sanctuary, 41, 44(nn 12, 13), 182
Careerism, 188–190
Categorization
   within immigration discourse, 88–89,
      93–96, 104(n8), 106(n21)
   Orientalism, 154–155, 170
   political asylum, 99–102
   sanctuary reinterpretations, 109, 127
   subordination through, 130(n16)
   during Tucson sanctuary trial, 131, 137,
      148–149
Central American church
   advocacy for poor, 24. *See also*
      Liberation theology
   solidarity with, 206–207
Central American organizations, 11
Central Intelligence Agency (CIA), 89
Change. *See* Personal change; Social
   change
Charity, 185–186
Chicago sanctuary movement, 39, 198(n9)
Chinese Exclusion Act, 94
Christians, 10–11, 71–78, 204, 207
Churches
   criticisms of U.S., 193–194
   gender of congregation members,
      173(n14)
   included in fieldwork, 6–9, 16(n1)
   sanctuary arrangements, 117–118